The law and
the public's health

Issues and problems in health care

Paul R. Torrens, M.D., M.P.H., Series Editor

School of Public Health,
University of California,
Los Angeles

The law and
the public's health

Kenneth R. Wing, J.D., M.P.H.

Formerly of the School of Public Health,
University of California,
Los Angeles

Saint Louis

The C. V. Mosby Company

1976

Library of Congress Cataloging in Publication Data

Wing, Kenneth R   1946-
    The law and the public's health.

    (Issues and problems in health care)
    Bibliography: p.
    1. Public health laws—United States.   I. Title.
KF3775.W5   344'.73'04   76-6074
ISBN 0-8016-5601-X

TS/M/M   9   8   7   6   5   4   3   2   1

Preface

Since this book crosses the lines between two distinct disciplines, it requires a little introductory explanation. This book is written primarily for students and others with some exposure to public health but with little or no background in law. Its primary goal is to describe public health law in a way that is relevant to the needs of students and professionals in the public health fields.

As such an overview, the book by necessity treats some topics rather superficially and some points of law not at all. Even within the topics that are covered in depth, it is impossible in the context of a book like this to completely describe all of the details of the law as it relates to each issue. For example, it was absolutely essential that the basic principles of constitutional law be described in this book; but it was practically impossible to do so within the confines of an introductory textbook. To put it another way, in order to cover public health law and the various issues that are critical to it, I have occasionally had to rely on simplified working definitions of legal principles, skeletal outlines of what are much more complicated processes, and an occasional fiction that is necessary to bridge an unimportant gap.

My only defense is a simple one: I wanted to write a book that would be an overview of and an introduction to the law as it relates to the public's health, not a definitive treatise on public health law.

For the reader who wants to supplement these materials, I have tried to indicate at the end of each chapter some appropriate references.

In this book I have addressed nine broad topics relevant to public health law that are both important in their own right and demonstrative of broad principles of the law applicable to a variety of legal issues.

Chapter 1 describes the law and the legal system and introduces some basic ideas that are prerequisites to understanding the remainder of the book.

Chapters 2 through 5 examine various aspects of the same critically important issue: the legal rights that exist between the individual and the government in matters relating to the public's health. Chapter 2 is a description of the breadth of the government's authority in matters involving the public's health, focusing on the state government's authority. Chapter 3 examines the limits on the government's exercise of authority using as a demonstrative example the civil commitment of the mentally ill. Chapter 4 discusses an individual right of particular importance to public health issues, the right to privacy, and how the law has resolved the conflict between that right and the government's authority to regulate family planning decisions. Chapter 5 also examines the rights between the individual and the government, but concentrates upon a unique type of legal right, a statutory entitlement to benefits, using as examples the Medicaid and Medicare programs.

Chapters 6 and 7 involve a different set of issues, the rights that exist between an individual patient and a private provider of medical care. This basically involves the legal rights between two private individuals, but the rights between private individuals are somewhat different when one of those individuals is a provider of medical care. Chapter 6 explains the basic principles behind the liability of providers for malpractice and the nature of what is known as the malpractice problem. Chapter 7 examines the meaning of the term "patients' rights" and some of the more fundamental legal principles defining the relationship between the patient and the provider.

Chapter 8 returns to the legal relationship between the government and private individuals, but in this case the individual is an institutional provider of medical care. This chapter examines the legal basis for the exercise of governmental control over health facilities and some of the programmatic approaches that the government has taken in the past and may take in the future.

Chapter 9 is conceptually distinct from all of the previous chapters. It examines certain legal rights that exist between private individuals and private providers of health services because of the quasi-public nature of the provider institution. That is, because these institutions are either involved with or subsidized by the government, for some purposes they take on the responsibilities of the government. Several examples are presented of such responsibilities, with particular focus on the public responsibilities of nonprofit hospitals.

Taken together, these nine topics represent a broad range of legal issues relevant in the public health context. Certainly there are some specific issues omitted and some areas of public health law that are mentioned only briefly. But most of the important legal principles are explained; I am convinced that it is an understanding of these principles, not any particular application of the law, and the process by which these principles are defined and enforced that should be important to people interested in understanding the law and the public's health. Although there are certainly particular topics not covered, most of the important legal principles are explained. The understanding of general principles of law that is the necessary prerequisite to the understanding of the law and the public's health will be demonstrated throughout this book, not their application in any particular context.

I would like to acknowledge and thank the many people who have assisted me in the preparation of this book. Most particularly I would like to express my appreciation to Paul Torrens for his guidance and editing. I would like to thank Patricia Butler and Steve Axelrad with whom I co-authored Chapter 5 and Chapter 9, respectively. I would also like to thank the staff, past and present, of the National Health Law Program; anyone familiar with NHeLP's work will recognize that I have drawn heavily from that program's experience in this book. I would also like to express my appreciation to the faculty of the Department of Health Education at the University of Oregon for giving me the time and encouragement to complete this book while I was in residence there.

I would like to thank all of the various people who read the material as it was developed, but particularly Ray Correio, Stan Price, Ruth Roemer, Dan Strouse, and Pam Waldman for their encouragement and criticism—usually in that order.

Kenneth R. Wing

It is the basic right of every citizen to have available to him adequate health care.

RESOLUTION OF THE AMERICAN
MEDICAL ASSOCIATION, 1969

Our entire society, then, has a direct stake in the health of every member. In carrying out its responsibilities in this field, a nation serves its own best interests, even as it demonstrates the breadth of its spirit and the depth of its compassion.

RICHARD M. NIXON, 1971

Experience should teach us to be most on guard to protect liberty when the government's purposes are beneficent. Men born to freedom are naturally alert to repel invasion of their liberty by evil minded rulers. The greatest dangers to liberty lurk in insidious encroachment by men of zeal, well meaning but without understanding.

JUSTICE LOUIS BRANDEIS, 1927

Contents

Introduction

Kerr White, writing in the introductory article to Scientific American's *Life and Death and Medicine,* begins with the question: "Why, at this time, are medicine and the provision of health care rapidly becoming a major focus of debate in almost every industrialized society?" White cites as one reason the enormous costs of delivering health care. He also finds the explanation inherent in the tremendous technological advances in medicine that have developed through the last few decades; these advances have created the potential for tremendous progress as well as a series of problems, among them the need to readjust our political and social institutions in light of this potential and the need to make the difficult policy choices created as a result.

To understand the relative importance of health care at this unique point in time, it is absolutely necessary to view our current situation in this sort of historical perspective. A few thousand years ago Hippocrates wrote what were then the most profound observations about the health of man; today it seems impossible that anyone could ever accept such inaccurate and primitive ideas. A mere hundred years ago John Snow made what was at that time an incredible medical breakthrough: he counted deaths from cholera and noticed that it somehow was related to the water that people drank. These events mark only the evolution of man's understanding of his health. The ability to actually treat disease or injury is even more recent. We still taunt the medical profession with the estimate by one Harvard professor that it was the year 1912 when "for the first time in human history, a random patient with a random disease consulting a doctor chosen at random stood better than a 50-50 chance of benefiting from the encounter."

The technological progress of the last 50 years has been so rapid and accelerated that it is impossible to characterize anecdotally. Today medicine can do such incredible things that near-miracles are commonplace. Perhaps the key to the understanding of why medicine and health are so important today is that we have come to expect so much. At least in this country, good medical care is no longer a luxury; it is something we demand. We expect medicine to be available to treat us and to do so successfully. When our expectations are not met, we focus our demands on our social and political institutions.

In short, we are at a point in time where health, particularly the delivery of medical care, has emerged as a critically important public issue. It is not the first time that health has become a public issue. For example, national health insurance has been debated and seriously considered a number of times;

it was part of Theodore Roosevelt's campaign platform in 1912 and was strongly urged by social reformers within both the Franklin Roosevelt and Truman administrations. But never before has the public's health become so important as a political issue, and never have our political institutions been so apparently willing to respond.

This book is not intended to be an analysis of public health from a political or social perspective. It is a book about the law. The outline above, however, is a necessary introduction. It explains why the law as it relates to public health is so important at this point in time. Not only are the legal rights and responsibilities relating to the public's health currently being examined, reevaluated, and in some cases altered, but quite literally new law is being created at an ever-increasing rate and in ever more complicated forms.

At all levels of government there has been a response to this emerging public issue. At the federal level, particularly, an entirely new role has evolved for the federal government in the delivery of health care and in the maintenance of health. In the last 10 years there has been an ever-increasing investment of federal dollars in health and a seemingly endless number of federally funded health-related programs and institutions. Not only is the government involved directly in financing and delivery of health care, it is also inextricably involved in financing health facility construction, medical research, and training and educating health care manpower. The logical progression of this federal government financial investment should be realized in the very near future with the passage of some kind of mandatory national health insurance scheme.

Furthermore, health care delivery is becoming an industry subject to various kinds of governmental regulation. Traditionally, the states have confined their role to that of assuming responsibility for the licensure of manpower and health care facilities. In addition to these functions many states have now enacted legislation requiring a "certificate of need" prior to the construction or operation of health facilities. There is some serious discussion, although no state has yet attempted it, of similar regulation of the distribution of manpower. The federal government has also taken on responsibility for the regulation of institutions that participate in governmentally financed health care programs and has recently begun a program similar to the state certificate of need programs to regulate the construction of facilities. Even more recently the federal government has started to implement the controversial PSRO system, a program that hopes to directly monitor a system of peer review over the quality of care delivered under federally financed health care programs in all institutional and, eventually, noninstitutional settings.

All these activities involve new law, both in the sense of the increasing complexity of the legal relationships among these various actors, institutions, programs, and dollars and in the sense that each year there are new laws being enacted. The more complex the system (or perhaps it is more correct to refer to the delivery of health care in this country as many fragmented systems or a nonsystem), the more complex its legal structure.

Undeniably, public health law, or to turn it around, the law as it relates to public health, must be understood by anyone who deals with the critical issues involving the public's health that face our society today. If for no other reason, the law is a set of constraints on behavior. To operate in the public health field, one must know what can and cannot be done. More importantly, the law is one important determinant of the public's health and the health care delivery system, and it is therefore a means for causing change. In the field of public health adjustments in the law are prerequisites for almost any change and one of the most important tools available to anyone interested in producing major change. Accordingly, the objectives of this book are to facilitate those in the field of public health to understand the law they must deal with and to use the law and the legal system to achieve their purposes.

CHAPTER 1 The law and the legal system

Before one can understand the law as it relates to the public's health, one must have a basic understanding of the legal system and the law in general. This chapter will be a short description of the American legal system and an explanation of some of the basic legal concepts that underlie that system. Hopefully it will establish a language that can be used throughout this book in explaining the substance of public health law. To some readers this chapter may appear to be no more than a basic civics lesson, and to a large extent that will be true. However, it is surprising, and unfortunate, to find that the vast majority of people in this country still have major misunderstandings about the ways in which our legal system operates and the nature of their legal rights.

The meaning of "the law"

The first thing that has to be understood is that there is no truly comprehensive way to define the law. Aside from a few not-worth-quoting one-line epigrams, the law in its entirety has rarely been described in a meaningful, accurate manner. There are the treatises that have been written attempting to summarize in relatively short statements what the law has been interpreted to be. These are written on a specific subject, for example, Prosser's *Restatement of Torts,* but they are always written by lawyers for the use of lawyers. This could be done for the subject of public health law, but it would be relatively boring to read—and to write. Furthermore, it is doubtful that anyone but the most scholarly ever reads these treatises, at least in their entirety. More importantly, it would be inappropriate and misleading, as will be explained on the following pages, to prepare a book in treatise form for an audience not formally trained or experienced with the law.

The fact of the matter is that the law on a given subject cannot be defined in a series of short statements; nor is the law simply a set of principles from which specific answers can be easily drawn to cover questions that arise in specific situations. Certainly there are principles worth drawing, and in some situations relatively clearcut statements can be made of "what the law is" or "what I can or cannot do." However, in most important situations this is not possible. This is particularly true when dealing with the law relating to current public issues where the law has not had the time to grow and evolve into a relatively settled form. It would be misleading to try to present the law of public health in that manner, particularly to the lay (meaning non-lawyer) reader. That is not the character of the law; it is quite different and, in some respects, much more.

The law is, of course, literally the sum, set, or conglomerate of all of the laws in all of the various jurisdictions: the constitutions, the various statutes, the traditional principles of justice that we refer to as the common law, and the judicial opinions that interpret all three. The law is also the legal profession and its shortcomings, prejudices, ideas, and language, as well as the roles lawyers play. To understand what the law is, something must be known of lawyers and how they think; a way to understand the "legalese" with which they speak so freely must be developed.

The law is also the legal process—how laws are made, enforced, and interpreted. From one perspective, there is the theoretical framework of this process that must be understood in order to understand the law. It includes notions such as the divisions of power between the branches of government, the separate roles of trial and appellate courts, and the difference between findings of fact and conclusions of law. One must understand the interrelationship of statutes and regulations, the meaning and role of judicial opinions, and the role of individual procedural rights in ensuring that the process is not only efficient but satisfies notions of "justice."

At a second level, there is the legal process, meaning the practical realities of the system: the legislatures and their politics, the somewhat archaic judicial system, and the innumerable institutions that make up the executive branch of our government and its ubiquitous administrative agencies. An understanding of the legal process must include both the theoretical and the practical. For instance, it must include the notion that legislatures make and amend laws, but also that some citizens and some institutions can influence legislatures more easily than others. It must include the recognition that there is a right to a jury trial in many instances, but that right should be considered in light of the kinds of people that actually end up sitting as jurors in our society. Above all, the legal process must be understood as having an economic component. It costs money to make, enforce, or interpret the law. It will cost most people something—probably more than they can afford—to enforce even their most basic legal rights. For large portions of our population, this in essence means that the legal process is virtually inaccessible and totally overwhelming when caught up within it. These are the kinds of theoretical and practical things that must be first understood in order to understand the legal process, which is a necessary part of any description or explanation of the law.

Not only is the law not easily described, but there is a traditional barrier between lawyers and nonlawyers that makes describing the law even more difficult. The legal profession has for centuries done many things, with both the best and worst of intentions, to surround the law with a mystical aura. Much as the medical profession would have us believe that there is something almost sacred about medical judgment and that only a physician can understand it, lawyers have perpetuated the only partially justified myth that there is something called legal judgment that only someone with the proper mix of formal education, practical experience, and appropriate vocabulary can make.

It does take training to read and understand the law, particularly judicial opinions, but it is not as difficult as the profession would have the lay public believe. The various rules of research must be mastered, a certain disciplined diligence must be employed, and there must be a certain familiarity with the concepts of the law; the more practice one has in these skills, the better. But what are often passed off as legal judgments are sometimes more accurately described as educated guesses, some of which are really experienced bluff. It is the difference between the judgments, the guesses, and the bluffs that ought to be understood, but that is often confused and obscured by lawyers with their conveniently obscure vocabulary. The law is sometimes contradictory, often complex, and almost always vague. There are vast gray areas between the black and the white rules where even the best of the profession cannot read "what the law is." Some lawyers would have us believe that it is the ability to decipher the seemingly contradictory nature of the law and the ability to fill in the missing coloration of the apparently gray area that are the quasi-mystic skills that place lawyers one step above mere mortals and the law beyond the layperson's understanding. Such notions are the unjustified part of the mystique and major barriers to an understanding of the law.

How, then, can the law be best described? How can all of these various aspects of the law and the legal system, the theory and the practice, be accurately explained?

The approach that will be taken in this book will be to enunciate and describe the background and general legal principles for each of a series of topics in public health law and the application of these principles to a series of critical—and generally unanswered—problems concerning the public's health. This description will not be in the form of a series of straightforward statements of what the law permits or prohibits in each problem situation. In some instances there will be rather specific declarations of what the law is, but in most situations it turns out that the best description admits that the law is little more than a series of rather vague guidelines and uncertain predictions of what legal decision makers will do the next time they are faced with a given situation. In those situations it is better to acknowledge the vagueness and the uncertainty than it is to impose a more certain reality that is not there. Thus the most accurate approach to an important problem in public health usually involves defining the broad legal principles that are relevant to that problem and some of the factors that are considered in the application of those principles, while above all, focusing on the theory and the reality of the decision-making processes by which this strange thing called the law has been—and will be in the future—made, enforced, and interpreted.

Laws: statutes, constitutions, regulations, judicial opinions

What are laws?

Most people think of laws in terms of statutes. Statutes are written laws passed by legislatures at any level of government. Before passage, pending statutes are called bills or occasionally propositions, terms which are often used inappropriately in common language when referring to an enacted statute. There are federal statutes, state statutes, and the equivalent of statutes passed by city and county governments that may be called ordinances or municipal laws. Statutes can govern any of the variety of human endeavors, ranging from the distribution of property to the definition of criminal conduct, limited only by the jurisdiction—the sphere of influence—of the legislative body that enacts them.

Statutes are only one form of law. Constitutions are also laws and are the written legal documents establishing the government. There is, of course, the United States Constitution, which defines the various powers of the federal government and the function of its branches. There are also state constitutions in each state, which have comparable provisions relating to each state's government. The U.S. Constitution is often referred to as the supreme law of the land because any law, be it state or federal, that is in conflict with the Federal Constitution is invalid. Similarly, any state law in conflict with that state's constitution is invalid.

In addition to statutes and constitutions, there are regulations that are also laws for most intents and purposes. A statute that relates to a complex activity may be worded in very general terms, with the specific details of the legislation not determined by the statute, but delegated to some governmental agency or official to define and enact. This is very common with regard to health legislation. For example, all states have statutes allowing the state to commit people who are mentally ill. Many state commitment statutes either imply or state that the term "mentally ill" will be defined by regulation as determined by some state administrative agency, but the term is not defined in the statute itself. Other examples are the federal health benefit programs. Great portions and almost all programmatic details are left to the determination of the Secretary of Health, Education and Welfare according to appropriately enacted regulations.

The first important thing to note is that because they are authorized by statute and implemented under a statutory law, regulations are part of that law and have the full force of law. The second thing to remember is that the term regulation has a very specific legal definition. Regulations must be enacted by the designated agency of the state according to a specific process. Usually there is a requirement that regulations be published in proposed form and that there be opportunity for public input or a hearing. They may be challenged in court if they are enacted without the proper procedures or if their content goes beyond their statutory mandate. Occasionally there will be rules employed by governmental agencies that are referred to internally as regulations (incorrectly), where actually they do not have the force of law of legally valid regulations.

In theory regulations permit legislatures to delegate authority to administrative agencies that have great expertise in that particular area of the law. It would be cumbersome and to a certain extent inappropriate for the legislature to pass statutes that defined every little detail of a government program or activity. This is particularly true in the field of health where the legislatures have by statute mandated a large number of programs and agencies that require for their implementation the understanding of a great amount of technical information that an administrative agency might have. Because of this, the regulations can become the most critical part of the legal basis of a governmental health program. However, the application of this theory in practice must be constantly reevaluated. The wisdom of the delegation of power by the legislature that allows nonelected officials to make important public decisions has frequently been questioned and has led to a number of problems and issues that will be discussed in various parts of this book.

Another form of law that is at first encounter confusing is the judicial opinion. Appellate courts (and some trial courts) write legal opinions giving the basis for their decisions in individual cases. Since all legal principles and all laws are by their nature general statements, courts have to apply these general principles to specific situations and, in effect, interpret the law by their decisions. These interpretations of law in the form of judicial opinions are recorded and published and have the force of law in the particular court's jurisdiction. The most important opinions are those of the United States Supreme Court, since the opinions become law for all other courts, both state and federal. Courts incorporate into their opinions interpretations of regulations, statutes, and constitutions, but also principles of law that have traditionally been applied in our legal system. These latter principles are known as the common law. The reader should be warned that this definition of the common law is vastly oversimplified, but is a sufficient explanation of the term for the purposes of this book. It would also be misleading to assume the above is a complete explanation of the content and role of judicial opinions. What is important is to remember that they are laws, just as a statute is a law. Anyone who desires to have any real feel for the law and its application will have to know something of how these opinions are made, how to find these opinions, and will have to become accustomed to reading them. As was discussed in the introduction, only a good lawyer can make an exacting legal judgment, but much of the law can be understood by nonlawyers with just a basic understanding of the law and its components. Being able to locate judicial opinions and understand their role is one way that this can be done.

These are the primary forms of law: statutes, constitutions, regulations, and judicial opinions. Their implications and complexities will become clearer as the reader continues through the substance of this book.

In addition to an understanding of these various kinds of law, it is necessary to know something of how these laws are found.

Statutes are codified, arranged according to subject matter, in sets of volumes or codes that are periodically updated to reflect recent changes. Statutes are also available in a form indexed in the chronological order of their enactment.

Judicial opinions are much harder to find, but are published in a variety of sets, called reporters, arranged by state, region, or jurisdiction of the court, and are in chronological order. Since one is generally concerned with the subject matter of an opinion, there are techniques for locating cases utilizing various published indices and the case summaries and footnotes that are found preceding most judicial opinions; this is a relatively difficult art to attempt and exceedingly difficult to master.

Regulations are also published according to subject matter and in chronological order of their enactment. At the federal level they are relatively easy to find; but some state governments are seriously negligent in making regulations available in a timely fashion and, sometimes, in making them available to the public at all.

At first glance at legal material, it must appear that the legal profession is extraordinarily preoccupied with references and cross-references to the point that legal literature is particularly cumbersome to read. Actually the vast amount of material encompassed by the law does justify this preoccupation and a basic understanding of legal references and citations can be very useful in both understanding and finding the law.

Although statutes can be referred to by their title (if they have one), e.g., the Administrative Procedures Act or the Social Security Act, they are most often cited by the section and volume of their code; in the case of the Administrative Procedures Act, that would be cited as 5 U.S.C. § 1000, meaning volume (or "title") 5 of the United States Code at section 1000; for state statutes, the citations are basically the same, although most state statutory citations refer to a section or chapter or title within the state code, e.g., N.Y. Gen. Bus. Law. § 352, meaning New York General Business Laws, section 352; Cal. Wel. and Inst. Code, § 1400, would refer to the California Welfare and Institutions Code, section 1400.

Regulations are cited similarly. All federal regulations are codified in the Code of Federal Regulations by their volume and section number; for example, 42 C.F.R. § 562 is volume 42, section 562. State regulations are usually codified in the same way, e.g., 22 Cal. Ad. Code § 50000 is volume 22 of the California Administrative Code, section 50000.

Judicial opinions are more uniform in their citations. They will almost always be referred to by the page in the particular volume in which they appear; 182 U.S. 427 (1901) is a U.S. Supreme Court case decided in 1901 that appears on p. 427 of volume 182 of the United States Reports. 459 F.2d 6 (1st Cir. 1972) is a 1972 case, decided in the First Circuit Court of Appeals, that can be found on p. 6 of volume 459 of the second series of the Federal Reports.

About the only real difficulty is understanding the rather complicated system of abbreviations that has developed over the years; one also has to be aware of the fact that most judicial opinions are published in more than one source and sometimes several citations to different sources of the same material may be given. In terms of actually locating the material from a citation, the only real skill is being able to transcribe the citation exactly. All law libraries have reference librarians to assist in the interpretation of citations—a service used quite frequently by lawyers as well as lay people.

The legal system

As has been indicated throughout this chapter, it is important to understand the legal process and the legal system. Here again, as with many other legal concepts, there is often a great discrepancy between the actual system and public perceptions of it, even at the most basic levels.

To begin with, the American governmental structure is traditionally described as having three branches: the legislative, the executive, and the judicial. This description applies to the federal government as well as state governments and, in most cases, local governments, except where occasionally these functional branches are merged at the local level into one or two bodies. The legislative branch is usually defined as the branch that makes law; the executive branch enforces the law; and the judicial branch interprets law. However, that is not really descriptive; judicial interpretations in some sense make law as well as interpret it, and the executive branch and its administrative agencies make, as well as enforce, the law through administrative regulations. Similarly, one can argue that the executive branch in some ways interprets laws as it enforces them, subject to the ultimate interpretation and review of the courts. In any event, this is the traditional definition of our basic legal structure: the legislature, the executive branch, and the courts, however rough the delineation of their function may be.

More important than the overlap of function is the appreciation that the administrative agencies that are, in the traditional theoretical model, part of the executive branch really are a separate "branch," sometimes called the fourth branch of government. Over time and with the growing complexity of society and the government that serves it, the enforcement of law and the administration of the executive branch has led to the formation of what are in reality autonomous agencies that are only to a limited degree under the control of the chief executive. Public health may be the archetype example: as the government has become more involved in matters affecting the public's health, there has been an expansion of the executive branch to include the administrative capabilities to enforce public health laws and to handle the various health-related programs. The practical result of this has been the formation of great bureaucratic institutions having all the good and bad connotations that the term "bureaucracy" suggests. Anyone looking with a detached perspective at the constitution that established our state, and particularly our federal, governments would have to comment that it is unlikely that the framers of those constitutions contemplated a system wherein the administrative agencies played such an independent and powerful role in the creation, interpretation, and enforcement of the law.

The judicial branch merits separate and more detailed attention. Understanding the nature and function of the various courts that make up the American judicial system can be a surprisingly complex undertaking. In the first place, there are two separate judicial systems. In addition to the federal judicial system, each state has its own judicial system, which varies drastically from state to state.

Some states establish different courts for different kinds of legal disputes. For example, in addition to the courts of general jurisdiction (i.e., courts that can hear any kind of legal dispute) a state may also have courts of special jurisdiction that deal with such things as probate, juvenile matters, and small claims. In addition, courts of general jurisdiction will usually divide administratively into divisions (or departments or sessions) handling only criminal matters, civil matters, or matters in equity.

Because of this interstate variation it is probably unwise to consider any state's judicial system typical of the rest. One should remember that there are basically two types of court that make up any state judicial system—appellate courts and trial level courts. All states' judicial systems have at least a supreme appellate court; many have intermediate appellate courts. These courts hear appeals from their trial courts. All states have many trial level courts.

Trial courts hear all cases first, hear oral testimony, take other evidence, and interpret the law as it applies to the facts established by all the evidence. Most people are somewhat familiar with trial courts and the trial process, thanks to our age of mass media, particularly television. People are less familiar with appellate courts, which only review the legal interpretations of trial courts. In essence they consider and hear only legal arguments and generally take no evidence. They make their decisions based on the factual conclusions of trial courts and their own interpretations of the law. Appellate courts do write opinions, and it is the opinions of appellate courts (and a few trial courts) that are reported and that become part of the law.

In terms of scenario, a trial court judge sees witnesses, hears evidence, and considers the arguments of two lawyers. An appellate court hearing involves only the judge considering the arguments of two lawyers; usually nothing more is presented.

The federal judicial system consists of the U.S. District Courts, the federal trial courts; U.S. District Courts of Appeals, the intermediate level federal appellate courts; and the U.S. Supreme Court, the supreme appellate court of the legal system.

The federal judicial system handles cases that involve disputes over federal law. They also handle cases involving disputes over state law, if the disputing parties are from two different states. There is also something known as pendente jurisdiction, which means that if a case involves both a violation of state law and federal law, the federal courts will decide both issues. The state courts, on the other hand, have jurisdiction over all legal disputes in their state, whether the disputes involve violations of state or federal law. Therefore, at times a case may be brought in either the state or the federal judicial systems. If a case is brought in the state judicial system and it involves federal law, in addition to the appeals to the state appellate courts, there is also the possibility that the case may be appealed to the U.S. Supreme Court, since in matters involving federal law, particularly the U.S. Constitution, the Federal Supreme Court is the ultimate authority.

When a federal court is considering a case that involves state law, the federal courts are extremely hesitant to overrule a previous interpretation of that state's law by its own state courts, and in theory they do not have the power to overrule an interpretation of the state's constitution by its own state supreme court.

The function of law: legal rights

To understand that laws can be in the form of opinions, statutes, constitutions, or regulations and to understand some of the framework that makes up our legal system is only the beginning of a conceptual understanding of the law and the law as it relates to public health. One must also understand the real function of the law.

To put it as simply as possible, the function of the law is to establish legal rights, and the purpose of the legal system is to define and enforce those rights. But what does it mean to have established (or enforced) a legal right? To put these short statements into more meaningful terms and to develop a definition of this critical term "legal right," it is probably best to consider an example: the freedom of speech.

Without much argument, everyone would agree that American law establishes for its citizens the legal right to the freedom of speech (at least in theory). Every American civics lesson taught makes reference to that right; it is a foregone conclusion. But what does it mean?

As a teaching exercise to consider this question, I once posed to a class of graduate public health students this hypothetical question: "Suppose that one of the rules of the class is that anyone criticizing the President of the United States or his political party, either in class or out of class, during the pending semester, will be given a failing grade despite his or her performance on the class exams. Would that be illegal?" Of course everyone realized that such an outrageous edict would be impossible to apply and most everyone thought it was probably an illegal rule, but none of the students was immediately sure why. After some discussion the class agreed that it is a violation of the constitutional right to free speech, which most people (although not all) remembered was part of the first amendment of the U.S. Constitution.

Most were also surprised to find that a reading of the first amendment did not immediately support that conclusion. It reads:

> Congress shall make no law respecting an establishment of religion, or prohibiting the free exercise thereof; or abridging the freedom of speech, or of the press; or the right of the people peaceably to assemble, and to petition the Government for a redress of grievances.

No doubt that establishes a legal right to the freedom of speech, but all that it apparently does is establish that "Congress shall make no law." Why does that limit the restrictions a teacher can place on the conduct of students?

The ensuing class discussion of the hypothetical question and the ultimate explanation cannot be detailed here, but the conclusion can be. As it turns out, the students were quite right. Such a rule would be a violation of their legal right to free speech as it is established by the first amendment. However, one could hardly expect them to be able to recite the legal analysis that leads to that conclusion. It is the fourteenth amendment that includes the critical provision that can prohibit a teacher from interfering with the free speech of his or her students. The fourteenth amendment includes a provision that states: "nor shall any state deprive any person of life, liberty or property without due process of law." Since this due process clause is rather vague, courts have looked to the first ten amendments of the U.S. Constitution as guidance in determining what kinds of actions would be deprivations of liberty within the meaning of the fourteenth amendment. Over the years the courts have established (by judicial opinion) that the prohibition of the first amendment must apply to the states as well as the federal government because of the terms of the fourteenth amendment. They also have established that this prohibition in the first amendment should be interpreted to mean all branches of government, not just a prohibition on the Congress or legislative branch. To complete the analysis, as an agent of a state-financed institution, a teacher is, in effect, standing in the shoes of the state government and, as is the state government, is prohibited by the first and fourteenth amendments from interfering with the legal right to free speech of the citizen-students.

Admittedly, and in fact, intentionally, this is a complicated example. It is the first of many lessons on how the law can be interpreted in somewhat complicated, if not surprising, ways. However complex the legal basis for this right, it also illustrates a number of fundamental and important points about the nature of a legal right.

First, in order for there to be a legal right, there must be a specific law that recognizes that right—in this case, the U.S. Constitution and the judicial opinions that have interpreted it. Had there not been some specific law establishing the freedom of speech, it would not be a legally enforceable right no matter how cherished the freedom of speech was as a societal value or how many people thought it important.

Second, rights do not exist generally but apply to specific people or institutions and place responsibilites on specific people or institutions. If the courts had not interpreted the first amendment so broadly, it could have been only a prohibition on congressional action, not on state government or on a teacher in a state-financed school. Consider for the moment if the person imposing the restriction were not an agent of the state or federal government, but a teacher in a private college or even the student's next-door neighbor threatening to exclude the student from a social club. Are private individuals precluded by law from interfering with the freedom of speech? There may be other laws prohibiting such conduct, but one thing is clear: the specific legal rights established in the first amendment do not prohibit such conduct. The first amendment defines the right to free speech, and it defines it as a rather specific relationship between the people and the federal or state government.

Third, a legal right is a relationship that tends to benefit some specific individual(s) and at the same time imposes a responsibility on some other specific individual(s). The constitutional right to free speech is a benefit enjoyed by the people, and it is the responsibility of the government to respect the enjoyment of that benefit.

"Games" similar to our hypothetical situation can be played with other legal rights, and these elements will also be illustrated. Conversely, these elements will make it easier to analyze the nature of the legal right at stake in most situations. For example, what are the legal rights preventing people from doing bodily harm to one another? First, criminal laws define such conduct as criminal and give the state the right to punish the offender. Civil laws give the offended party the right to sue the offender and recover damages. Each is a very specific relationship between two or more parties that exists because it is defined by the legal system and enforced by the sanctions of the legal process. If someone is the victim of a physical attack or battery, it is his or her legal right to sue the attacker for any damages caused; it is the state's legal right to punish and incarcerate the criminal.

Legal rights, then, are the relationships between two or more specific entities established by law and defined and enforced by the legal system. These entities can be individual people or institutions. They confer a benefit on at least one of the entities and create a duty or responsibility on the other.

This definition of legal rights is the primary concept used throughout this book to describe public health law. To really understand the law as it relates to public health and to be able to use that law to promote change, one should look at public health law as a set of specific relationships, i.e., legal rights.

This definition of legal rights is not meant to imply that there are not other relationships that may be appropriately called rights. Certainly there are other relationships that are important and relevant to public health, and there should be a way to relate them to the discussion of public health law.

First of all, some rights, meaning relationships between two or more specific entities, are enforced and defined not by (or in some cases, not only by) the legal system, but by the force of the prevailing ethics. Loosely, ethics can be defined as formal principles of conduct recognized and enforced by whatever sanctions are employed by one's associates or professional peers. In many cases ethics are only nominally recognized and are not enforced in any sense of the term. Conversely, many professions, including physicians, have what can only be described as "informal codes of ethics" that are also enforced. Sometimes ethics are vigorously enforced, and, particularly with regard to medical care providers, the sanctions available to one's professional association can have drastic personal and economic impact. For example, as will be seen in the section on patients' rights, an action interpreted to be a breach of confidence by a physician's peers, though not always a violation of the patient's legal rights, may be a violation of the patient's ethical rights if the physician's peers choose to enforce their ethical codes and apply available sanctions. This can have an important effect on physician conduct.

Similarly, there are certain things that each of us individually feels so strongly about that it is considered a right despite the fact that it is not legally enforceable or enforceable under any ethical code. There is nothing more than the power of moral suasion to enforce these rights or relationships, but these moral or human rights do exist. It is helpful in talking about the law to speak not just of legal rights, but occasionally of their interface with something called ethical rights and moral rights. However, these materials will be primarily concerned with existing, legally enforceable rights, and it will be important to focus on the various elements of a legal right as a language to use in discussing the various legal issues relating to public health and in analyzing their implications.

Perspectives on the law

There is at least one other observation that ought to be made about the law in general before proceeding to specific topics in public health law. There are a number of different perspectives that one can take in looking at the law. One can look at the law in terms of what it is in theory—the responsibilities the law imposes or the benefits it confers, if and when it is perfectly enforced. One can also look at the law with a firm awareness that the law is imperfectly enforced: law enforcement is discriminatory along a number of parameters, the courts are slow to act and expensive to gain access to, and many violations of legal rights go undetected or unenforced. With this realistic perspective one can see the law in terms of what one can or cannot get away with or what one can get, despite what one is entitled to. One can also step back and look at the law and compare it to one's own notions of right and wrong. What should be the law? What is just?

To a certain extent, the choice of perspective depends on the reader's purpose. Lawyers are generally asked to give their opinion based on the "what I can get away with" perspective. Indeed, many people look at the law with that in mind. In advising their clients, however, lawyers should also be aware of what their rights are in theory, if for no other reason than to discover and criticize and, maybe someday, change the imperfections that prevent the theory from becoming the law.

The first two perspectives would seem to be particularly appropriate in the field of public health. Certainly the law as it relates to the public's health should be looked at in theory as well as in practice. The most striking observation that can be made after considering these perspectives is that the law as it relates to public health generally in theory promotes and protects the public's health, but the law as it is applied and practiced often frustrates those goals.

The third perspective mentioned above is also important. What the law should be is as important a question as what the law is. Certainly one has to ask that question when looking at the realities of the law, the inequities and injustices that it does not correct, and those that it tends to perpetuate. That same question should also be asked of the law in theory: to promote or protect the public's health is a laudable, critical, and extremely important goal, but unless the definition of the public's health is very broad, that is not the only goal of a society or of its legal system. There are other notions of justice that will occasionally conflict with the promotion of the public's health: there is the idea that there are means that the legal system or the government cannot employ, even for the end of improving the public's health, and there are notions of individual privacy and dignity and notions of free choice of the individual, even where that choice may be contrary to the individual's best interest. It is important to identify these conflicts, just as it is important to identify the gap between the law in theory and the law in practice.

References

Black, C.: The occasions of justice, 1963.

Butler, S.: Erewhon, 1922.

Friedman, L.: A history of American law, 1973.

Freund, P.: On law and justice, 1968.

Fryer, W., and Orentlieher, H.: Legal method, legal system, 1967.

Fuller, L.: The morality of law, rev. ed., 1969.

Gardner, J.: Grendel, 1972.

Hayt, E., Hayt, L., and Groeschel, A.: Law of hospital, physician, and patient, Part I, ed. 3, 1972.

Hill, C.: Rights and wrongs, 1969.

Llewellyn, K.: The common law tradition: deciding appeals, 1960.

Pollack, E.: Fundamentals of legal research, ed. 3, 1967.

Pollack, E.: Human rights, 1971.

Price, M., and Bitner, H.: Effective legal research, ed. 3, 1969.

Redman, E.: The dance of legislation, 1973.

Reich, C.: New property, Yale L.J. **73**:733, 1968.

CHAPTER 2

The power of the state governments in matters affecting the public's health

This chapter and the three that follow it will focus on one major set of legal rights relating to public health: the legal rights that define the relationship between the people and their government. The present chapter will be primarily concerned with the legal rights of the state governments—generally referred to not as the state's rights, but as the state's powers—to control the conduct of individual people in matters relating to their own or the public's health.

Federal constitutional authority

To define the powers of the government at either the state or the federal level, one should start with the constitutions that establish the basic legal framework of the state and federal institutions.

The U.S. Constitution sets out the explicit enumerated powers of the federal government. All other powers not granted explicitly to the federal government by the U.S. Constitution are retained by the state governments or by the people themselves. This is true because historically the original state governments preceded the formation of the federal government and took on all of the powers traditionally held by governments. This is literally true. The colonists who settled early America and the settlers who expanded into the rest of the continent came as individuals and formed governments that eventually evolved into the states that exist today. It was only later that a federal government was formed. Some of the states were formed after the federal government was instituted, but the various territories first became states and only after statehood were they admitted to the federal union.

It was through the collective agreement that is the U.S. Constitution that the state governments decided to give up certain explicit governmental powers to a federal government of a higher authority. They did so reluctantly and carefully. By explicit provision of the U.S. Constitution all other governmental powers not explicitly granted to the federal government are reserved to the states. The tenth amendment to the U.S. Constitution reads:

> The powers not delegated to the United States by the Constitution nor prohibited by it to the States, are reserved to the States respectively, or to the people.

Because of this principle, any federal government activity must be explicitly allowed by one of the enumerated powers of the Constitution.

It is worth noting that in some ways this is not very descriptive of the role that the federal government has actually taken, particularly since the American depression of the 1930's.

As a response to the greater demands of a more complicated society, the federal government has taken on a far more active role in the governing of our nation than was probably contemplated at the time of the drafting of the U.S. Constitution. This more active role has occurred through amendments to the Constitution, but also through interpretation of the enumerated federal powers in ever-expanding terms. For example, the explicit power of the federal government to regulate interstate commerce has been expanded not just to include the power to literally regulate interstate commerce, but also to regulate goods after they have passed through interstate commerce as well as activities that are only indirectly related to people or goods that have previously passed through state borders. The courts have also interpreted the federal power to tax as including broad powers to regulate and control whatever federal tax revenues are spent for.

Notwithstanding these broad and expanding interpretations, the principle remains that the federal government must operate within enumerated powers, and federal government activities must be justified in terms of one or more of the explicit provisions of the U.S. Constitution. This is and will be an important issue in public health and will be raised again in subsequent chapters. One need only compare this principle to the active role the federal government has taken in the last 30 years in promoting and maintaining the public's health and to the variety of current proposals for national health insurance, manpower redistribution, and facility regulation to see how questions might arise. No matter what the advantages of the active federal role or the merits of the various proposals, each will have to be justified as within explicit, constitutionally permissible federal governmental power.

State constitutional authority

In direct contrast to the federal government's explicit powers, the state governments have extremely broad, inherent powers to act; they are not limited to the exercise of power explicitly defined by the state or federal constitutions. Under our legal system the state governments may exercise all powers traditionally inherent in government itself.

As mentioned above, groups of individuals came to this country and formed governments that later became states. It can be argued that therefore there may be areas of human conduct that are inherently beyond the reach of the state's broad powers and withheld by the people themselves. Certainly the tenth amendment implies that there are such inherent rights reserved to the people. However clear that implication is, it should be pointed out that this amendment has never been interpreted to support the existence of any individual right. No court has ever admitted to the existence of an individual right inherent in individual people, even though in theory all governments operate under powers granted to them by their citizens.

In describing the extent of the state's power, it is much more accurate to say that the states hold broad sweeping powers to act; they are the primary repository of powers and rights. The major constraints on the extent of that power are (1) the explicit powers granted to the federal government (or prohibited to the states) by the U.S. Constitution and (2) the individual rights of citizens explicitly enumerated in the federal and state constitutions.

Since the state's powers derive not from only constitutional provisions but also from inherent powers implied in the legal basis of our system, state's powers, known as police powers, are very difficult to define. In the broadest usage of the term the courts have defined the police powers to be all of the legitimate functions of government. This may be a complete definition, but it is not very useful. Other courts have added some specificity and used the definition that the police powers of the state are powers inherent in the state to prescribe, within the limits of the state and federal constitutions, reasonable regulations necessary to preserve the public order, health, safety, and welfare.

The police powers that are relevant to public health exemplify the nature of police powers in general. Throughout the years, with the almost endless ways in which the state legislatures have chosen to exercise their police powers, these legislative enactments and the implementation of these enactments by the executive branch of the state governments have almost always been upheld by the courts as proper exercise of power as long as they could somehow be justified as providing for the public's health. This broad power over matters affecting the public's health has also been delegated from the state to local and municipal governments, particularly with regard to enforcement of public health laws in the local area. This delegation by the state legislature to another level of government has also almost always been upheld.

Although there is no specific definition of police powers in matters of public health, the courts have found that there are two basic purposes that justify the state's actions with regard to public health: (1) actions for the protection of the health of a given individual and (2) action's for the protection of society at large. That is, under our legal system it is a legitimate purpose of government to protect the health of an individual even when, in some instances, it is over his or her own objection. As the cases to be described later will illustrate, the logic is apparently that the state can act with strictly paternal motives to prevent the individual from eventually becoming a burden on society. It is not necessary that the individual present a direct risk to the health of anyone else before the state can intervene in the individual's life.

Limitations on governmental authority

It is obvious that either of the above purposes, if carried to its extreme, could justify any number of things that should be repugnant to a free society and, as will be shown, are not properly within the state's powers. State governmental actions are not simply valid because they are intended to protect any one individual's health or to protect the health of the public. There are some important limitations.

The first major category of limitation on the state government has been mentioned above. The state cannot perform certain functions that have been prohibited by the Federal Constitution or granted to the authority of the federal government. The second major category of limitations are individual rights, rights secured to individual people by either the state or federal constitutions. It is helpful to think of these individual rights as falling within two subcategories—procedural and substantive rights.

When either the federal or state government acts, even if the action is within their valid governmental power and within the proper purposes, there are still limits on *how* the government must act and by *what means.* The basic sources of these procedural limitations are the due process clause of the fifth amendment (prohibiting the federal government from depriving any person of life, liberty, or property without due process of law) and the fourteenth amendment (imposing on the states a similar requirement of due process). In most state constitutions there are also requirements that the state provide its citizens with due process of law.

The specific meaning and requirements of due process will be explored in a number of different contexts and in great depth in Chapter 3. For initial purposes, it is probably best to think of due process as requiring different specific procedures depending upon the circumstances under consideration but requiring generally that whatever the government does it must do so using fundamentally fair procedures.

Substantive individual rights refer to the various individual rights that have been interpreted to be in the state or federal constitutions, primarily those in the first ten amendments to the U.S. Constitution, the Bill of Rights. Examples of these are the freedom of speech, the right to be free from cruel and unusual punishment, and the right to privacy. Where the exercise of the state's police powers causes too great of an infringement on one or more basic individual rights, that exercise of power may be checked or limited. As one court put it, "the [police] power is for the security of liberty and not for oppression."

As with so many other important legal concepts, it is hard to define with any precision the exact circumstances under which the security of liberty becomes oppressive. The only way to describe it other than by a series of examples is to say that in a conflict between the state government exercising its (valid) police powers in matters involving the public's health and an individual claiming that individual constitutional rights are being violated by that exercise of power, the courts often weigh the purposes of the state against the importance of the individual's rights; either the state or the individual may prevail. Almost by definition any exercise of the state's police powers in the field of public health restricts someone's individual rights in some way. As will be shown, sometimes the infringement of individual rights is quite drastic, yet the courts have upheld the state's power. As the state's justification becomes less convincing and the individual rights involved become more drastically abridged, the exercise of power may be invalidated. It is the relative importance of the state's basic purposes of protecting the health of a given individual and of society as a whole and this "weighing process" that the courts must go through to compare the state's purposes to the individual rights involved that must be understood to understand the nature of the state's powers in matters relating to the public's health.

The archetypical case involving an examination of the state's powers in matters affecting the public's health is *Jacobson v. Massachusetts,* 197 U.S. 11 (1905).

In 1902 a man named Jacobson refused to comply with a Massachusetts statute that required compulsory smallpox vaccination (for all adults). His argument was that the statute invaded his personal liberty and that:

> . . . a compulsory vaccination law is unreasonable, arbitrary and oppressive, and, therefore hostile to the inherent right of every freeman to care for his own body and health in such a way as to him seems best; and that the execution of such a law against one who objects to vaccination, no matter for what reason, is nothing short of an assault upon his person.

Jacobson's arguments fell on deaf ears in the state trial court and in his appeal to the state supreme court. Jacobson then appealed to the U.S. Supreme Court claiming that the state was exercising authority beyond its constitutional powers and in violation of his individual constitutional rights.

The Supreme Court denied his appeal. The opinion of the court found that the state was very clearly within its legitimate authority:

> The authority of the State to enact this statute is to be referred to what is commonly called the police power—a power which the state did not surrender when becoming a member of the Union under the Constitution. Although this court has refrained from any attempt to define the limits of that power, yet it has distinctly recognized the authority of a State to enact quarantine laws and "health laws of every description"; indeed, all laws that relate to matters completely within its territory and which do not by their necessary operation affect the people of other States. According to settled principles the police powers of a State must be held to embrace, at least, such reasonable regulations established directly by legislative enactment as will protect the public and public safety. . . . The mode or manner in which those results are to be accomplished is within the discretion of the State, subject, of course, so far as Federal power is concerned, only to the condition that no rule prescribed by a State, nor any regulation adopted by a local government agency acting under the sanction of state legislation, shall contravene the Constitution of the United States or infringe any right secured by that instrument.

This is one of the clearest overall summaries of the breadth of the state's power in the field of public health and the wide latitude given to the states in implementing those powers. The state may enact "health laws in every description" and "such reasonable regulations established directly by legislative enactment as will protect the public health and the public safety." Within these wide bounds, the only limitations on the state's power suggested by the court were where the exercise of power interfered with a power of the federal government or where it interfered with an individual constitutional right. There was no claim that federal power was being interfered with. As for Jacobson's claim that the statute interfered with his personal liberty and his "right to make personal decisions about his person," the court found that in the face of the obvious public interest in preventing small pox, these rights must be subordinated. Although there is a "sphere within which the individual may assert the supremacy of his own will and rightfully dispute the authority of any human government," the court held:

> . . . the liberty secured by the Constitution of the United States to every person within its jurisdiction does not impart an absolute right in each person to be, at all times and in all circumstances, wholly freed from restraint. There are manifold restraints to which every person is necessarily subject for the common good . . .

. . . (liberty) is only freedom from restraint under conditions essential to the equal enjoyment of the same right by others. It is then liberty regulated by law.

This is not to deny the existence of a personal right to liberty; it is the judgment that, at least in this particular situation involving compulsory vaccination of the public against smallpox, that right is subordinated to the state's power and its purpose of protecting the public.

The broad range of state authority in matters relating to the public's health

The courts have upheld the validity of the state's exercise of power in matters relating to the public's health in a variety of similar situations. The power of the state to examine, quarantine, and, in some cases, treat people suspected of carrying contagious diseases, has been consistently recognized. Compulsory medical examinations and treatment, e.g., vaccination, of children prior to and during school attendance has been held to be valid, as has compulsory examination of people getting married or engaging in certain occupations where they will be exposed to the public. Likewise, the state may require compliance with fire, safety, and sanitation laws, in both private and public buildings. The state's power has also been interpreted to include the right to fluoridate the public water supply. Why are all these actions valid? Because it is clearly within the state's power to act when the purpose of the action is related to the protection of the public's health. Not only is it within the state's power, but the state is given broad discretion in choosing its approach and the circumstances for its activity.

Another broad area within which the state has proper authority to act involves the civil commitment of certain categories of people. It has been recognized that the state may involuntarily confine the mentally ill, the mentally retarded, drug abusers, or epileptics. This involves a very serious deprivation of liberty and an infringement of almost every individual right. Recently, this state power to civilly confine people has come under more rigid scrutiny in terms of the validity of the procedures that are used and the realities of the confinement. Both these aspects of civil commitment will be treated in some depth in Chapter 3, and further analysis will be deferred. Notwithstanding these developments, there is no doubt that civil commitment, using proper procedures and within certain circumstantial constraints, is a valid exercise of the state's police powers.

Compulsory sterilization

The state's police powers have been allowed to do more than confine and provide treatment to the mentally ill and other related categories of people. It has been upheld that the state has the power to require the compulsory sterilization of the mentally ill. In *Buck v. Bell,* 274 U.S. 200 (1927), the Supreme Court upheld the Virginia law allowing the state to sterilize mental patients under certain circumstances. The opinion summarizes the facts and the reasoning better than any paraphrase:

Carrie Buck is a feeble minded white woman who was committed to the State Colony above mentioned in due form. She is the daughter of a feeble minded mother in the same institution, and the mother of an illegitimate feeble minded child. She was eighteen years old at the time of the trial of her case in the Circuit Court, in the latter part of 1924. An Act of Virginia, approved March 20, 1924, recites that the health of the patient, and the welfare of society may be promoted in certain cases by the sterilization of mental defectives, . . . that the Commonwealth is supporting in various institutions many defective persons who if now discharged would become a menace but if incapable of procreating might be discharged with safety and become self-supporting with benefit to themselves and to society; and that experience has shown that heredity plays an important part in the transmission of insanity, imbecility . . .

. . . In view of the general declarations of the legislature and the specific findings of the Court, obviously we cannot say as a matter of law that the grounds do not exist, and if they exist they justify the result. We have seen more than once that the public welfare may call upon the best citizens for their lives. It would be strange if it could not call upon those who already sap the strength of the State for these lesser sacrifices, often not felt to be such by those concerned, in order to prevent our being swamped with incompetence. It is better for all the world, if instead of waiting to execute degenerate offspring for crime, or to let them starve for their imbecility, society can prevent those who are manifestly unfit from continuing their kind. The principle that sustains compulsory vaccination is broad enough to cover cutting the Fallopian tubes. *Jacobson v. Massachusetts,* 197 U.S. 11. Three generations of imbeciles are enough.

This opinion would be remarkable enough if it were a lower appellate court and not the U.S. Supreme Court. It is even more remarkable since it is written by Oliver Wendell Holmes, not the least talented of the Justices who have served the Court. Since it is now nearly 50 years later, it can be argued that our more sophisticated knowledge of the etiology of imbecility (and even the use of the term) might be used to challenge Mr. Justice Holmes' conclusions, but at least at this point in time, no one has done so successfully. The case still stands as a valid interpretation of law. Many states still have laws allowing for the compulsory sterilization of mental patients, and some involuntary sterilizations are being performed. Oregon, for example, reported doing "only" a few dozen in 1973.

The interpretation of the state's police power to involuntarily sterilize people has been narrowed since the decision in *Buck v. Bell,* both with regard to mental patients and similar laws that are less frequent today but that still exist in some states and allow involuntary sterilization of "habitual criminal offenders." Some lower state and federal courts have found specific state sterilization statutes within legitimate state police powers, but not properly implemented. Thus where a statute failed to provide notice or an opportunity to be heard to the person whose sterilization is proposed, the law was held to be unconstitutional as a violation of due process. Another statute was held to be cruel and unusual punishment and violative of the eighth amendment in a case where the sterilization was apparently for punishment as much as for the prevention of procreation. Despite its holding in *Buck v. Bell,* the Supreme Court later declared unconstitutional an Oklahoma statute, *Oklahoma v. Skinner,* 316 U.S. 535 (1942), that allowed the compulsory sterilization of a "habitual criminal" because the statute violated the requirements of the equal protection clause of the fourteenth amendment. That statute permitted the sterilization of anyone who was convicted on three successive felonies, but it exempted felons convicted of the violation of the prohibitory laws, revenue acts, embezzlement, or political offenses. (Could the members of the legislature who wrote the law have been protecting themselves?) This kind of arbitrary distinction between two categories of felons without any apparent rationale is a violation of the requirement of equal protection of the laws. (For further explanation, see Chapter 3.) By relying on such narrow grounds for declaring the law unconstitutional, the court intentionally avoided reexamining the validity of the state's power to sterilize "undesirables" and avoided reviewing the underlying assumption of the state law that criminality is hereditary. In a concurring opinion one of the Justices of the Court outlined the questions left unanswered in the *Skinner* case:

> I also think the present plan to sterilize the individual in pursuit of a eugenic plan to eliminate from the race characteristics that are only vaguely identified and which in our present state of knowledge are uncertain as to transmissibility presents other constitutional questions of gravity. This court has sustained such an experiment with respect to an imbecile, a person with definite and observable characteristics, where the condition had persisted through three generations and afforded ground for the belief that it was transmissible and would continue to manifest itself in generations to come. *Buck v. Bell,* 274 U.S. 200.

> There are limits to the extent to which a legislatively represented majority may conduct biological experiments at the expense of the dignity and personality and natural powers of a minority—even those who have been guilty of what the majority defines as crimes. But this Act falls down before reaching this problem, which I mention only to avoid the implication that such a question may not exist because not discussed . . .

Almost every compulsory sterilization statute, be it for the mentally infirm or the habitual offender, can be challenged as somehow violative of the requirement of equal protection of the law; several in addition to the Oklahoma statute discussed above have been struck down. However, many have been upheld and still exist.

Hopefully, no one would seriously argue today that criminality is heritable. Those statutes still existing that provide for the compulsory sterilization of criminal offenders will eventually be invalidated on that basis. But is imbecility or any other kind of mental disability hereditable? If so, at least some courts, including the Supreme Court, have been in the past willing to recognize a police power inherent in the state to conduct such "biological experimentation" as compulsory sterilization of those, who along with their potential offspring, present a risk to our health, safety, or welfare.

Compulsory medical treatment of incompetent people: children

Another way in which the state has exercised its police powers relating to public health has involved the compulsory medical treatment of certain categories of people who are adjudged to be not capable of making their own decisions with respect to their health. This differs from the involuntary treatment of the mentally ill and other related categories of people in that the individual is considered incompetent by age or mental condition to make the necessary decision. It is not strictly speaking involuntary treatment in the same way that involuntary civil commitment is considered involuntary. (Not all mentally ill people are also incompetent, as explained below.)

One situation in which medical treatment is given to legally incompetent people is where the state uses its power to take children, who are by law considered incompetent to make decisions relating to their medical care or many other matters, from the custody of abusive or neglectful parents and provide them with compulsory (at least compulsory to the parent) medical care.

The law has always respected the autonomy of the family unit under most circumstances and recognized parents as being the primary custodians over their children. However, in situations where the health, well-being, or life of a child is jeopardized, state governments have recognized powers—if properly implemented by state legislation—to take custody of a child and provide for the child, including necessary medical treatment. Laws have also been upheld that provide for the criminal punishment of the neglecting parent(s). This is an example of what is known as the state acting in loco parentis (in the place of a parent) or parens patriae (the sovereign's power of guardianship over persons under disability). In effect these terms are little more than a specific characterization of the state's police powers, the inherent powers of a state to, among other governmental functions, act as a parent to neglected or disabled people.

Under these circumstances, children have been removed from the custody of neglectful or abusive parents or simply put under temporary guardianship while the guardian consents to the needed care. In some cases temporary guardianship is little more than a fiction, existing only long enough for the guardian to consent to a single procedure or even a single vaccination.

Medical care provided to children over the objection of the parent(s) is valid even when the parent is not neglectful or abusive in any real sense but, perhaps misguidedly, distrustful of physicians and/or hospitals, and even when the objection is based on firm religious belief. For example, the courts have repeatedly ordered blood transfusions to the children of Jehovah's Witnesses despite the fact that their religious tenets forbid any such procedure.

However, parental judgment and preference is not overlooked and is heavily weighted in applying the law. The courts are reluctant to require medical treatment for a child over the objection of his or her parent(s) except where immediate action is necessary or the potential harm is rather serious. To do otherwise would interfere with the individual rights of parents to, within limits, decide what is best for their children. This would put the courts in the uncomfortable role and oppressive position of constantly supervising parental decision making.

A good example of how this state power is recognized but weighed and balanced against the individual rights of the parent(s) is *In the Matter of Martin Seiferth*, 309 N.Y. 80, 127 N.E.2d 820 (1955).

In that case a 12-year-old boy had what was described as a massive harelip and unrepaired cleft palate. It not only detracted from his personal appearance, but it also severely limited his verbal skills. There was no real risk of physical harm, but the conditions presented a serious risk to his social and psychological growth. The boy's father thought that only the forces of the universe should work on one's body and that medicine or surgery would only interfere with those forces; the boy concurred with his father's opinion.

The county health department did not agree. Under a state statute delegating authority from the state to the county, they petitioned the local court for the custody of the child for purposes of consenting to restorative surgery. After an evidentiary hearing, the trial court denied the petition. On appeal to an intermediate appellate court, the decision was reversed. The boy's father appealed to the supreme appellate court of that jurisdiction.

After considering the evidence compiled by the trial court relating to the potential harm to the boy, the purposes justifying the country's proposed actions (as representative of the state), and the nature of the parent's objection, the court concluded that there was neither an emergency nor a serious threat to health or life. The court weighted heavily the fact that it was the boy, albeit a minor, who was objecting to the operation, not just the parent, and also considered relevant the fact that there would be time for the boy to change his mind as he grew older.

This was, however, a close case. The specific facts of the situation were as determinative of the decision as were the legal principles that the case illustrates. The case could easily have gone the other way, and the court could have ruled in favor of the county and the state's power. In fact, of the seven members of the appellate court, three dissented and would have voted to allow the county to take temporary custody of the boy. Their dissenting opinion was vigorous in its opposition:

> It is quite true that the child's physical life is not at peril as would be the situation if he had an infected appendix or a growth on the brain, but it may not be questioned, to quote from the opinion below, "What is in danger is his chance for a normal, useful life . . . "

> . . . it is the court which has a duty to perform [citation omitted] and it should not seek to avoid that duty by foisting upon the boy the ultimate decision to be made. Neither by statute nor decision is the child's consent necessary or material, and we should not permit his refusal to agree, his failure to cooperate, to ruin his life and any chance for a normal, happy existence; normalcy and happiness, difficult of attainment under the most propitious conditions, will unquestionably be impossible if the disfigurement is not remedied.

> . . . The welfare and interests of a child are at stake. A court should not place upon his shoulders one of the most momentuous and far-reaching decisions of his life. The court should make the decision, as the statute contemplates, and leave to the good sense and sound judgement of the public authorities the job of preparing the boy for the operation and getting him as adjusted to it as possible. We should not put off decision in the hope and on the chance that the child may change his mind and submit at some future time to the operation.

Compulsory medical treatment for incompetent people: adults

The *Seiferth* case suggests a similar but far more difficult situation. To what extent is the state allowed to require compulsory medical care for people who are legally incompetent, not because they are minors, but because they are determined to be mentally incompetent and not capable of making decisions with regard to their own health care?

The declaration of an individual as mentally incompetent and the concomitant appointment of a guardian occur in a number of situations. Basically the state has the power to intervene into the life of any person not capable of conducting his or her own life and affairs. The state can appoint some other person that will, as the agent of the state, make that incompetent individual's decisions. A guardian can have power over an individual or his or her property (and money) or both; the breadth of the guardian's power is defined in the court order appointing the guardian and is supposed to be tailored to the needs of the incompetent person. The determination of who is competent to make his or her own decisions is obviously based on rather vague and somewhat subjective standards, and unfortunately there are numerous instances where this power of the state has been subverted and abused.

Mental patients are usually committed under a standard that calls for a finding that they are in need of treatment. They are not automatically considered legally incompetent. Commitment is a judicial determination that the patient is, in effect, incompetent to volunteer for psychiatric treatment, but commitment does not require a finding of general incompetency. In order for someone to involuntarily provide a mental patient with nonpsychiatric medical care, a separate incompetency proceeding has to be initiated and a guardian appointed for that patient. (The guardian would then have the choice of consenting or not; as a practical matter, the guardian almost always does consent.) Similarly, an incompetency determination would have to be made following the proper legal procedures before a mental patient's control of his or her property is given to a guardian.

It is this power to appoint a guardian over allegedly incompetent people that is the means by which the state provides involuntary medical care to adults under certain circumstances. Clearly the state has the power to do so: providing for the medical care of incompetent people is little different than providing psychiatric care to mental patients, providing necessary medical care to children over the objection of their parent(s), or requiring people to submit to compulsory vaccinations. However, whereas the powers over an individual are generally based on the state's authority to protect some members of society from others, e.g., to protect the society from the mentally ill or children from their parents, the state's powers exercised over incompetent people are usually to protect these individuals from themselves. To deny an individual the rights to freedom, privacy, and self-determination may be easily justified by the threat of dangerous conduct or the risk of exposing others to contagious disease. To interfere with these rights simply to protect certain individuals from themselves is not an easily accepted justification. In fact the justification stands or falls on the reality of the incompetence. Is this really a person who is not just refusing treatment, but one who by mental deficiency is unable to make a rational choice? Understandably, the law has not always upheld the state's power to involuntarily provide medical care when the individual involved is not in the strict sense incompetent. This can be demonstrated by the following case.

In 1973 the brother of a 60-year-old woman filed a petition in a New Jersey court asking that his sister be declared incompetent and that he be appointed her guardian. The purpose behind the request was to give him the power to consent for his sister to undergo diagnostic and corrective surgery. The woman was a mental patient diagnosed as a schizophrenic, chronic undifferentiated. Her physician believed that she may have had breast cancer and recommended surgery, but she refused. At first she objected because of her fear that she might die. She believed, incorrectly, that her aunt had died during similar surgery. By the time that the case got to court, her fears were also based on her delusions that the surgery would interfere with her genitals, that she would lose her ability to have a baby, and that her chances for a movie career would be lost.

Apparently her specific delusions were not typical of her general condition. Nonetheless, her physician testified that she was incompetent to make the decision with regard to surgery. The court was faced with the dilemma of balancing the state's powers and legitimate purposes against her individual rights to freedom, self-determination, and privacy. The court concluded:

> In our opinion the constitutional right of privacy includes the right of a mature competent adult to refuse to accept medical recommendations that may prolong one's life and which, to a third person at least, appear to be in his best interests; in short, the right to privacy includes a right to die with which the State should not interfere where there are no minor or unborn children and no clear and present danger to the public health, welfare, or morals. If the person was competent while being presented with the decision and in making the decision which she did, the Court should not interfere even though her decision might be considered unwise, foolish or ridiculous.

> The testimony of the caseworker with respect to her conversations with [the woman] in December, 1972, convinces us that at that time her refusal was informed, conscious of the consequences and would not have been superceded by this Court. The ordinary person's refusal to accept medical advice based upon fear is commonly known and while the refusal may be irrational and foolish to an outside observer it cannot be said to be incompetent in order to permit the State to override the decision.

> The obvious difficulty in this proceeding is that in recent months [the woman's] steadfast refusal has been accompanied by delusions which create doubt that her decision is the product of competent, reasoned judgement. However, she has been consistent in expressing the fear that she would die if surgery were performed. The delusions do not appear to us to be her primary reason for rejecting surgery.

The court then concluded that she was entitled to make her competent but irrational decision to refuse surgery. The court clearly recognized the state's power over medical decisions of incompetent people, but did not extend that power to include people who make irrational choices.

Other courts in other jurisdictions have delineated the state's powers in very much the same way. Courts in several jurisdictions have ordered medical treatment in the form of blood transfusions to adult competent patients who refuse to consent to the transfusion based on religious beliefs. In each of these cases the courts have scrupulously avoided recognizing a broad power of the state to act in the best interests of competent adults and have justified these particular interventions on the basis of special circumstances. One court justified its ruling on the grounds that the transfusion would save the life of a yet unborn child. Another court argued that by saving the parent it was protecting the interests of the dependents of that parent. Another court simply said that in an emergency the courts must act first to protect life, especially when the law is not clear. Most every court that has faced squarely the issue of whether the state has the power to compel treatment of a competent—but arguably foolish—adult has ruled that there is no general state power to do so, but many courts have found elaborate ways to sidestep the logical consequences of that conclusion.

This may be the furthest extent of the state's power over the individual in matters involving the public's health. When the state's purpose is solely for the individual's benefit, and the individual is competent and defines his or her interest differently, the right of the individual to exercise that choice appears to be dominant. On the other hand, the courts have been quick to find exceptions to this rule, as discussed above, and other grounds for exceptions do exist. For example, if the woman refusing breast surgery had been 20 years old instead of 60, a court inclined toward allowing surgery might have cited her potential capacity to be a productive member of society. As alluded to in *Buck v. Bell,* it has been traditionally recognized that a society does have some interest in securing able-bodied people to maintain and defend itself. It might be that a "right to die" or at least risk death is something the law will more easily allow to those who are older and to whom the circumstances and dignity of death are more relevant considerations. Such a social utility argument has never been openly articulated in the law, but it is interesting that the cases that have allowed people to refuse medical treatment and disallowed compulsory medical treatment by the state have tended to involve older people and people with no societal obligations.

Yet if social utility is the measure, it would be a rather drastic affront to a number of important individual legal rights. Would not most people's sense of justice be offended if the government had the power to interfere with their life simply because the government or some one person working for the government disagreed with the way in which that life was being conducted?

Conclusion

Whatever the actual specific limits on the state's police powers in matters affecting the public's health, the most important thing is to understand the general principles that determine the specific cases. The state has broad, sweeping powers to act in matters affecting the health, safety, and welfare of the public. In implementing these powers the states have to act within certain procedural limitations, as will be more fully explicated in the next chapter. The law also recognizes certain individual rights such as privacy and the exercise of religion. A valid state purpose will often justify the deleterious impact that the state's action may have on these individual rights, but that is not always the case. The courts often find themselves weighing those valid state purposes against the rights of individual people, and at some point the importance of those rights requires that limitations be put on the extent of the state's powers and the means that the state can use to implement them. This process of balancing and the points at which the scales dip in either direction are issues that defy simple explanation. However, these are the key issues that will be involved throughout the entire discussion of the rights that exist between the government and the individual.

References

Curran, W., and Shapiro, E.: Law, medicine, and forensic science, ed. 2, 1970.

Grad, F.: Public health law manual, ed. 3, 1973.

Power of courts or other public agencies, in the absence of statutory authority, to order compulsory medical care, Annot., 9 A.L.R.3d 1391 (1966).

Related cases

Application of President and Directors of Georgetown College, 331 F.2d 1000 (C.A.D.C. 1964).

Barsky v. Board of Regents of the University of the State of New York, 347 U.S. 442 (1954).

Schuringa v. The City of Chicago, 30 Ill.2d 504, 198 N.E.2d 326 (1964).

Slaughter-house Cases, 83 U.S. 36 (1872).

United States ex rel. Siegel v. Shinnick, 219 F. Supp. 789 (E.D.N.Y. 1963).

United States v. Omar, Inc., 91 F. Supp. 121 (D.Neb. 1950).

CHAPTER 3 **The state's police powers
and involuntary civil commitment**

Given the overview of the state's police powers in the previous chapter, this chapter will focus on one specific area within those powers and in this way try to further elucidate the legal rights that exist between the individual and the government.

As stated previously, it has been firmly recognized in the law that the state has broad powers to civilly commit, meaning involuntarily confine and treat, the mentally ill, as well as other categories of people such as drug addicts and the mentally retarded. This is legally justified as serving the legitimate state purpose of protecting the health and safety of the society and of the individual involved. Despite the fact that commitment is clearly within the state's powers, as with other legitimate state police powers there are limitations on the extent of this power, and there are some major procedural limitations that the state must observe in implementing this power.

The various forms of civil commitment

Confinement and treatment of the mentally ill is considered "civil"; this is to be distinguished from the criminal process by which the state punishes people who are found to be guilty of crimes. In theory civil confinement is more benevolent than criminal confinement; this has certain legal implications that will be explained throughout this chapter.

To begin with, one must distinguish between the various kinds of civil commitment. For the most part, civil commitment means the process by which people are declared in need of treatment, confined, and treated. This basically requires a finding that a person is mentally ill. Two other processes also exist that result in civil commitment; both involve people who have been first accused of a crime.

Accused criminals may be committed prior to their criminal trial if they are found to be incompetent to stand trial. The question is not whether they are mentally ill, but whether they are incompetent, meaning in this situation that they cannot assist in their defense and do not understand the nature of the proceedings against them. The theory is that it would be unfair to force someone to stand trial who is incompetent and who with treatment might regain competency; however, it is somewhat ironic that in the name of fairness people are confined civilly for treatment to avoid the risk that they might be confined criminally.

Another form of civil commitment results when an accused individual is found not guilty of a crime by reason of insanity. Here the question is not the presence of mental illness or the individual's present competence, but the mental condition of the individual at the time of the crime; in general if an individual is found to be unable to distinguish between right and wrong at the time of a crime, he or she is technically not guilty of the crime, even if in fact he or she did commit the crime. In most states this not guilty defendant is then civilly committed, but this automatic commitment is particularly questionable in light of the *Jackson* case, which will be discussed on p. 45.

This chapter will be concerned primarily with the first category of civil commitment, although the legal issues to be discussed will be applicable to all three types of commitment.

The importance of civil commitment as a legal issue

It is important to focus on this particular state police power when examining public health law. As an example of the state's police powers, civil commitment dramatically illustrates the legal issues involved. On the one hand, a mentally ill person can be clearly in need of treatment and/or present a direct threat to the safety of society. On the other, civil commitment involves the most serious abridgment of individual rights imaginable—the total denial of freedom and privacy, often for long periods of time and often under abhorrent conditions. It is a good example of how the state's purposes must be balanced against the individual's rights. But not only is civil commitment a good illustration, it is itself no small problem. Estimates of the number of people hospitalized in mental institutions in this country range between one-half million and 700,000; many of these people are involuntarily confined. That is at least twice the number of people in jails and prisons. Compared to the system for providing medical care services, the system for providing psychiatric services is still relatively large and larger than many people realize. Approximately 40% of the hospital beds in this country are used for psychiatric patients.

What is probably more dramatic and certainly more shocking is that civil commitment is a topic in public health law that demonstrates the legal system at its very worst. Despite the fact that important legal rights are at stake in civil commitment and the courts' proper function would be to interpret these rights and balance the state's interests against those of the individual, until recently, most courts have been little more than rubber stamps for physicians' decisions. This behavior still characterizes the judiciary in many parts of the country.

It is quite proper that courts should turn to the medical profession for psychiatric evaluations and opinions, but courts have very often deferred the decision to commit entirely to the medical decision maker. This is in effect allowing the medical opinion to make two decisions: (1) the medical justification of the commitment and (2) the legal justification of the commitment. It is the latter decision that the courts have often failed to question. This can almost be quantified. Regardless of the literally millions of people who have been involuntarily civilly committed, extremely few decisions have ever been appealed; consequently, very few judicial opinions exist that interpret the state's power to civilly commit mentally ill individuals. This can only be characterized as a failure by the courts to play their proper role in the interpretation and enforcement of the law.

By far the most important reason for this failure of the judiciary to play its role is economic. Our entire legal system is based on an assumption of the financial ability to gain access to it. The civil commitment process is no exception. Courts rely on the adversary system to function properly. Consequently, only people who can afford legal counsel have a meaningful opportunity to protect and enforce their rights. Our legal system simply does not work when it comes to protecting the rights of poor people, and, at least in public mental institutions, people involuntarily committed are almost always poor. Even with the advent of governmentally sponsored legal services programs for indigent people, mentally ill individuals are usually precluded by their condition or by their confinement from reaching even the few legal services programs that are available for the poor.

The focus of the blame should not be entirely on the judiciary for failing to protect the rights of individuals in civil commitment. Many state legislatures have passed civil commitment statutes with glaring constitutional inadequacies reflecting a similar lack of concern for individual rights and a willingness to allow virtually unchecked authority for committing people to be placed in the hands of the medical profession. As an example of a statute of this type, one should consider the civil commitment statute that existed in South Carolina until 1973.

The Code of Laws of South Carolina Title 32, sections 32-954 through 32-970, provides for four separate procedures by which an individual may be civilly committed to a mental hospital in that state.

Under the procedure provided by sections 32-954 and 32-955, any individual may be summarily committed without a judicial hearing upon (1) the application to the hospital by any person, (2) the certification "by two designated examiners" that the individual is mentally ill and either in need of hospitalization and unable to recognize that fact or likely to injure himself or others, and (3) the endorsement of the certificate by a probate court judge.

Under sections 32-956 and 32-957, any individual may be summarily committed without judicial hearing upon (1) the application by any person, (2) the certification by a physician that he or she has examined and found the individual to be insane and likely to injure himself or others, and (3) the endorsement by a probate court judge.

Under section 32-958, an individual may be committed but only after (1) the application by any person; (2) the certification by a licensed physician certifying that the individual is mentally ill (or a written statement that the individual has refused to be examined); (3) notice of the proceedings to all interested parties, including the individual; (4) examination by two designated examiners; (5) a judicial hearing prior to commitment before the probate court wherein (a) testimony is heard by the judge, (b) all interested parties can attend and cross-examine witnesses, and (c) counsel, appointed at the expense of the court if necessary, is present to represent the individual; and (6) opportunity to appeal to the circuit court. Not unexpectedly, this procedure has rarely been used. The first two procedures, relying almost entirely on the decisions of physicians and devoid of legal procedures, have been used to commit several thousand people each year.

The fourth procedure is related to the commitment of individuals charged with crime.

The South Carolina statute is fairly typical of the commitment law in most states until recently as well as the law as it still exists in many states. The last two decades have, however, marked the beginning of a period of reexamination of these laws.

The 1960's brought a number of changes to the legal system that involved an increased concern for the rights of individuals with respect to governmental power. Among the most important developments was the recognition and enforcement of the constitutional rights of the criminally accused, particularly the right of the accused indigent individual to appointed legal counsel. Courts started examining more critically the procedures by which accused criminals are tried and confined, and attorneys become available to advocate the rights of accused people. Some courts and some attorneys brought attention to the analogous situation of the "civil" process by which people accused of being mentally ill are confined and treated.

This period of reexamination has only begun, and the answers to many of the long-overlooked questions are yet to be determined. The attitudes of the courts, the legislatures, and even society in general have not changed to any great extent, and, of course, there is still the problem that the legal system relies heavily on financial access to it. Consequently, even the legal rights that are recognized are not always respected and enforced. But the law in theory and in practice as it relates to civil commitment is changing relatively rapidly. In the next decade many questions that are today unanswered will be litigated, and predictably one of the results will be that the state's powers to civilly commit will be in some ways limited.

The reexamination of the state's powers to civilly commit the mentally ill has not been and probably will not be directed at the legality of that power itself. Civil commitment is clearly one of the state's legitimate police powers. The thrust has been in two somewhat different directions: (1) an examination of the adequacy of the procedures used in the commitment process and (2) an examination of the purposes of civil commitment in light of the realities of the resulting confinement. Each of these trends will be discussed separately.

The constitutional adequacy of civil commitment procedures

The first trend in the reexamination of civil commitment involves the procedures used, the means by which the state government carries out this public health related police power.

Constitutional limitations on civil commitment procedures

What are the procedures that a state must follow in civil commitment in order to conform to the law? To state the same question in different terms, what are the procedural rights of the individual in the civil commitment context? Given the nature of this book, it is probably justified to digress slightly in answering these questions to the general concepts outlined in Chapter 1. When considering what the law is, it is important to remember the various kinds of laws. An easy trap to fall into is to think of legal rights only in terms of constitutional rights. Actually, as a practical matter, constitutional rights, though critically important, are the hardest and the most expensive to enforce. To answer the questions above one should look first at the state statute that authorizes civil commitment and see what procedures are required by the statute; then one should look to any administrative regulations promulgated under the authority of that statute to see what procedures are required by regulation. To be complete, one should also look at state and possibly federal judicial interpretations of these statutes and regulations; then, and only then, would one look to state and federal constitutional law, by applying to the statute and regulations judicial interpretations of the constitution(s) and by direct application of the various constitutional provisions.

With regard to state governmental activities in this particular area of the law, the constitutionally defined legal rights become very important because the procedures that have been provided by statute and regulation and interpreted by the courts over the years are woefully inadequate. This would not be necessarily true in other areas of the law that involve the exercise of governmental power over individuals. With regard to civil commitment, however, constitutional rights are extremely important. Of the various constitutional rights relating to procedures that must be used by state governments when dealing with individuals, the most important are the requirements of due process and of equal protection of the laws guaranteed by the fourteenth amendment to the U.S. Constitution and included in the provisions of most state constitutions. The fourteenth amendment reads:

> All persons born or naturalized in the United States, and subject to the jurisdiction thereof, are citizens of the United States and of the State wherein they reside. No State shall make or enforce any law which shall abridge the privileges or immunities of citizens of the United States; nor shall any State deprive any person of life, liberty, or property without due process of law; nor deny to any person within its jurisdiction the equal protection of the law.

(The federal government must also provide due process and equal protection in its exercise of power over individuals under the fifth amendment.)

The requirement of due process

The requirement that the state provide individuals with due process is the single most important mandate of the U.S. Constitution. But what does it mean when specifically applied to any one of the thousands of relationships between the government and an individual? An attempted answer to this question could be in the form of an encyclopedia of the thousands of cases that have interpreted this clause as applied to specific sets of facts. To generalize, it is the requirement of basic fairness in the exercise of power by the government. Among other things it requires that the government use fundamentally fair procedures in exercising its police powers. To be more specific than that requires an analysis of the specific power under consideration.

In the criminal context the requirement of due process has been interpreted in a vast number of situations, and consequently the procedures that are constitutionally required by the due process clause in a criminal proceeding are relatively well defined and generally well known; for example, the right to counsel in a criminal proceeding, the right to jury trial, and the right to "Miranda" warnings when held in custody are considered fundamentally fair procedures in the criminal context. With regard to civil commitment, it is not as easy to specifically define what due process means because the due process clause has not been applied to the civil commitment context very frequently. The law has for many years neglected these proceedings, and few courts have addressed themselves to the issues they raise.

One can draw an analogy between the individual accused of being mentally ill and the individual accused of a crime. One might imagine that the law would simply take those procedures that it requires as fundamentally fair in the one context and require them in the other. However, that has not been done and will not be done in the future. Although the due process requirement of fundamentally fair procedures has and will require in civil commitment that the state follow some of the procedures required in the criminal process, even modern courts have always allowed the states more leeway in committing the mentally ill. Courts scrutinize the procedures used in a civil process less rigorously. To some extent it is because some of the procedures used with accused criminals would be inappropriate for individuals accused of being mentally ill (e.g., a jury trial before any confinement when the individual is actively psychotic). This is also done because of the persistent notion that civil commitment is civil—intended at least in part to help the confined individual—as distinguished from the criminal process, where the emphasis is on deterrence and punishment; rehabilitation of the criminal is only a secondary goal, if it is a goal at all. When the state has the more benevolent purposes, the law is not so rigid in its enforcement of limitations on the state. From a practical point of view this is a debatable distinction, but the law has always made it nonetheless. In applying the due process clause to civil commitment, it is necessary to assume that this civil/criminal distinction will always be one of the factors distinguishing the specific reqirements of fundamentally fair procedures in one situation from those specific procedures required under the same principle in another situation.

Referring to the South Carolina statute as an example of a traditional state civil commitment statute, does the due process clause require that those people committed under sections 32-954 and 32-955 or sections 32-956 and 32-957 be provided with a judicial hearing despite the fact that the statute does not require one? Does the requirement of due process mandate that these individuals be provided with legal counsel if they can not afford one? Each of these questions would require a court to examine whether or not the procedures are fundamentally fair in conformance with the requirements of due process. At this point in time there have been few definitive answers, although these are exactly the sorts of questions that are now coming before the courts. Predictions of what specific procedures will be required would at this point be little more than educated guesses anticipating future court decisions. The general principles of due process will be applied, however, just as they would be in any relationship between the government and the individual.

The fundamental requirements of notice, hearing, and counsel

Although the specific requirements of fundamentally fair procedures depend on the circumstances under consideration, in all cases the general principles of due process wil require some kind of notice to the individual involved, some kind of hearing, and almost always representation of the individual by legal counsel. Notice, hearing, and counsel are the foundation of the adversary system and are usually regarded as the minimum requirements for fair procedures. Clearly the two summary procedures for civil commitment allowed by the South Carolina statute will be found to be unconstitutional and violative of due process. At no point before or after the actual confinement is the allegedly mentally ill individual given an opportunity for a hearing. Also, for that hearing to be fair, it would have to be preceded by advance notice to the individual. Moreover, to make the defense meaningful, the individual would have to be represented by his or her own legal counsel. It should be pointed out that the right to *appointed* counsel at the expense of the court is an extension of the basic right to be represented by counsel if one has (and can afford) counsel. In anything as crucial to individual liberty as civil commitment it is safe to predict that due process will require not only the right to counsel, but the right to court-appointed counsel as well, in order for the process to be considered fundamentally fair.

In understanding these basic requirements of due process and applying them to specific situations such as civil commitment or any of the other areas of state police powers, it is important to understand why they are considered so basic and essential.

Why are the requirements of notice and hearing so important? Notifying the individual is the first step in giving an individual the opportunity to defend against the charge. Notice informs the individual of whatever opportunity to defend is available and of the state's allegations, and it gives the individual an opportunity to prepare that defense. Thus the concept of notice involves not only a communication of information, but it also implies notification sufficiently in advance to allow a reasonable amount of preparation. It is obviously unfair not to tell someone what to defend against or to deny an opportunity to do so. Furthermore, that opportunity, whatever it is, would be meaningless unless the affected individual is informed of it and informed in advance to allow time for preparation.

A hearing is that opportunity to defend. Hearings can take a number of forms ranging from an informal discussion with the decision maker (which is all that is required by due process in some situations) to a full-blown jury trial (which is required in situations where the rights at stake are very important). Whatever the form of the hearing, it is an opportunity to confront the decision maker and to advocate the interests of the accused person. In the most basic sense a hearing is a safeguard against errors. It is an opportunity to present the decision maker with evidence or argument that shows that the contemplated decision is based on incorrect information, is poorly conceived, or, possibly, is not within the legal authority of the decision maker. This is true whether the decision maker is a judge in a criminal trial or a public official in an administrative agency's hearing.

Not only is a hearing a safeguard against errors, it also serves the purpose of forcing the decision to be made publicly. Hearings are open to at least some members of the public (at the very least the individual involved represents the public). The assumption is that an openly made decision is not only better conceived and less likely erroneous, but not as easily corrupted or abused. If the decision maker knows that his or her decision and the reasons for it are open to public examination, it is predictable that the decision will be made more carefully and more honestly.

Beyond that, there is also the notion that it is just to require that the government make decisions publicly. The Kafkaesque notion that the government could make secret decisions that affect the lives of its citizens is itself offensive to most people, apart from whether or not the decision itself is good or bad. People simply like to participate, even as observers, in things that affect their lives. This is a good illustration of one aspect of justice underlying the theory and hopefully the practice of our legal system; whatever justice is, it has at least a somewhat dual nature. It is not merely a good, fair, or equitable end; it requires that the law achieve these ends by good, fair, or equitable means. Justice must be served by the process just as it should be served by the outcome. The requirement of some form of hearing and a publicly made decision, as well as the requirement that this opportunity be preceded by notice to those who will be affected, illustrates that aspect of justice; this is part of the reason that the law holds these procedural requirements as essential to fundamental fairness.

Why is legal counsel so often considered an essential requirement of due process?

A lawyer can assist the individual involved in a number of ways. Obviously, in most situations only a lawyer can explain to the individual involved the relevant legal issues, and only a lawyer can make the proper legal arguments that may be available to defend the individual. Lawyers also have skills that go beyond their abilities to research and interpret the law. Lawyers are skilled in argument and in presenting facts in their most convincing manner; anyone who has ever seen a skillful attorney cross-examine a witness will be convinced of that. This does not mean that all attorneys are that skillful or that some people are not able to defend themselves. However, it is important to note that the law has recognized that ours is an adversary system relying on an effective advocate for each side. Because of this, due process requires that in most situations an individual can be represented by legal counsel, and in many important situations due process requires the government to pay for legal counsel for people who cannot afford one. This is, in effect, recognizing one practical reality in our legal system: the law in theory may give you certain rights, but the law in practice may predicate the enforcement of those rights on your representation by counsel; and this depends on the lawyer's skills and on your ability to pay for them. This reality is so well accepted and so critical that the right to legal counsel has been interpreted as one of the specific requirements of due process in most situations.

The requirement of equal protection

The other important requirement of the fourteenth amendment that often acts as a procedural limitation on the state is the equal protection clause. As with the requirement of due process, equal protection is both an extremely important limitation and, at the same time, difficult to explain in other than general terms. Basically, equal protection requires that the government treat similarly situated individuals equally unless there is a sufficient justification for a distinction between them. It is a prohibition against certain kinds of governmental discrimination. Beyond that it is hard to explain without reference to a specific set of facts.

The legal analysis is extremely complex, considering a number of interrelated factors, and further complicated from a layman's point of view by the tendency of courts interpreting equal protection to rely on legal terms of art. In the example of the South Carolina statute, some equal protection violations are clear. The procedures outlined by the statute are lacking with respect to the requirement of due process, but there is also a rather obvious problem with the disparity between the way South Carolina allows some people to be committed rather summarily while others are committed by a process that includes a much more elaborate set of procedural safeguards. There is no apparent difference between the people who might be committed under the summary procedures of sections 32-954 and 32-955, sections 32-956 and 32-957, or the lengthy procedures of section 32-958. This is a clear violation of equal protection—similarly situated categories of people being treated quite differently under the law.

Independent of whether a state has to provide certain procedures under the due process clause, it cannot allow certain procedures to some people and deny them to others unless there is a valid reason for this discrimination. Unfortunately, the application of the equal protection requirement is not always as clear as it is in this example, but there will be opportunity to elaborate further on this basic concept with other examples in this chapter and throughout this book. (See *Jackson v. Indiana, infra.*)

Judicial enforcement of constitutional limitations

In some states the more obviously unconstitutional statutes like that in South Carolina have been successfully attacked in the courts. There has been a general trend toward the recognition of procedural rights for people accused of being mentally ill. However, these rights are not implemented everywhere. Furthermore, many legal questions have not been answered about the process of civil commitment, and a number of complex issues remain for the courts to unravel. For example, if a state must be fundamentally fair in the process it uses to commit people, must it allow an individual accused of being mentally ill the right to remain silent after being accused? Assuming that the individual is entitled to a hearing before a judge, must that hearing also be held before a jury? And must the hearing precede any commitment, or can temporary commitment be ordered pending the hearing or trial? All these procedural questions and many others will require that the courts examine the state's purposes in commitment, the specific factual situation presented by civil commitment, and the principles of law, statutory and constitutional, that limit the government's actions. Like all areas of the law, it will require that many specific questions be answered by the courts on a case-by-case basis before these broad principles of law begin to form definable patterns and predictable guidelines.

Legislative reform of civil commitment procedures

In addition to judicial reformation of civil commitment procedures, some state legislatures have in anticipation of these challenges taken the initiative and reformed their state law by statutory revision. A good case in point is California. In 1966 California passed the Lanterman-Petris-Short Act, completely revising the preexisting commitment statute that was in many ways similar to the South Carolina statute described earlier in this chapter. As it now stands, the California statute is one of the more progressive civil commitment statutes in the country. It merits some detailed examination of the manner in which California has attempted to balance the state's purpose in civil commitment against the rights of the individual while trying to stay within constitutional guidelines.

In order to be committed as mentally ill in California, a person must fall into one of three categories: he or she must be mentally ill and dangerous to others, mentally ill and a danger to himself or herself (suicidal), or mentally ill and gravely disabled, meaning unable to feed, clothe, and protect oneself. The procedures and length of commitment for each category differ slightly.

When an individual is in the opinion of a peace officer or a certified mental health professional mentally ill and dangerous to others, the individual can be involuntarily committed for 72 hours for examination. If based on that examination the individual is found to be mentally ill and dangerous, the confinement can be extended for 14 days of intensive treatment. This all occurs without any intervention by legal process, but at least the procedures for examination and intensive treatment are strictly defined in terms of who can commit and on what basis and in terms of the length of the resulting confinement. Any commitment beyond 17 days—3 days examination and 14 days of intensive treatment—requires rather elaborate judicial procedures to be followed. During the 14-day period of intensive treatment the individual receives notice of the right to contest any further confinement, the right to a trial by jury, and the right to appointed legal counsel. An additional 90 days of intensive treatment can be ordered, but only after a jury trial finding that the individual is still mentally ill and dangerous to others.

A similar set of procedures allows for the commitment of people accused of being mentally ill and dangerous to themselves. Again, an individual can be committed for 72 hours examination by a peace officer or a mental health professional. If the diagnosis is confirmed by the examination, 14 days of intensive treatment can be ordered. At the end of 17 days, if the individual is still dangerous to himself or herself, an additional 14-day confinement can be ordered, but a person mentally ill and dangerous to himself or herself can only be held for a maximum of 31 days and must then be released.

A third set of procedures is available for the commitment of people accused of being mentally ill and gravely disabled. After a 72-hour period of examination and a 14-day period of intensive treatment following the same procedures outlined above, no further involuntary confinement can be ordered. However, the state may request a court to appoint a conservator for the individual. In that case the individual is notified of the proceedings, given an opportunity to request a jury trial, and appointed legal counsel. If the trial results in the appointment of a conservator, the appointment lasts for 1 year and expires unless renewed by a court order based on another trial. An appointed conservator almost always exercises the authority to "voluntarily" commit the individual involved. In effect the appointment of a conservator for an individual who is mentally ill and gravely disabled is an involuntary commitment for a 1-year period.

The civil commitment process enacted by the Lanterman-Petris-Short Act represents a number of interesting policy decisions; among other things it provides for a set of procedural limitations on the exercise of the state's commitment power, which can only be described as a compromise. In some ways the California law protects individual rights very carefully. For example, indefinite involuntary commitments are no longer legal. Jury trials are available if anything longer than a temporary confinement is contemplated. On the other hand, the California process allows the power to temporarily confine people to be wielded quite freely. There is no prior notice, and the courts are not involved in this decision for a relatively long period of time. With one category of mentally ill people, those accused of being dangerous to themselves, the temporary confinement without opportunity to oppose the decision can last 31 days; with the other two categories it lasts 17 days. The only real limits of the temporary confinement allowed under the statute are the strict definition of the categories of people who can be committed and the fixed periods of involuntary confinement allowed. None of the basic safeguards, e.g., notice, hearing, or counsel, is available to an individual until the state intends long-term commitment. At that point the procedures that must be followed are rigorous, including a full jury trial and the right of the accused to appointed counsel.

Examining this compromise in terms of the two constitutional principles discussed earlier, a number of legal questions can be raised about this process. In the first place the state is apparently treating one category of mentally ill people, those dangerous to themselves, differently than it does others. Does this violate equal protection? The state will have to argue that these are not equally situated categories, but that mentally ill people who are dangerous to themselves are sufficiently different to warrant a different kind of treatment. The state will also argue that even though the temporary confinement is up to 14 days longer, there is never any long-term commitment of this category of mentally ill; therefore, the circumstances being compared are slightly different. It is not worth developing this argument beyond this sketch, but it is important to point out that this issue can be raised and this statute can be questioned on equal protection grounds.

A more complex set of issues can be raised by asking the question of whether this statute meets the constitutional requirements of due process. Is it fundamentally fair to confine someone for 17 (or 31) days without any opportunity to challenge that decision? The essential elements of notice, hearing, and counsel are present, but their availability is delayed.

If the statute does in practice limit involuntary confinement as strictly as it does in theory, then the focus of civil commitment will be on short periods of intensive treatment. Since all procedural safeguards are by their nature time-consuming, perhaps they would only delay the termination of what would be only a short period of confinement to begin with. As a practical matter, scheduling and preparing for a judicial hearing can take weeks.

Nonetheless, 17 days is a long time, and ardent civil libertarians are convinced that the Lanterman-Petris-Short Act is unacceptable; California is allowing individual liberty to be abridged for several weeks at a time without any meaningful recourse for the confined individual and without the basic elements of fairness generally considered essential. There could easily be some sort of initial review, like an arraignnment in criminal proceedings, that would examine the legality of the initial confinement and that would be something less than a full evidentiary hearing on the wisdom of the commitment itself. Given the history of abuse of the power of civil commitment in this country, that would not be a totally unreasonable requirement.

Whatever the challenges made to this statute, even the most severe critics must admit that the Lanterman-Petris-Short Act is a vast improvement in the procedures traditionally used in this country to commit the mentally ill and a more rational approach to the legal dilemma of balancing the state's legitimate purposes in civil commitment against the individual's personal rights. The California statute, as well as the more traditional statutes like the South Carolina law, will have to be tested in the courts against constitutional standards. Whereas laws similar to that of South Carolina will obviously be found to violate such principles as the requirement of due process and equal protection, the California statute will present much closer questions.

The importance of procedural limitations on governmental authority

Whether considering procedures required by statutes and regulations or those required by constitutional provisions, the importance in the law of procedural limitations on the state's powers to civilly commit the mentally ill or any other state police power cannot be underestimated. Procedural limitations are safeguards against errors. In the civil commitment context, procedural limitations on the state must be observed in order to assure that people committed are actually mentally ill, dangerous, or whatever the standard being decided. These procedures check commitment decisions for factual accuracy and balance the state's intentions in light of the underlying legal authority. As mentioned earlier in this chapter, procedural limitations imposed by the law also reflect the underlying notion that justice in our legal system is both a means and an end. It is easy, particularly in dealing with something as humanitarian as health care, to slip into the erroneous logic that our purposes are noble, and, therefore, the means by which we achieve them are relatively unimportant. Hopefully in post-Watergate America no governmental activity will be allowed again to proceed on that assumption. In terms of civil commitment the state cannot simply justify a process for civil commitment on the need to treat mentally ill people or even the need to protect society from them. It must also justify the procedures used as both accurate and fair. Fairness must include a realistic opportunity for anyone subject to civil commitment to challenge the purposes and legality of the confinement. Fairness requires that opportunity even where it is perfectly clear to the rest of us that the confinement is both justified and legal. Similarly, the state must exercise its power in a way that does not discriminate unfairly or violate a rather complex principle of law and justice known as equal protection of the law. Just as society suffers a loss when someone in need of treatment does not receive it, society loses when we commit someone, even someone in need of treatment, using procedures that are offensive to a free society. The law requires that we justify not only what we do, but also how we achieve it.

In theory principles such as due process and equal protection are easy to accept. In practice we almost predictably fall short of actual acceptance. With regard to civil commitment, historically we have failed miserably. It remains to be seen whether or not we will be willing to adjust our traditional practices to incorporate these legal principles and to extend to people subject to civil commitment all of the legal rights to which they are theoretically entitled. This adjustment of practice will require more than courts recognizing that certain procedures must be incorporated into each state's civil commitment process or enlightened legislatures revising their statutes to conform to constitutional principles. It will take enforcement of those decisions and revisions on a day-to-day basis. For the legal system, this will require what it has not done in the past: it will require the protection of the rights of people who generally cannot afford access to the legal system. For the health care system and the mental health professionals within it, it will require at the least an awareness of the law and its limitations as well as a willingness to act within them.

The most important and yet the most difficult part of the law to accept for a mental health professional involved in the civil commitment process is the fact that the professional is not just a physician, therapist, or provider of services; he or she is also exercising the police powers of the state government. Under the law that means the professional is an agent or extension of the government. This imposes on the professional all of the limitations we have through our legal system imposed on the government. It is hard to accept these limitations. For that matter, mental health professionals have never been trained to do so. It is not really human nature to treat another human within the confines of rules like due process or even equal protection. But in order for the law to be enforced and for the law in theory to become the law in practice, the people who are representatives of the government will have to accept their roles and the accompanying legal limitations. That is why it is so important to understand the law both in terms of its specific requirements and its underlying principles.

Justifying civil commitment in terms of the realities of the resulting confinement

The second major trend in the recent period of reevaluation of the state's power to civilly commit the mentally ill involves a more direct examination of the extent of that power. The legal system has started to examine the purposes justifying civil commitment in light of the realities of the resulting confinement.

Treatment: the purpose of commitment

Most traditional civil commitment statutes simply allow for the commitment of people believed to be mentally ill and in need of psychiatric treatment for indefinite periods of time. There is no assurance within these statutes that the length or conditions of confinement will relate to the original purpose for the commitment or to the specific needs of the individual. Of course there is no civil commitment statute that explicitly prohibits a state that is implementing the statute from considering these factors. In fact it would seem like nothing more than common sense for a state to administratively require that the civil commitment powers authorized by statute be implemented in such a way that people are only confined for appropriate lengths of time and under conditions relating to their specific needs. Unfortunately, that has not been the case in most states. Indeed, the practice in most states has been exactly the opposite: thousands of people are involuntarily committed each year without any specific finding as to their needs or as to the appropriate length for their confinement. At least until very recently, civil commitment has far too often resulted in long-term confinement to large, custodial mental institutions that are typically poorly staffed and underfunded. If the legal basis for the state's power to civilly commit is examined, it will be found that treatment is our justification; if the realities are examined, indefinite confinement without any real treatment is the actual result. This could not happen under a legal system that perfectly enforced its laws.

It is not a sufficient justification that the mentally ill present a danger to society and that therefore we confine them not just to treat them, but to protect ourselves. To begin with, such an excuse would not apply to all people civilly committed. Very few mentally ill people are actually dangerous; but more importantly, civil commitment is a "civil" process. The police powers of the state do allow the state to protect its citizens from people who are dangerous. We arrest and confine people who commit crimes, not just to punish them, but to protect society. In some cases states have arrested people, not only on the basis of what they have done, but on the basis of what they might do, e.g., the confinement of the sexually dangerous or the "defective delinquent" statutes. It is not clear whether the state can legally justify arresting people who are dangerous without their first committing a crime. That is also a question that is now being decided by the courts; even if it is, what is clear is that these are *criminal* processes; they require very strictly defined procedures and very carefully protected safeguards. As mentioned before, civil processes do not. Civil processes must be fundamentally fair, be applied equally, and meet other basic requirements, but they are not as strictly defined under our legal system as is the criminal process. One need only think of the differences between an arrest and trial of a criminal, in terms of time and procedure, and the civil commitment of the mentally ill. Therefore, civil commitment by definition cannot be simply for the protection of society. If it were, it would no longer be civil; it would require elaborate procedures, those used to arrest and try criminals. This would be neither appropriate nor workable in the situation involving someone who is mentally ill. (And all this might not be enough. It is not clear that the state's police powers will be ultimately interpreted to include the criminal confinement of people who are dangerous prior to their commission of a dangerous act or crime.) Civil commitment must be for the purpose of treatment, yet the legal system can only be described as having failed to assure that this is carried out. It is hard to believe that we have allowed the difference between the law in theory and the law in practice to become so marked. It is also hard to believe that the thousands of people civilly committed for indefinite—and very often very long—periods of time might not have been just as well off with short periods of high-quality intensive treatment, or at least with the same treatment they received, but given on an outpatient or day-care basis. It is necessary to acknowledge that our current abilities to actually treat mental illness far exceed our abilities in the past, but that only raises the same question: if we were not treating people civilly committed, what has been the justification for their confinement in the first place?

Judicial reform of the conditions of confinement

As with the reexamination of the procedures used in civil commitment, one of the results of this concern for the differences between the purposes of the commitment and the realities of the resulting confinement has been the revision of some state statutes. The Lanterman-Petris-Short Act is again the best example and is cited often as a model for other states to follow. By defining involuntary commitment as for intensive treatment and by strictly limiting these periods in duration, California has tried to specify the purposes of commitment in a way that is more consistent with the legal authority of the state. Further, by providing for an initial examination and periodic reconfirmation of this initial diagnosis, the statute has made some attempt to require that the purposes will actually be carried out and that the whole process will not result in long-term custodial confinement. The requirements of a hearing and, particularly, the right to counsel at these hearings ensure that these requirements are adhered to. California is, however, the exception, and not all states' legislatures are likely to follow this example unless forced to do so.

There are some indications that the courts are concerned with the problem and that they may indeed force the states to revise their current practices. In 1972 the U.S. Supreme Court decided several cases that indicated that that court is, for the first time, interested in examining the power of the state to civilly commit the mentally ill. In fact in the most important of these decisions, *Jackson v. Indiana,* 406 U.S. 715 (1972), Mr. Justice Blackmun, speaking for the Court, expressed both his willingness to examine the law as it relates to civil commitment and his dismay that the legal profession had not brought this issue before the Court more often. He observed: "Considering the number of persons affected, it is perhaps remarkable that the substantive constitutional limitations on this power have not been more frequently litigated."

In the *Jackson* case, a deaf-mute who was described as mentally "defective" was charged with two counts of robbery. (The total value of the stolen goods was five dollars.) He was civilly committed after examination by two physicians and a hearing on the matter, in which he was found incompetent to stand trial on the robbery charges. Indiana law also provides for the civil commitment of insane persons (comparable to what other states call mentally ill), and the civil commitment of feeble-minded persons (comparable to the mentally retarded). Both of these other processes differ from the process for the commitment of people like Jackson as incompetent to stand trial in a number of ways, including (1) commitment under either of the other two statutes would have been according to a stricter standard of proof of the relevant mental condition; (2) release under the other civil commitment statutes would have been easier to attain; and (3) the treatment received under either statute would have been different and arguably better for Jackson.

Jackson claimed that his commitment violated his rights under the fourteenth amendment to the U.S. Constitution. The Supreme Court agreed, holding that the commitment of Jackson as incompetent to stand trial under the Indiana law denied him equal protection of the law and due process of law.

In finding that Jackson's commitment was a violation of equal protection, the Court was extending to a new situation a principle previously applied in a 1967 case, *Baxtrom v. Herold,* 383 U.S. 107 (1967). In *Baxtrom* the Court held that the state of New York had denied Johnnie Baxtrom, a convicted criminal, equal protection of the law when, near the expiration of his prison sentence, he was summarily transferred after a very brief hearing from prison to a hospital for the criminally insane to serve indefinitely until considered sane. In effect he was civilly committed while a prisoner. All other people civilly committed under New York state law are entitled to a jury trial; when they are committed to the facility where Baxtrom was confined, it was required that the jury find that the individual was both mentally ill and dangerous. The Court found that this denial of procedural rights to Baxtrom was a violation of equal protection. A distinction based on Baxtrom's status as a prisoner is not a rational basis upon which to justify a discrimination between Baxtrom and all other people subject to civil commitment. The Court applied this logic to Jackson's situation. "If criminal conviction and imposition of sentence are insufficient to justify less procedural and substantive protection against civil commitment, then the mere filing of criminal charges can not suffice." In other words, in order to satisfy the requirements of equal protection the state must show a rational basis for any process that deprives the committed person of substantial rights that would be available to other committed people. The Court rejected the argument by Indiana that Jackson's pending trial on the criminal charges was sufficient basis and rejected the argument that the commitment was only temporary, i.e., until Jackson recovered to stand trial, since based on the facts, that was unlikely to happen.

The Court's ruling on the due process issue had more far-reaching implications. The Court examined the proceeding used to commit Jackson and the reasons cited by the state as justifying his confinement and compared them to the treatment that Jackson would receive. While withholding explicit statement or definition of the exact basis upon which justification for commitment could be based, the Court very bluntly stated:

> We need not address these broad questions here. It is clear that Jackson's commitment rests on proceedings that did not purport to bring into play, indeed did not even consider relevant, any of the articulated bases for exercise of Indiana's power of indefinite commitment. The state statutes contain at least two alternative methods for invoking this power. But Jackson was not afforded any 'formal commitment proceedings addressed to (his) ability to function in society,' or to society's interest in his restraint, or to the State's ability to aid him in attaining competency through custodial or compulsory treatment, the ostensible purpose of the commitment. At the least, due process requires that the nature and duration of commitment bear some reasonable relation to the purpose for which the individual is committed.

> We hold, consequently, that a person charged by a state with a criminal offense who is committed solely on account of his incapacity to proceed to trial cannot be held more than a reasonable period of time necessary to determine whether there is a substantial probability that he will attain that capacity in the foreseeable future.

The Court further required that any continued confinement of Jackson as not competent to stand trial would have to be based on a probability that he would return to trial and could only be justified by progress toward that goal. It is violative of due process to confine someone as incompetent to stand trial when there is no hope for his or her return to competency. This is not to say that the state might not be able to confine and treat people who are found to be unable to care for themselves, e.g., the gravely disabled; it means that whatever the purpose for the commitment, the actual confinement, in terms of duration and treatment available, must be reasonably related to that purpose. Thus due process might not have been violated by proper procedures committing Jackson after finding him mentally ill and in need of treatment, or even by procedures committing Jackson temporarily while he recovered his competency, but even these commitments would have to have been justified by comparing their purpose to the conditions and the duration of the resulting confinement.

In the same term that the Supreme Court decided *Jackson v. Indiana*, it also decided another case that recognized the need to examine the purposes of a civil commitment in terms of the actual confinement. In *McNeil v. Director Paxutent Institute,* 407 U.S. 245 (1972), Edward McNeil, originally convicted on two counts of assault and sentenced to 5 years in prison, was sent to a mental institution during his criminal sentence for examination and observation. The purpose was to determine whether McNeil should be confined under the Maryland defective delinquent law; in effect it was a temporary commitment for observation prior to the defective delinquent proceedings, much like Jackson's "temporary" commitment. McNeil flatly refused to talk to the institution's psychiatrists during his confinement, and when his original prison sentence expired, no decision to initiate the defective delinquent proceedings had been made. The state tried to extend the period of observation, and McNeil filed suit claiming his confinement was no longer valid.

The Supreme Court agreed with McNeil. Specifically, the Court held that it is a denial of due process to continue to hold a person in a mental institution on the basis of an administrative decision to have the person observed. Citing the *Jackson* decision, the Court said that since this was clearly a long-term commitment (it had lasted several years), the state must commit McNeil like it would have any other person using the proper procedural safeguards, or strictly limit the confinement so that it is in reality a temporary observation.

Parenthetically, the Court took great pains to avoid deciding whether McNeil had a right to remain silent—just as a criminal defendant does—or, conversely, whether the state could interpret that silence as evidence that he was a defective delinquent. Therefore, the right to remain silent issue surfaced before the Court, but was not decided.

The implications of the above cases are that the Supreme Court is now willing to scrutinize the justifications and purposes behind civil commitment. It is unlikely that his will result in that court or any lower court ruling that any of the purposes traditionally cited as justifying civil commitment will now be declared unconstitutional. However, at least those purposes will be made explicit and will be examined closely. What is the real purpose in this commitment? What are the limits imposed by the Constitution on that kind of commitment? These are the kinds of questions that will be asked. Similarly, the courts will compare the answers to these questions with the length and conditions of confinement. The Supreme Court would not allow Indiana to justify Jackson's commitment as serving the purpose of holding him until he recovered, since it was unlikely he would recover. Nor would the Court accept the argument that McNeil was being held for observation, since the confinement had lasted several years. The nature and duration of any form of civil commitment will be required to bear some reasonable relation to the purpose for which the individual is committed.

The evolution of the right to treatment

Even before the Supreme Court decided the *Jackson* case, a series of lower courts had decided cases indicating a similar interest in an examination of the purposes of civil commitment in light of the realities of the resulting confinement. In 1975 the Supreme Court decided a similar case. These cases established what is known as the constitutional right to treatment. In various parts of the country both state and federal courts have taken a hard look at the public mental institutions in which the mentally ill are confined and have held that an individual involuntarily civilly committed has a right to receive at least minimally adequate psychiatric care.

There have been several bases for these holdings. In some cases the courts have held that this legal right is found in the state's statute; that is, they have found either explicit provisions in the statute or the strong implication that anyone committed under the statute had a right to receive adequate care while confined. The right can also be based on provisions of the U.S. Constitution. It is a violation of due process and is fundamentally unfair to confine people for treatment for their mental illness and then not provide them with the necessary treatment. This is almost more compelling than the similar argument accepted by the Supreme Court in *Jackson* and *McNeil.* Due process requires that the nature and duration of the confinement must relate to the purpose of the confinement. If that purpose is treatment, there must be some kind of treatment provided, not necessarily the best care available, but care that is at least minimally adequate. It can also be forcefully argued that to confine a mentally ill person without treatment is cruel and unusual punishment in violation of the eighth amendment to the U.S. Constitution.

This is essentially the right to treatment argument. It is as simple as it is compelling. But for the fact that the legal system neglected for many years the rights of people civilly committed, this right would have been recognized long ago. The problem, however, is not just the final recognition of this right by the legal system. The problem is also the enforcement of this right, the implementation of the courts' decisions. The development of this legal doctrine from its first recognition to its present status reveals not only the real meaning of the right to treatment but also a great deal about the problem of enforcing legal rights and the shortcomings of our current legal system.

As early as 1963 the Massachusetts Supreme Court recognized that people involuntarily confined to mental institutions had a constitutional right to treatment. In 1965 the Court of Appeals for the District of Columbia under Judge David Bazelon, who has been responsible for a number of decisions recognizing the rights of the mentally ill, came to a similar conclusion. Both of these cases encountered some practical difficulties, and there was never any real enforcement of those decisions.

However, the legal principle of the right to treatment was recognized in those and, eventually, in several other jurisdictions. In 1975 the Supreme Court recognized that at least nondangerous people who are civilly committed have a constitutionally-based right to treatment. In *O'Connor v. Donaldson* 422 U.S. 563 (1975), Donaldson sued the superintendent and the staff of the Florida mental institution where he had been confined for nearly 15 years. He claimed that he was neither dangerous nor mentally ill, and, even if he had been mentally ill, he had received no treatment. Thus he claimed that the defendants were depriving him of his personal liberty, and as a result, they were liable to him for compensatory damages. The federal court of appeals upheld a jury verdict in Donaldson's favor, awarding him $38,000. However, on appeal to the U.S. Supreme Court, that court remanded the case for further determinations relating to the legal basis for holding the defendants personally liable for damages. But the Court did rule that whatever the outcome of the case, it is a violation of the constitutional rights of nondangerous civilly committed people to hold them in mere custodial confinement. Some kind of treatment must be given. Where the state's purpose is only treatment, that treatment must be forthcoming, or the commitment is illegal—and the people confining the committed person may be personally liable for damages.

While withholding judgment on several broad issues raised by the parties to the *Donaldson* case, including whether all involuntarily confined mental patients have a right to treatment, the *Donaldson* opinion will become a landmark in the development of the rights of civilly committed people.

Of the various cases that have upheld the right to treatment, by far the most important in terms of the actual enforcement of that right has been *Wyatt v. Aderholdt,* 503 F.2d 1305 (5th Cir. 1974) (formerly known as *Wyatt v. Stickney*), which was brought as a challenge to the quality of care in the various public mental institutions in Alabama.

The central issue in a right to treatment case is an evaluation of that elusive but all-important quality of care. No one can give a perfect definition of this term, and no one is totally satisfied with any of the ways in which the quality of medical care in general and specifically psychiatric care has been measured. It is slightly easier to define and measure minimally adequate care, but it is still difficult, even for experts, let alone lawyers and judges. In Alabama in 1972, however, no one could dispute the fact that the quality of psychiatric care available to those who were civilly committed was abysmal. In the largest of the state's institutions there were 5000 patients for whom there were only seventeen physicians (three of whom had psychiatric training), twenty-one nurses, twelve psychologists (one of whom had a Ph.D.), thirteen social workers, twelve patient activity workers, and 850 psychiatric aides. These are the state's statistics. They tend to obscure a number of things, including the fact that most of the physicians were involved in administration of the hospital, not patient care. It was also found that Alabama ranked fiftieth in the nation in per patient per day expenditures. Thousands of geriatric and mentally retarded patients were indiscriminately mixed with the other mentally ill patients. The programs available for treatment were found to conform to no known minimum standards for the treatment of the mentally ill.

The federal district court in Alabama, notwithstanding the fact that this was virtually a precedent-breaking case, had no trouble in ruling that the treatment available in that state's mental institutions was totally inadequate and that this was a violation of the constitutional rights of committed mental patients. This left the court in a difficult position. Having found that the Alabama state mental health system was inadequate, the court was left with the problem of defining what would be legally adequate. More crucial than that, it is one thing for the judicial branch of the government to rule that the executive should not do something; that is fairly consistent with the division of powers among the branches. To tell the executive what it has to do, particularly with regard to a complicated administrative program, is something that is not within the role traditionally played by the courts. Moreover, if the court were to issue an order requiring the executive branch of the Alabama state government to improve the quality of care in the state's mental institutions, the court would be indirectly telling the legislature it must appropriate more funds for mental health, an even greater deviation from the traditional role played by the judiciary.

Consequently, the court in *Wyatt* took a very conservative approach. Rather than ordering the state to take immediate action, the court held that the conditions of confinement were unconstitutional and gave the state 6 months to develop a plan to improve the mental institutions and the care that was available. A report was filed by the state, but, after a hearing on the matter, it was found to be totally inadequate. By that time, a number of psychiatric professional groups had joined in the suit as amici ("friends" of the court), although the American Psychiatric Association was conspicuous in its absence. With the help of these groups and the expert witnesses that they provided, the court then took a more active course of action. Still wary that the quality of care is difficult to measure and that courts should only interfere with the administration of the state's executive branch when the executive fails to meet minimally acceptable standard, the court held that adequate treatment must include: (1) qualified staff in numbers sufficient to administer adequate treatment, (2) a humane physical and psychological environment, and (3) individualized treatment plans for each patient. The court did not want to evaluate actual treatment provided. It did not want to look at modalities of treatment or the amount or kind of staff-patient interaction, or even to look at whether the individual patient's plans were carried out. Nonetheless, even this limited ruling was not the sort of thing that courts are often willing to do, particularly with regard to something as foreign to them as medical care and more particularly with regard to something they have traditionally left completely alone—psychiatry.

Following that decision by the court, the plaintiffs, the defendants, and the amici tried to negotiate a set of specific standards implementing the three broad principles laid down by the court. The standards recommended by the plaintiffs and the psychiatric professional groups included elaborate specifications for the physical facilities, the conditions within those facilities, and the patient/staff ratios that would have to be provided. The recommended staff patient ratios included:

One psychiatrist for every thirty to fifty patients
One psychologist for every thirty to fifty patients
One physician for every 150 patients
One nurse for every twenty-five patients
One psychiatric aide for every three to five patients

The court adopted these recommended specifications and staff/patient ratios and (1) ordered their implementation, (2) ordered the establishment of a human rights committee in each Alabama institution to review all research and treatment programs to ensure that the dignity and human rights of all patients are preserved, and (3) ordered that the state file a report within 6 months on the implementation of these orders.

Alabama appealed the decision to the U.S. Court of Appeals for that district. The court of appeals heard oral argument on the appeal and, for reasons known only to the members of the court, sat on the case for nearly 2 years before issuing its decision. Finally, over 4 years after the original case was filed in the district court and after numerous hearings, negotiations, investigations, and reports, the court of appeals affirmed the lower court's finding that involuntarily civilly committed mental patients have a constitutional right to treatment and that in Alabama that right is being violated.

The enforcement of the right to treatment

Hopefully, Alabama will comply with this decision, although the state may choose to appeal still further to the U.S. Supreme Court. After the *Donaldson* case, the issues raised by *Wyatt* are still not settled, although it does seem that the Supreme Court is willing to recognize the right to treatment, at least in part. If there is no appeal, it is still not clear that the state will comply with the decision, or even that it can. With the number of patients currently confined in Alabama mental institutions, any improvement in the treatment programs will be very expensive and require a much larger staff than is presently available. Budgets and staffing can only be increased by the state legislature. What if the state legislature, in light of the extreme cost, refuses to cooperate?

The options that remain open to the court are limited. The traditional means by which a court enforces its orders is by use of its contempt power. If anyone, even a state official, refuses to obey a court order, he or she can be jailed or fined. Conceivably the court could hold any number of Alabama state officials in contempt for failing to implement the right to treatment decision. Is it even conceivable that the court would hold the whole state legislature in contempt? How would that be reconciled with the division of powers?

Another alternative open to the court is to appoint what is known as a special master to take over, on behalf of the court, the administration of the mental health system in Alabama. But without more money to spend, there might not be anything that even a special master could do to rectify the problem.

The basic problem is that our judicial system is not set up to deal effectively with these kinds of legal issues. There are various ways that the executive branch of government can be prohibited from doing something, but it is next to impossible to force the executive to take an action that it has expressly refused to do. To look at it from a different perspective, the responsibility to enforce legal rights under our legal system is given not just to the judiciary, but to the executive as well. It is very obvious that in Alabama legal rights are being violated. It is reprehensible that the executive created the situation in the first place. There is no excuse for the executive not to relieve the problem now that it has been declared illegal—even if the courts cannot force the executive to do so. But the absence of an excuse is not enough to compel an unwilling executive to act.

One possibility that has not been given much attention is that the state may be ordered to release some of the people it now confines. If one of the expenses of an adequate treatment program is caused by a required staff/patient ratio, then one way that costs can be controlled is by reducing the number of patients. This may be realistic; many of the people now confined in Alabama may be adequately cared for in nursing homes or on a day-care basis. In fact an improvement in the treatment program might itself reduce the patient population. Among other things, with better treatment the length of patient stays might be substantially reduced. But again, these programmatic changes are the sort of things that are hard for a court, even with the assistance of outside experts, to force on the administration of a state government. The executive branch of the state government should take the responsibility for seeing that they are done. Why have they not done these things before? Why did they, instead, oppose this lawsuit so vigorously?

The court may have difficulty in ordering changes in the state's programs that indirectly reduce the number of people confined, but it could order people released solely on the basis of illegal confinement. If the state administration refuses to develop an acceptable program and the state legislature refuses to appropriate sufficient funds, the court could opt to release the patients who are being illegally confined. However, this has not been a major consideration in the *Wyatt* lawsuit. It is interesting to contemplate the implications of that fact.

If a criminal defendant is illegally arrested, even if clearly guilty, he or she will be released. Can anyone imagine a criminal trial where it is discovered that a confession is coerced or that a search was made without a warrant, but the defendent is convicted and confined anyway—and the police are given 6 months to report on whether they have improved their arrest and interrogation practices? That is analogous to what happened in *Wyatt*. Why?

The answer lies in our attitudes, meaning the attitudes implied in the law and the attitudes of judges who enforce the law, officials who implement the law, and even the lawyers who try to advocate the law. When the issue involves a process that is considered "civil" we are somehow more lenient with the state and tolerate more illegal exercise of the state's power. The state is not threatened with the possibility that it may have to release people civilly committed if their rights are violated. The courts are hesitant even to declare the neglect of mental patients illegal and do everything possible to give the state an opportunity to make amends. We tend to forget that an abuse of civil power can be as violative of individual rights as an abuse of criminal police powers. Unfortunately, these attitudes have invited both the violation of the legal rights of the people we seek through civil commitment to help and have created a legal system where remedial measures are difficult to enforce.

There are a number of other right to treatment cases currently being litigated. Some involve the mentally ill; others involve other categories of civilly committed people such as the similarly-reasoned right to rehabilitation for the mentally retarded. The idea that the state must provide minimally adequate treatment to civilly confined people has a number of applications and will be developed in a number of ways. So far, the courts have only applied the principle to uphold challenges to the shockingly inadequate, primarily custodial mental institutions that unfortunately still exist in many states. In Alabama there was no doubt that the mental institutions were inadequate. It is not clear that courts would be eager to evaluate the quality of care in other institutions, e.g., community-based mental facilities, where the treatment available was arguably, but less obviously, inadequate. The courts that have recognized the right to treatment have been persuaded by a constitutional argument and a shocking set of facts. That argument could justify evaluating the care in other factual situations, but the courts may retreat into their traditional role. This would be understandable, given the practical problems in enforcing these kinds of decisions.

Although it is unlikely, in 10 years the nature and extent of the right to treatment could be a relatively settled issue. Certainly the cases now pending will be decided; hopefully, they will be enforced and resolved. However, the basic tension between individual rights and the state's police power will remain, and the difference between the law in theory and the law in practice will continue to be a problem. Likely as not, the exact nature of the right to treatment will not be settled in the coming decade, and if settled in theory, will not be entirely enforced. Thus the right to treatment will be one of several major issues in public health, representative of the broader issue of resolving the conflicts between the public health powers of the state governments and the individual rights of their citizens.

Conclusion

As mentioned earlier in this chapter, civil commitment is both an important public health related problem and a good example of the legal issues involved with the exercise of police powers by the state. The state's powers in matters relating to the public's health are very broad, but there are some limitations. One major limitation on the exercise of police power by the state is procedural. Even with a valid purpose, the state must use only constitutionally permissible and statutorily authorized means. Another limitation on the state involves an examination of the state's purpose. At the least, the state must cite a valid purpose for its exercise of power; the state must also be able to explain the relationship between that purpose and what it is actually doing. This chapter has examined the situation where the state has to rationalize in terms of its purpose the conditions and procedures by which it has civilly committed people for treatment and/or observation. The next chapter will concentrate on the limitations imposed on the exercise of police power when it involves the infringement of one of the basic individual rights, the right to privacy.

Throughout this chapter and the entire book one theme is repeated. Just as it is important to understand the principles behind the law in order to understand the law, it is important for the same reason to understand the legal system that enforces it. The legal system translates the law in theory into the law in practice. When it works, it represents society at its best; when it fails, it brings out our very worst.

References

Brakel, S., Rock, R.: The mentally disabled and the law, rev. ed., 1971.

Chambers, D.: Alternatives to civil commitment of the mentally ill: practical guides and constitutional imperatives, Mich. L. Rev. **70**:1108, 1972.

Developments in the law: civil commitment of the mentally ill, Harv. L. Rev. **87**:1190, 1974.

ENKI Research Institute: A study of California's new mental health law, 1972.

Hearing on Constitutional rights of the mentally ill before the Subcommittee on Constitutional Rights of the Senate Committee on the Judiciary, 91st Cong. 1st & 2d Sess., 1970.

Katz, J., Goldstein, J., and Dershowitz, A.: Psychoanalysis, psychiatry, and the law, 1967.

Subcommittee on Mental Health Services of the Assembly Interim Committee on Ways and Means, California Legislature: The di-

lemma of mental commitments in California, ed. 3, 1972.

Symposium: Mental disability and the law, Calif. L. Rev. **62**:397, 1974.

Szaz, T.: The myth of mental illness, 1961.

Wing, K., and Carman, R.: Mental commitment cases of the 1971-1972 Supreme Court Term, Clearinghouse Rev. **6**:659, 1973.

CHAPTER 4

The right to privacy and governmental control over family planning decisions

The government's powers (or rights) in matters involving the public's health are extensive. As described in earlier chapters, the state government has what are known as police powers, giving the state broad authority to act, inherent in the constitutional basis of the government. The federal government can also act in matters relating to the public's health, although its authority is somewhat more prescribed. At least its authority must be based on one or more of the explicit provisions of the U.S. Constitution.

The relationship between the government and the individual in matters relating to public health is not entirely one-sided. In Chapter 2 situations were illustrated in which the state's purposes were held not to outweigh certain substantive individual rights. In Chapter 3 using civil commitment as an example, other limitations on the government's exercise of power were discussed: the individual's procedural rights that the government is required to observe and the right of the individual to require that the government show that its purposes are actually being fulfilled.

In this chapter the focus will be on the development of one substantive individual right in the public health context, the right to privacy. In Chapter 2 the conclusion was drawn that in certain situations the legal system must weigh a valid governmental purpose against certain individual rights. At some point the individual's rights become so important that limitations must be put on the government's exercise of power. This chapter will examine the right to privacy and how it has been interrelated with attempts by state government to exercise authority over sexual conduct and family planning decisions. This should illustrate both the nature of the right to privacy and further elucidate the manner in which the legal system tries to balance individual rights in general with governmental exercise of power.

The origins of the right to privacy

The concept of privacy is difficult to define. It involves at the least a notion of the individual's right to be left alone and free to make certain personal decisions without outside interference. Whatever its exact nature, privacy probably has always been a cherished human value; certainly it has been in American society. Yet with the advent of a more complicated, institutionalized society, privacy has become even more important and essential to the maintenance of individual integrity. There were once areas and activities into which one who sought privacy could escape, but increasingly these outlets are becoming unavailable. In fact, many of our economic and social activities are direct threats to individual privacy, and this has created a series of conflicts often pitting the objectives of society (or one group within the society) against the individual's objective of preserving privacy. It is in this type of societal conflict that the law often becomes one means by which resolution is attempted.

The importance of privacy has been recognized in the law in many ways. The legal rights that define the relationship between one individual and another individual often reflect a purpose of protecting privacy. The legal recognition of private property is a prime example. The law recognizes the right of the individual to control the possession and use of certain tangible and intangible things—a house, a business, or even an idea. It recognizes this right by keeping other people away from this property or imposing penalties on those who do interfere. The law of torts (see Chapter 6, *infra*) also recognizes and protects privacy in a variety of circumstances; the fact that one individual can sue another for personal assault or defamation is in part based on a notion of privacy. In many jurisdictions any "invasion of privacy" may be an actionable tort and a basis for civil liability.

Although privacy can be threatened in situations involving two individuals, e.g., data collection by credit bureaus or private insurance companies, issues of privacy most often arise out of governmental activities. Yet a legal right to individual privacy, meaning a legally enforceable relationship between the individual and the government, has not always been recognized. The major reason for this is that there is no explicit provision recognizing the right to privacy in the Constitution. (At least one state, California, has such a provision in its state constitution.) There are, of course, a number of federal constitutional provisions that protect certain aspects of privacy. The first amendment protects the freedom of association and the free exercise of religion from governmental interference; the fourth amendment prohibits governmental searches and seizures unless certain conditions exist; even the rarely remembered third amendment recognizes the importance of individual privacy by prohibiting the mandatory housing of soldiers in citizens' homes. However, it was not until 1965 that a general constitutional right to privacy was recognized. Before that time privacy was protected from governmental interference only under certain circumstances and in some indirect ways, but privacy had never been recognized as an individual right defining a general relationship between the people and the government.

Consequently, the right to privacy and its ramifications are of recent origin and are still unfolding.

The right to privacy: use of contraceptives by married people

The landmark case that established for the first time the constitutional right to privacy was *Griswold v. Connecticut,* 381 U.S. 479 (1965).

In 1961 the Planned Parenthood League of Connecticut opened a center in New Haven for the distribution of birth control information. After only 9 days of operation, Estelle Griswold, the Executive Director of Planned Parenthood, and the medical director of the clinic were arrested. They were charged with giving information, instruction, and medical advice to married people for the purposes of contraception. In Connecticut at that time it was a crime to use contraceptives:

> Any person who uses any drug, medicinal article or instrument for the purpose of preventing conception shall be fined not less than fifty dollars or imprisoned not less than sixty days nor more than one year or be both fined and imprisoned.

Griswold and the medical director were tried for aiding and abetting this crime and found guilty. They appealed through the state court system to no avail and eventually to the U.S. Supreme Court, which accepted jurisdiction. The basic thrust of their appeal was that the law prohibiting the use of contraceptives was in violation of a constitutional right to privacy.

The individual members of the Supreme Court were rather divided as to the reasoning for their decision, but by a 7-2 decision (two separate concurring opinions and two separate dissenting opinions were written in addition to the majority opinion), the Court reversed the criminal convictions and declared the Connecticut law as applied unconstitutional.

Justice William Douglas wrote the majority opinion. He cited a long list of constitutional rights that had been recognized and protected by the Court, despite the fact that these rights were not explicitly mentioned in the provisions of the Constitution. From these precedents he reasoned:

> The foregoing cases suggest that specific guarantees in the Bill of Rights have penumbras, formed by emanation from those guarantees that help give them life and substance. . . . Various guarantees create zones of privacy. The right of association contained in the penumbra of the First Amendment is one, as we have seen. The Third Amendment in its prohibition against the quartering of soldiers "in any house" in time of peace without the consent of the owner is another facet of that privacy. The Fourth Amendment explicitly affirms the "right of the people to be secure in their persons, houses, papers, and effects, against unreasonable searches and seizures." The Fifth Amendment in its Self-Incrimination Clause enables the citizen to create a zone of privacy which government may not force him to surrender to his detriment. The Ninth Amendment provides: "The enumeration in the Constitution, of certain rights, shall not be construed to deny or disparage others retained by the people."

> The Fourth and Fifth Amendments were described . . . as protections against all governmental invasions "of the sanctity of a man's home and the privacies of life." We recently referred . . . to the Fourth Amendment as creating a "right to privacy, no less important than any other right carefully and particularly reserved to the people. . . ."

> We have had many controversies over these penumbral rights of "privacy and repose.". . . These cases bear witness that the right of privacy which presses for recognition here is a legitimate one.

> The present case, then, concerns a relationship lying within the zone of privacy created by several constitutional guarantees. And it concerns a law which, in forbidding the use of contraceptives rather than regulating their manufacture or sale, seeks to achieve its goal by means having a maximum destructive impact upon that relationship. Such a law cannot stand in light of the familiar principle, so often applied by this Court, that a "governmental purpose to control or prevent activities constitutionally subject to state regulation may not be achieved by means which sweep unnecessarily broadly and thereby invade the area of protected freedom. . . ." Would we allow the police to search the sacred precincts of marital bedrooms for telltale signs of the use of contraceptives? The very idea is repulsive to the notions of privacy surrounding the marriage relationship.

We deal with a right older than the Bill of Rights—older than our political parties, older than our school system. Marriage is a coming together for better or for worse, hopefully enduring and intimate to the degree of being sacred. It is an association that promotes a way of life, not causes; a harmony in living, not political faiths; a bilateral loyalty, not commercial or social projects. Yet it is an association for as noble a purpose as any involved in prior decisions.

Justice Douglas' opinion was not unusual in its logic; it was fairly straightforward. He recognized that the proper role of the judiciary was not to interfere with the legislative process unless it was necessary to protect a constitutional right. The state should be allowed wide discretion to regulate most economic and social activities, particularly those that relate to public health. In fact the opinion specifically recognized the right of the state to regulate the use of contraceptives, at least in some ways. However, where the exercise of authority by the state interferes too greatly with a constitutional right, "sweep[s] unnecessarily broadly," it infringes on that right, the exercise of power is beyond constitutional limits, and the courts must intervene. This is another example of how the courts balance the state's power against the rights of an individual; in this case, the decision upholds the individual right as predominant.

The unusual nature of the opinion was that it created, or at least recognized for the first time, a new constitutional right *and* a new concept of constitutional analysis. Not only did the *Griswold* case create a right to privacy with far-reaching implications, it also suggested the possibility that other rights might be found in the penumbral light of the specific guarantees of the Constitution. Although in many situations the Court has had to look to the implications of the explicit provisions of the Constitution in order to apply those provisions to a given set of circumstances, rarely has any case been so explicit—or so graphic—in finding that there are rights implied in the Constitution.

What exactly is the nature of this right to privacy recognized in *Griswold?* The majority opinion speaks generally of "zones of privacy" and specifically of one of these zones, sexual activity between married people. The opinion does not claim that the state cannot invade this zone of privacy in any way; it implies, at least, that the state could regulate the sale or manufacture of contraceptives; however, the state cannot prohibit the use of contraceptives since by doing so it interferes too greatly with the privacy of married people. Beyond holding that this Connecticut statute is unconstitutional as applied in this case, *Griswold* actually gives little guidance to what the state can and cannot do in related situtations. The opinion did little more than open the door to the right to privacy and to the future examination of these "zones of privacy."

The right to privacy: giving contraceptives to single people

The *Griswold* case had a nationwide impact. Many state legislatures realized that they must change their state statutes to conform to the *Griswold* opinion. Among these states was Massachusetts.

Prior to the *Griswold* decision, among the "Crimes Against Chastity, Morality, Decency, and Good Order" defined in the Massachusetts criminal statutes, was the following:

(anyone who) . . . sells, lends, gives away, exhibits, offers to sell, lend or give away . . . any drug, medicine, instrument, or article whatever for the prevention of conception or for the causing of unlawful abortion, or advertises the same, or writes, prints, or causes to be written or printed a card, circular, book, pamphlet, advertisement or notice of any kind stating when, where, how, of whom, or by what means such article can be purchased, or obtained, or manufactures or makes any such article shall be punished by imprisonment in the state prison for not more than five years or in jail or in the house of corrections for not more than two and one half years or by a fine not less than one hundred nor more than one thousand dollars.

After the *Griswold* case that statute was amended by the state legislature to make an exception for contraceptives given to a married individual by a physician or a pharmacist with a prescription. In effect contraceptives were to be treated as prescription drugs available only to married people.

A fair reading of the *Griswold* case immediately after its decision might have led to the conclusion that the Massachusetts law as amended might still be valid. Certainly Douglas' glittering praise of the marital relationship left a clear impression that it was sexual conduct within the association of marriage that was the zone of privacy protected by the Constitution. There was the implication that the state could regulate contraception in some ways, including the use by unmarried people. But such an inference, however reasonable, would have been wrong, as was proven a few years later in *Eisenstadt v. Baird,* 405 U.S. 438 (1972).

William Baird is a man whose name has been associated with a number of social causes, and in the late 1960's he was renowned in Massachusetts for his crusades to free birth control from the strict legal restraints imposed in that state. His method was direct confrontation. He openly violated these laws and eventually forced his own prosecution in order to challenge their constitutionality.

Thomas Eisenstadt was also a man with a cause, but in his case the purpose was to further his own political career. As the elected sheriff of a county with a large Irish-Catholic population, it was only natural that he would be eager to prosecute Baird.

In May of 1967 Baird gave a lecture on birth control at Boston University. His presentation included exhibits and displays of contraceptive devices, and after his address he invited members of the audience to help themselves to available samples. Baird was approached by an unmarried woman, and he personally handed her a can of vaginal foam. At that point Sheriff Eisenstadt's conveniently placed police officers arrested Baird.

Baird was charged with both exhibiting contraceptives and giving contraceptives to an unmarried person in violation of the statute cited above. He was tried and convicted. He appealed through the state court system; the Massachusetts Supreme Judicial Court reversed the conviction for exhibiting contraceptives as violative of Baird's right to free speech secured by the first amendment to the U.S. Constitution. The court upheld his conviction for the giving of contraceptives.

Contending that the conviction was a violation of the right to privacy, Baird filed a writ of habeus corpus in federal court. (This is one means of appealing a state court conviction on the grounds that it violates the U.S.

Constitution.) His appeal was dismissed in the federal district court, but in the federal circuit court of appeal Baird was successful, and the court ordered him released. Sheriff Eisenstadt then appealed to the Supreme Court, which accepted jurisdiction over the case.

This case presented a different set of circumstances to the Court than those considered earlier in *Griswold v. Connecticut.* Baird was asserting the right to privacy of unmarried people and asking for an extension of the reasoning exhibited in *Griswold.* However, the legal analysis in both cases is very similar; the Court was asked to weigh the extent of the ability of the state to exercise its police powers against certain individual rights protected by the Constitution.

Mr. Justice Brennan, writing the majority opinion, first analyzed the state's authority. In order to establish the nature and importance of the state's authority to act, the opinion first established the purpose of the statute. If the purpose of the Massachusetts statute was to regulate dangerous health-related devices, one of Eisenstadt's claims, not only would the statute be based on the erroneous assumption that all contraceptive devices can be dangerous, but there would be the patent absurdity that only unmarried people are protected from the danger. The statute would be therefore both unnecessarily broad and discriminatory.

If the purpose of the statute was to deter premarital sex, which was a second claim, there would also be some inherent contradictions in the statute. First of all, it would be rather strange to try to deter premarital sex by punishing those who commit the act with pregnancy. In addition the Court added,

> Aside from the scheme of values that assumption would attribute to the State, it is abundantly clear that the effect of the ban on the distribution of contraceptives to unmarried people has at best a marginal relation to the proffered objective.

This was a rather candid acknowledgement of the fact that contraceptives were readily available to unmarried people in Massachusetts, despite the illegality.

The Court also pointed out the irony of a contraceptive law that proposed to regulate premarital sex, but apparently did not discourage extramarital sex. In addition, the Court pointed out that contraceptives were legal in Massachusetts as long as they were used for the prevention of disease but not when they were used to prevent conception.

Finally, the Court pointed to perhaps the most ludicrous aspect of the statute. In Massachusetts fornication is only a misdemeanor punishable by a thirty-dollar fine or 90 days in jail. If the purpose of the contraceptive law was to prohibit premarital sex, it is rather absurd that aiding the crime is a serious felony while the crime itself is a misdemeanor.

In short the Court held that the real purpose of the statute was an attempt to prohibit contraception itself. The statute was a codification of the value held by some members of the society that contraception is immoral; the only reason the statute was directed only at premarital sexual relations is that the state was constitutionally forbidden, after *Griswold,* from extending this prohibition to married people. The question for the Court was, given this purpose, can the state prohibit the use of contraceptives by the unmarried?

The Court then turned to the individual rights at stake. It concluded that there was a constitutional right involved:

> If the right of privacy means anything, it is the right of the individual, married or single, to be free from unwarranted governmental intrusion into matters so fundamentally affecting a person as the decision whether to bear or beget a child.

In effect this is a recognition that the right to privacy found in the penumbra of the Constitution includes another zone of privacy, sexual conduct between unmarried people. The issue before the court then was much the same as that before the Court in *Griswold*—to what extent can the state regulate contraception given the effect of the state's action on this constitutionally protected zone of privacy? The federal court of appeals was prepared to rule that the state cannot regulate contraception at all. The Supreme Court, however, made a somewhat narrower decision relying on an equal protection argument, although the practical impact is very much the same. The court held:

> We need not and do not, however, decide that important question in this case because, whatever the rights of the individual to access to contraceptives may be, the rights must be the same for the unmarried and the married alike.

The Court ordered Baird's conviction reversed and his release from prison.

Eisenstadt v. Baird shed further light on the constitutional right to privacy by defining another zone of privacy, sexual activities between unmarried people. The case also stands as a further example of how the courts will impose limits on the exercise of governmental power where that exercise interferes with the right to privacy. The opinion in *Eisenstadt,* however, stopped short of preventing any governmental regulation of contraceptives; similarly the opinion in *Griswold* indicated that some kind of regulation might be permissible. However, the state cannot prohibit the use of contraceptives, the giving of contraceptives, or their exhibition and, presumably, any other transfer of information. In addition, whatever it does, the state cannot discriminate between married and unmarried people.

Does this leave open the possibility that a state could require all (or some kinds of) contraceptives to be available only on prescription? Or could a state regulate the quality of available contraceptives by imposing standards on their manufacture?

With such a recent legal development as the right to privacy, it is difficult to answer these questions with any certainty; however, the abortions cases that followed *Griswold* and *Eisenstadt* went a long way toward answering those questions and further developed the meaning and importance of the right to privacy in the sexual activity/family planning context.

The right to privacy: the abortion cases

It is not surprising that soon after *Eisenstadt* was decided, the issue that arose was the extent of the state's power to regulate abortion decisions.

In the late 1960's and early 1970's in several parts of the country there were a number of legal attacks on the various state laws that attempted to prohibit or greatly restrict the availability of voluntary abortions. Some of these suits were successful; others were not. All were controversial. Finally in 1972 the issue found its way to the Supreme Court in the companion cases of *Roe v. Wade,* 410 U.S. 113 (1973) and *Doe v. Bolton,* 410 U.S. 179 (1973).

In *Roe v. Wade* a single woman suing under the assumed name of Jane Roe challenged the constitutionality of the Texas abortion statute, which made procuring or attempting an abortion except for the purpose of saving the life of the mother a felony. Roe claimed that the statute infringed on her constitutional right to privacy, citing the analogous decisions in *Griswold* and *Eisenstadt* as support. The state defended its statute with the argument that the prohibition of all but "medically necessary" abortions was a valid exercise of the state's police powers in matters relating to the public's health. Once again the Court was faced with the task of balancing the exercise of state authority against the allegation that it infringed on an individual constitutional right.

Much as it had in its earlier right to privacy decisions, the Court in *Roe* began its decision with an analysis of the extent of the state's authority and the purposes achieved by the statute. Mr. Justice Blackmun, writing for the majority, started with a long account of the legal controls that have been exercised over abortion decisons throughout history, beginning as early as the Persian, Greek, and Roman empires; tracing these controls through their development over the centuries in the English common law; and comparing these controls to the legal restraints imposed in many states. In every case he found that abortions were much more freely available in other times and other societies than under American criminal abortion statutes, of which Texas' was typical. Blackmun then detailed the official opinions on abortion of the American Medical Association, the American Public Health Association, and the American Bar Association and their criticisms of the restrictive policies reflected in those criminal statutes.

Blackmun was not, of course, suggesting that the law of other societies or the opinions of professional associations have any direct precedential effect on interpretations of American law. He was, however, making the point that the restrictions placed on abortion in states such as Texas are neither traditional, based on long experience, nor above criticism. Furthermore, since the police powers of the state are defined as those powers traditionally considered inherent in government (see Chapter 2), it is at least relevant to look at these other societies and, particularly, the English common law from which our legal system developed.

But more than anything else, Blackmun's long historical introduction was probably an acknowledgement of the obvious emotional and political overtones of this case; with the extent of public attention drawn to this case, it is understandable that the opinion would go into excessive and somewhat unnecessary detail to demonstate that the decision was given very careful consideration by the Court.

Having placed the issue in its proper historical perspective, the opinion then turned to the Texas statute and the purposes that could be cited as supporting this exercise of power. Blackmun found that there were two reasonable bases that could be cited as purposes for restricting abortion decisions: (1) protecting the mother from a dangerous risk to her health and (2) protecting prenatal life.

On the other hand, Blackmun found that the "zones of privacy" protected by the Constitution included the right of a woman to terminate her pregnancy and that, therefore, there was an important constitutional right at stake. Thus the Court was faced with the difficult problem of weighing the interests of the state against those of the individual. As Mr. Justice Blackmun posed the issue:

> We therefore conclude that the right of personal privacy includes the abortion decision, but that this right is not unqualified and must be considered against important state interests in regulation.

Given these conflicting interests, neither of which is absolute, the Court proceded with the following analysis:

> We repeat, however, that the State does have an important and legitimate interest in preserving and protecting the health of the pregnant woman . . . and that it has still another important and legitimate interest in protecting the potentiality of human life. These interests are separate and distinct. Each grows in substantiality as the woman approaches term and, at a point during pregnancy, each becomes "compelling."

> With respect to the State's important and legitimate interest in the health of the mother, the "compelling" point, in the light of present medical knowledge, is at approximately the end of the first trimester. This is so because of the now established medical fact that until the end of the first trimester mortality in abortion is less than mortality in normal childbirth. It follows that, from and after this point, a state may regulate the abortion procedure to the extent that the regulation reasonably relates to the preservation and protection of maternal life. Examples of permissible state regulation in this area are requirements as to the qualifications of the person who is to perform the abortion; as to the licensure of that person; as to the facility on which the procedure is to be performed, that is, whether it must be a hospital or may be a clinic or some other place of less-than-hospital status; as to the licensing of the facility; and the like.

> This means, on the other hand, that, for the period of pregnancy prior to this "compelling" point, the attending physician, in consultation with his patient, is free to determine, without regulation by the State, that in his medical judgement the patient's pregnancy should be terminated. If that decision is reached, the judgement may be effectuated by an abortion free of interference by the State.

> With respect to the State's important and legitimate interest in the potential life, the "compelling" point is at viability. This is so because the fetus then presumably has the capability of meaningful life outside the mother's womb. State regulation protective of fetal life after viability thus has both logical and biological justifications. If the State is interested in protecting fetal life after viability, it may go so far as to proscribe abortion during that period except when it is necessary to preserve the life or health of the mother.

This decision relies on two critical conclusions. The first is that the state's interest in protecting life is a protection of individual people, not the unborn or the "potentiality" of a person. This doesn't mean that the state cannot have an interest in protecting property and other "nonperson" interests, but in order to justify the infringement of an individual constitutional right, as in this case the invasion of a woman's right to privacy, the state must justify its exercise of power as for the protection of a living person.

The second critical conclusion is that a fetus becomes a living person only after it becomes viable, i.e., capable of life outside of the mother's womb; based on the current status of medical knowledge, this is generally accepted to begin after 24 to 28 weeks of pregnancy.

Based on these conclusions, the Court in *Roe* developed a series of guidelines for states to follow in regulating abortions. During the first trimester a state cannot justify regulation of a woman's right to terminate her pregnancy on any grounds. There is no viable fetus; there is no risk to her health; there are always some risks to any medical procedure, but in order to regulate this particular procedure, the state would have to have some grounds for regulating this procedure more strictly than it does other medical procedures; if anything, a first trimester abortion is safer than many surgical procedures—and, in fact, safer than the delivery of a baby.

After the first trimester of pregnancy, the state can regulate abortion in some ways, but, again, only if the regulation is reasonably related to the protection of maternal health. Thus, as Blackmun suggests, although prohibiting abortion would be overly broad and not a reasonable attempt to protect the mother, regulating the facilities where the procedure is performed or the qualifications of whoever performs abortions might be reasonable and constitutionally acceptable.

However, in the third trimester, the state can regulate abortion and prohibit it altogether, since at that point the fetus becomes viable and, therefore, a life, and the protection of the life of an individual person is a legitimate, if not a paramount, state purpose. The only exception listed by the Court is that a state may not proscribe abortion if it is necessary to preserve the life or health of the mother.

In the companion case of *Doe v. Bolton,* the Georgia criminal abortion statute was challenged by "Mary Doe." That law declared the performance of an abortion a crime unless perfomed by a physician and, "based on his best clinical judgment," the abortion was "necessary" because of (1) the risk of permanent and serious injury to the mother, (2) the likelihood that the fetus if born would have been physically or mentally defective, or (3) the fact that the pregnancy was a result of rape.

However, even with the consenting judgment of her physician, a woman was only allowed a legal abortion under Georgia law if a number of other conditions also were satisfied. These conditions included requirements that (1) two other physicians concur in writing with the first physician's judgment, based on independent medical examinations; (2) the abortion be performed in a hospital licensed by the state health department and accredited by the Joint Commission on Accreditation of Hospitals; and (3) the procedure be approved by a committee of the hospital of not less than three members of the hospital's staff.

The decision in *Roe v. Wade* held that any statute that prohibits abortion in the first two trimesters of pregnancy is unconstitutional. Therefore, the portion of the Georgia statute limiting legal abortions to those where the mother was endangered, the fetus defective, or the pregnancy a result of rape was invalid. The more difficult issue presented by the *Doe* case was whether the second portion of the Georgia statute requiring professional concurrence in the abortion and regulating the setting in which an abortion can take place was valid. In each of the previous right to privacy cases the Supreme Court had indicated that the state could exercise its power to regulate family planning decisions. Even where it interfered with individual privacy, regulation would be constitutional, as long as the regulation was reasonable and did not interfere too greatly with the constitutional right to privacy. In *Roe v. Wade* the Court had specifically upheld the right of the state to regulate abortion decisions and the conditions under which they could be performed, as long as the regulation was reasonably related to a legitimate state purpose such as the protection of maternal health.

That was exactly the issue before the Court in *Doe*. Were the conditions imposed on legal abortions in Georgia reasonably related to legitimate state purpose? How far would the Court go in examining the exact nature of an attempt to regulate abortion decisions? The message that was delivered in the opinion was very clear: the right to privacy is important enough that the courts will look rather closely at any exercise of state power that infringes on a protected zone of privacy. In this case, the conditions imposed by Georgia on abortion decisions were not reasonably related to any legitimate state purpose.

With respect to the requirements that abortions only be performed in hospitals that are licensed by the state and accredited by the Joint Commission on Accreditation of Hospitals, the Court in *Doe* held these requirements invalid. There was no reasonable relationship between these requirements and the state's legitimate interest in protecting the health of the mother and regulating the quality of medical care. JCAH accreditation only involves a general evaluation of a hospital and not an evaluation of the hospital's capabilities to perform abortions. Therefore, there was no reason to restrict abortions to only JCAH hospitals when other forms of nonabortion surgery are not similarly restricted. Going even further, the Court in *Doe* found no showing by the state that only licensed hospitals were suitable for abortions when, to the contrary, there was a great deal of evidence presented throughout the case that abortions under some circumstances could be performed in other licensed health facilities.

With respect to the requirement that the concurring approval of a hospital committee be obtained prior to an abortion in Georgia, the Court found no reasonable basis for this condition either. The Court again noted that there was no reason for treating abortion differently than other medical or surgical decisions. The Court concluded:

> We conclude that the interposition of the hospital abortion committee is unduly restrictive of the patient's rights and needs that, at this point, have already been medically delineated and substantiated by her personal physician. To ask more serves neither the hospital nor the State.

The Court then went on to the third condition imposed by the Georgia statute:

> . . . There remains, however, the required confirmation by two Georgia-licensed physicians in addition to the recommendation of the pregnant woman's own consultant (making

under the statute, a total of six physicians involved, including the three on the hospital's abortion committee). We conclude that this provision, too, must fall.

The statute's emphasis, as has been repetitively noted is on the attending physician's "best clinical judgment that an abortion is necessary." That should be sufficient. The reasons for the presence of the confirmation step in the statute are perhaps apparent, but they are insufficient to withstand constitutional challenge. Again, no other voluntary medical or surgical procedure for which Georgia requires confirmation has been cited to us. If a physician is licensed by the State, he is recognized by the State as capable of exercising acceptable clinical judgment. If he fails in this, professional censure or deprivation of his license are available remedies. Required acquiescence by copractitioners has no rational connection with a patient's needs and unduly infringes on the physician's right to practice. The attending physician will know when a consultation is advisable—the doubtful situation, the need for assurance when the medical decision is a delicate one, and the like. Physicians have followed this routine historically and know its usefulness and benefits to all concerned. It is till true today that "(r)eliance must be placed upon the assurance given by his license, issued by an authority competent to judge in that respect, that he [the physician] possessed the requisite qualifications." [citations omitted]

Future applications of the abortion cases

The decisions in *Roe v. Wade* and *Doe v. Bolton* had a tremendous impact on laws regulating abortion decisions. Nearly every state had to revise its statutes relating to abortions, and many statutes were totally invalidated by these decisions. Yet the controversy surrounding abortions is far from resolved —either as a public issue or as a matter of law.

There are still "abortion on demand" advocates who feel that a woman's decision to abort a pregnancy should not be regulated by the government in any way; at the other extreme, there are the "right to life" advocates, who have actively opposed the legalization and availability of abortions, even after the Supreme Court opinions in *Doe* and *Roe.* One measure of the strength and the fervor of the "right to life" movement, in fact, has been their political success despite *Roe* and *Doe.* Many states have passed legislation, of questionable validity, since those cases restricting the reimbursement under Medicaid for the performance of an abortion. At the federal level a number of antiabortion bills have been seriously debated, and several have been enacted, although their constitutionality is not clear. The amount of foreign aid money that can be spent for abortions has been limited; federally funded legal services attorneys have been forbidden by their authorizing statute from representing anyone seeking an abortion; and physicians and hospitals have been given the right to choose not to perform abortions as a matter of conscience. Furthermore, a direct attack on the Supreme Court abortion decisions has been launched by a proposed constitutional amendment that would give an unborn fetus the rights of a person under the U.S. Constitution, effectively reversing the *Roe* and *Doe* decisions.

In addition to these legislative activities, there is likely to be a series of related legal issues that are soon to be before the courts. Many commentators have characterized *Roe v. Wade* and *Doe v. Bolton* as having raised more questions than they settled. That is an unfair characterization of those cases. They certainly brought a great deal of clarity to the law as it relates to abortion decisions; but it is true that many legal issues relating to abortion remain unsettled.

One obvious problem concerns the Supreme Court's conclusion that viability is the point at which a fetus becomes a person, and the Court's definition of viability in technical terms of the current state of medical knowledge. Suppose, for example, that a new technique is developed that allows the maintenance of life and ensures the proper development of a fetus, even as early as the first trimester of pregnancy. Would a first trimester fetus then be considered to be viable—and a person? Or suppose that someday science develops the technology to raise a fertilized egg to development in an artificial environment. Would it be possible to argue that all fertilized eggs are viable? If these hypotheticals become realities, the courts will be faced with a series of difficult decisions; perhaps viability will be redefined to mean viability apart from the mother using no more than standard (or usual or reasonable) medical procedures to sustain life. However, even a close reading to these previous abortion cases gives little clear answer to these questions; they will have to be settled in future litigation.

Some of these issues have already been raised. In late 1974 a physician in Boston was tried and convicted for manslaughter after performing an abortion on a woman who was 20 to 28 weeks pregnant. The prosecution charged that the fetus that was removed was in fact viable and that the physician's failure to sustain life was manslaughter. In a trial that was marked by a highly emotional atmosphere and hints of racial prejudice, the jury found the physician guilty as charged. The conviction has been appealed, however, and undoubtedly several appellate courts will have to sort out the complicated legal issues involved in this case before the decision becomes final. In the meantime the trial will have an impact throughout the country. Whatever the eventual outcome of the case, many physicians will be hesitant to perform late-term abortions at the risk of being prosecuted. Already, other prosecutions have been initiated under similar circumstances, although the Boston case is the only one that has led to a conviction as of this date.

Another complex question suggested but not settled by the *Roe* and *Doe* cases involves the rights of a father to participate in abortion decisions. Given the decisions in those cases, can a man who has fathered a pregnancy claim he has a right to consent or withhold consent to an abortion of that pregnancy, or is it a decision only for the woman to make?

At first impression it might seem that the answer is straightforward. Such a requirement is unconstitutional. In *Roe* and *Doe* the Supreme Court spoke in terms of the woman's right to consent and right to privacy, not the rights of both parents. The only conditions that were allowed to be imposed on abortion decisions were those that served a legitimate state interest. If the father has no right to privacy that the state can claim it is protecting, then what purpose can justify the father's claim of a legal right to consent? It is critically important to understand that this is fallacious reasoning. The answer to this question is not clear at all and was certainly not settled by the decisions in *Roe v. Wade* and *Doe v. Bolton.* This question involves a very different set of legal rights. The relationship between a father and a mother of a fetus is one between two private individuals. *Roe* and *Doe* involved the relationship between a private individual and the government. The legal rights that make up the latter relationship are established by, among other things, the U.S. Constitution. One of the constitutional rights includes the power of the government to act to protect individual life and to protect the health of its citizens. Another of those constitutional rights is the right of the individual to privacy, including the right to choose to abort a pregnancy. *Roe* and *Doe* involved a balancing of those rights and a decision that analyzed the legal basis for those rights.

A suit between a woman seeking an abortion and a father trying to prevent that abortion would involve private legal rights. The constitutional right to privacy would be practically irrelevant—it established a relationship between the woman and the government, but not between two private individuals. The eventual decision in this controversy would be based on notions of property, torts, and other legal rights recognized between two private individuals (see Chapter 6, *infra*).

Of the few cases that have considered this question already, almost all have held that abortion is a decision for a woman to make and that a father's consent is not a necessary prerequisite. Yet the issue has not been clearly settled—and certainly it was not settled by the decisions in *Roe* and *Doe.*

Conclusion

In the relatively short span of 10 years an extremely important constitutional right, the right ot privacy, has developed in the law and has a substantial impact on a range of family planning decisions. The power of the state to regulate those decisions has been severely limited. But even more than its past impact, the right to privacy will be important for its future implications. As stated in the introduction to this chapter, whatever the exact meaning of privacy, it includes at least the notion that an individual has a right to be left alone and to be free to make personal decisions. In interpreting the legal right to privacy, the law has been extended to protect the privacy of a number of personal decisions. Contraception and abortion decisions fall within "zones of privacy" and are protected from unreasonable governmental interference; but almost all health-related activities involve equally personal decisions. Consequently, the extent of the right to privacy will be a relevant question that will be asked in regard to virtually all public health issues.

It is impossible to predict how the right to privacy will be interpreted under each new set of circumstances. Certainly the evolution of the right to privacy from its first narrow recognition in *Griswold v. Connecticut* to its application in the abortion decisions illustrates this point. The reasoning in each of the right to privacy cases was consistent, and each case was related to the precedents, but the specific outcomes were not always predictable. That is why it is so important to understand the underlying legal principles of an issue and to understand the legal process that is involved in their interpretation; the individual decisions answer certain specific questions, but the principles behind those decisions should be more important guides for future behavior.

The courts, and particularly the Supreme Court, have exhibited a willingness to jealously guard the individual right to privacy. Interference with that right even under the guise of the state government's police powers is not easily tolerated. This is part of the role that the judicial branch is supposed to play under our legal system: the courts must enforce individual constitutional rights, even when it requires that the judiciary invalidate decisions by the legislative or executive branch. However, it would be inaccurate to generalize from the example used in this chapter to the conclusion that where a constitutional right is infringed, the state's authority is usually limited. As shown in Chapters 1 and 2, if anything, the contrary is more often true.

In the cases described in this chapter the state legislation involved was practically rewritten by the courts. In other situations even the Supreme Court has been less willing to interfere so deeply with legislative decision making, even where constitutional rights are at stake. Perhaps this only highlights the importance of the right to privacy. Alternatively, this might indicate that with these particular cases, the Supreme Court felt it necessary to settle a very explosive set of issues in a very definitive, albeit extraordinary, manner.

In any event individual rights are one important limitation on the exercise of governmental power. The right to privacy is just one example of such a right. It is an individual right that has gone through a very recent period of evolution, and one that will be very relevant to future developments in the field of public health.

References

Abortion and the law, Newsweek **86:**18, March 3, 1975.

Butler, P.: The right to abortion under Medicaid, Clearinghouse Rev. **7:**713, 1974.

Gutman, J.: Can hospitals constitutionally refuse to permit abortions and sterilizations? Fam. Plann./Population Rep. **2:**146, 1973.

Krouss, E.: Hospital survey on sterilization policies, March, 1975 (American Civil Liberties Union pamphlet).

Warren, S., and Brandeis, L.: The right to privacy, Harv. L. Rev. **4:**193, 1890.

Related cases

Doe v. Rampton, 366 F. Supp. 189 (D. Utah 1973).

Parrish v. County of Alameda, 66 C.2d 260,425 P.2d 223 (1967).

Wyman v. James, 400 U.S. 309 (1971).

CHAPTER 5

Government entitlement programs: Medicaid and Medicare

Previous chapters have examined the legal rights that exist between the government and the individual primarily in terms of the constitutional basis for governmental authority and the individual constitutional rights that may impose limitation on the exercise of that authority. This chapter will examine this same set of legal rights, those between the government and the individual, but with a different emphasis. The focus will be on the legal rights established when the government enacts a statutory benefit or "entitlement" program. Specifically, this chapter will be an examination of two federal government programs: Medicaid, the medical assistance program for the poor, and Medicare, the health insurance program for the elderly and the disabled.

Development of social welfare programs

To understand the Medicaid and Medicare programs, one must first have a basic understanding of the structure of the American welfare system.

Prior to the 1930's, some individual states had limited programs that provided financial and/or medical assistance to the poor. However, during the depression when the inadequacies of these programs became apparent, the federal government took for the first time a major responsibility for maintenance of an adequate social welfare system. In 1935 Congress enacted the Social Security Act, 42 U.S.C. section 301 *et seq.* Included in this legislation were (1) a welfare program by which federal funding was given to states that would provide financial assistance to three categories of the poor: the blind, the elderly, and families with dependent children (a fourth category, the disabled, was added in 1950), and (2) a social security insurance program by which wage earners paid a monthly payroll deduction and received financial assistance when they retired or were disabled. Whereas the welfare program was primarily administered by each state, the social security program was entirely federally administered. This distinction between "welfare" for the poor and "social security insurance" for the former wage earner has persisted throughout the history of the programs, with all of the social and psychological differences suggested by those two terms.

Between 1935 and 1965 these programs were gradually expanded to include payments for medical care as well as financial assistance. First, some state welfare departments began to make payments for medical care to people on welfare, in the form of a "special needs" allowance to the recipient or in the form of direct payments to the provider of medical care. In 1960 Congress enacted the Kerr-Mills program of medical assistance for the elderly, administered by the states with financial support from the federal government. The theory behind the Kerr-Mills program was that since medical expenses consumed such a large portion of the income of many of the elderly, it was necessary to expand public medical assistance to the many elderly people who were not poor enough or who were otherwise ineligible for welfare assistance. Some states choose to participate in the Kerr-Mills program, but by and large it was neither popular nor successful.

By 1964 the concept of comprehensive medical insurance for the elderly had gained a great deal of political support. The central issue in the congressional debate was not whether there should be a program, but whether it should be—like social security—an entirely federal program or—like the welfare programs—primarily state administered with federal financial assistance. The result was a compromise: in 1965 Congress enacted a federally administered program of health insurance for the elderly or disabled social security recipient, financed by the Social Security payroll deductions (Medicare Part A), a federally administered supplemental insurance program that Medicare recipients could purchase (Medicare Part B), and in addition, a program of medical assistance for welfare recipients and other poor people administered by the state (Medicaid). Thus Medicaid was actually conceived in a hurried congressional compromise. While the controversy over Medicare had been intensely waged for several years and its details tediously debated, the Medicaid program was almost thoughtlessly appended to the Medicare bill, and Congress, ironically, gave it relatively little consideration. These two new programs, Medicare and Medicaid, became the new Titles XVIII and XIX, respectively, of the Social Security Act (42 U.S.C. section 1395 and 42 U.S.C. section 1396).

Thus by 1965 the Social Security Act provided for (1) four welfare programs admistered by the state: Aid to the Totally Disabled (ATD), Aid to the Blind (AB), Old Age Security (OAS), and Aid to Families with Dependent Children (AFDC); (2) a social security program for the retired or disabled wage earner; (3) Medicaid for welfare recipients and (some) other poor people; and (4) Medicare for social security recipients. The only subsequent change in this structure came with the Social Security Amendments of 1972, which "federalized" ATD, AB, and OAS. These programs are now known collectively as the Supplemental Security Income program (SSI). SSI payments come from the federal government. The level of payment to recipients by the federal government is uniform throughout the states and is higher than that paid by many states before SSI. States may pay eligible recipients supplementary benefits; states that previously paid recipients of ATD, AB or OAS at a level higher than that paid under SSI are required to make a supplementary payment in order that the total assistance received by an SSI recipient is at least as high as it was before SSI.

For purposes of clarity it is necessary to point out that the entire system of state and federal welfare is much more complicated than can be detailed here. There are a number of federally financed programs that could also be considered part of the total welfare system. Among these is the federal food stamp program for the poor. There are also the federally financed, state administered programs of unemployment compensation for the recently unemployed. In addition there are some states and local governments that maintain their own welfare or medical assistance programs for the poor who do not qualify for any of the federally funded welfare programs, e.g., adults with no children.

Medicaid and Medicare have grown enormously in the last decade and now account for a major portion of the total welfare budget. Medicaid costs about 11 billion dollars a year and provides benefits to 27 million poor people. Medicare costs about the same amount and provides benefits to about 23 million elderly or disabled people.

The administration of Medicaid and Medicare

Medicaid is best described as a cooperative federal-state medical assistance program for the poor. All states participate, although in theory each state has the option of participating or not. The federal government contributes 50% to 83% of the cost of the program, depending upon the relative wealth of the state. At the state level the program must be administered by a "single state agency," usually the welfare department or the state health department. At the federal level the program is monitored by the Medical Services Administration of the Department of Health, Education and Welfare (DHEW).

DHEW is, however, decentralized to some extent into ten regional offices. Medicaid regulations and policy decisions are made in Washington, but actual enforcement of the federal law is the responsibility of each regional office, which is required to monitor each state's compliance with the federal law. The state Medicaid agency must submit to its regional DHEW office a "state plan" describing its Medicaid program; this document must be legally authorized by the state Medicaid statute and regulations, but its form is prescribed by DHEW and the federal law. The state plan forms a contract between the state and federal government in which the state promises to provide the outlined services to given people and the federal government agrees to pay part of the costs of the program. This contract is enforceable by Medicaid beneficiaries, who can challenge in court a state's failure to conform to the federal requirements. DHEW has its own little-used procedure to enforce compliance with its requirements—a notice that the state is out of compliance with federal law, a hearing on the issues, and the power to withold payment of all federal funds to the state Medicaid program.

Medicare administration is exclusively federal, conducted by the Social Security Administration (SSA) of DHEW. SSA makes extensive use of insurance companies (usually Blue Cross and Blue Shield)—called fiscal intermediaries—to administer payment to medical providers and practitioners. Some state Medicaid agencies also use such intermediaries. SSA also delegates to state licensing agencies its responsibility to certify that institutional providers of care meet federal quality standards.

Eligibility for Medicaid and Medicare

The Medicaid program as originally written was intended to cover all people eligible for welfare (ATD, AB, OAS, and AFDC) *plus,* at the option of the state, other poor people not eligible for welfare, i.e., the aged, the blind, the disabled, or dependent children whose incomes were slightly over the welfare level. However, as the program grew to be more expensive than originally predicted, legislative amendments were enacted that were intended to limit the costs of the program, usually by altering the eligibility requirements that a state must impose. Thus the current Medicaid program is a product of two conflicting legislative policies, and the eligibility requirements are so complicated that they nearly defy understanding.

1. *Categorically needy—mandatorily eligible.*

First of all, certain groups of people are mandatorily eligible. That is, if a state chooses to have a Medicaid program, it must provide Medicaid to at least these groups of people.

All people actually receiving aid under the state plan for AFDC must be eligible for Medicaid. Eligibility must also be extended to all people under 21 who would be "dependent" children under AFDC plans were it not for age or school attendance requirements, plus all families receiving AFDC in at least 3 of the 6 months immediately preceding the month in which the family became ineligible for assistance because of increased hours of, or income from, employment. If employment continues, such family members are eligible for Medicaid for 4 additional months beginning with the month of ineligibility.

In addition all people who were receiving Medicaid in December 1973 when the ATD, AB, and OAS programs were federalized into SSI must continue to receive Medicaid.

However, after December 1973, for the first time states are no longer required to provide Medicaid to all adult people receiving ATD, AB, or OAS, although all AFDC recipients must be eligible.

The 1972 Social Security amendments to the Medicaid law gave states the option (after December 1973) of providing Medicaid to one of the following three groups: (1) all people receiving aid under SSI; (2) any or all people receiving benefits under SSI or a state supplementary program; or (3) SSI recipients meeting the adult welfare eligiblity criteria (age, disability, or blindness), and income or resources standards used by the state on January 1, 1972. In determining whether an individual meets the criteria used in 1972, the state must subtract SSI and state supplementary payments and incurred medical expenses from the individual's income and compare that figure with the January 1972 income eligibility standard. In other words states choosing this option to restrict Medicaid eligibility for SSI recipients must apply a "spend-down" for Medicaid eligibility (see explanation of "spend-down" *infra* p. 75).

This provision in the law permitting states to restrict their Medicaid eligibility was enacted to ease the burden upon state Medicaid programs that Congress assumed would occur because of increased eligibility of adults for aid resulting from SSI income levels, which are higher than previous state welfare income levels. Several states have taken the restrictive option and do not permit all SSI recipients to be automatically eligible for Medicaid.

States must also provide Medicaid to the following two groups of people:

(1) people who would be eligible for aid as AFDC or SSI recipients except for an eligibility condition specifically prohibited by Medicaid and (2) persons protected by specific congressional action from losing their Medicaid because of the August 1972 Social Security benefit increase.

Obviously a thorough understanding of the groups of people that are mandatorily eligible would require a working knowledge of the number of people who fall into the various subcategories and the kinds of exclusions and eligibility requirements built into welfare programs by federal and state law. A slightly oversimplified explanation would be that the states are required to offer Medicaid to the "categorically needy," roughly equivalent to all welfare recipients. However, recent amendments to the Medicaid statute allow states to restrict the eligibility of those people who qualify for SSI: the blind, the aged, and the totally disabled.

2. *Optional categorically needy.*

Ever since the enactment of Medicaid in 1965, DHEW has, without any actual statutory authority, permitted states to provide Medicaid to optional groups, which it calls "optional categorically needy." This is important since it provides an intermediate step that states may take before undertaking the expense of a full-scale medically needy program. The optional categorically needy groups that a state may cover are: (1) people meeting all conditions of eligibility for aid under AFDC, SSI, or state supplementation but who have not applied; (2) people in medical facilities (primarily nursing homes) who would be eligible for welfare if they left such institutions (these people may also be treated as medically needy if the state has a medically needy program); (3) persons who would be eligible for AFDC, except that the state AFDC plan imposes more stringent eligibility conditions upon applicants than those required by the Social Security Act; (4) all persons under 21 years of age who qualify on the basis of financial eligibility but not as dependent children under the state's AFDC plan; (5) "caretaker" relatives of AFDC children who are ineligible for welfare because of age or school attendance requirements; (6) persons who would be eligible for welfare if their work-related childcare costs were paid by earnings rather than by a service expenditure by the welfare agency.

Permitting states to provide Medicaid to these subcategories of people is, of course, commendable from the point of view of the recipients who are made eligible for Medicaid, but it is a good example of "agency legislation." Strictly speaking, DHEW has violated a mandatory requirement of the Medicaid statute. If a state provides Medicaid to persons who are not welfare *recipients* (such as any of the groups of persons who listed in the preceding paragraph) then it is supposed to provide a full-scale medically needy plan. Interestingly enough, even Congress has never reprimanded the agency for amending the legislation in this way. In fact, if faced with a challenge to DHEW's practice, a court might invoke the doctrine that by not criticizing DHEW, Congress has implicitly acquiesced in this broad administrative interpretation and thereby validated this apparently illegal exercise of administrative power.

3. *The medically needy.*

As mentioned earlier, the original concept behind Medicaid was that it would provide medical assistance coverage for all people on welfare and would permit states to cover people not receiving welfare whose income and/or resources are somewhat higher than the welfare eligibility levels, but who otherwise met the physical criteria for welfare eligibility—the medically needy. The thought behind this was that many people with high medical bills (which would not be considered in their application for welfare) should not be forced onto welfare or into bankruptcy. This medically needy program was enacted to prevent such destitution caused by medical expenses; it had a unique and important feature, making it a sort of catastrophic health insurance program. Although Congress required that DHEW establish income levels somewhat higher than the income and resources levels of the welfare programs, an individual with income above the medically needy eligibility level was not automatically ineligible for Medicaid but could become eligible when his or her income, *reduced by actual medical expenses,* fell below the medically needy eligibility level. This concept came to be called "spending down" or "satisfying the medically needy liability." Theoretically, this provided the opportunity for people with high incomes to become eligible for Medicaid when their medical expenses were sufficiently high to reduce their net incomes to the medically needy eligibility level. This feature was not originally built into the categorically needy program, but as mentioned above, it now applies if the state chooses the "restrictive option." DHEW initially set the floor for the medically needy income eligibility level at the highest welfare standard in the state, so that people with incomes above any welfare level could become eligible for Medicaid.

Since the medically needy program was open-ended, it became very expensive in the early years of Medicaid; in the first 2 years of operation the Medicaid program more than quadrupled its projected costs. Congress felt compelled to adopt a ceiling on the medically needy income level at $133^1/_3\%$ of the welfare payment level in the AFDC program, which in most states is the lowest of all the welfare program payment levels. This statutory limitation sets an artifically low ceiling on medically needy Medicaid eligibility. In many states this is lower than the SSI payment levels for the aged, blind, and disabled. Such a limitation directly contravenes the original idea that the medically needy program would have an income level higher than that of all the welfare programs. For example, in California, the SSI level is $259 for an adult over 65 years of age. The spend-down level for the medically needy program is $221, which is 133% of the California state AFDC welfare payment level for a single person. An individual who is receiving Social Security, supplemented by SSI, may become ineligible for SSI when he or she receives one of the almost annual increases in Social Security benefits; then instead of being eligible for Medicaid by paying back the increase, he or she must pay substantially more, spending-down to the artificially low medically needy income eligibility level.

In spite of this bizarre legislative inconsistency, the medically needy program provides an important concept in the theory of publicly financed medical care. It operates on the assumption that an individual should not need to be eligible per se for welfare in order to become eligible for publicly funded medical assistance. States that cover the medically needy, currently one-half of the states, must cover all groups of people as medically needy that correspond to the covered categorically needy groups. In other words, states must include the aged, the blind, the disabled, and dependent children plus any of the "optional categorically needy" groups mentioned above for which the state has chosen to provide Medicaid.

States with medically needy programs must establish a uniform medically needy income eligibility level, subject to the $133^{1}/_{3}\%$ of the AFDC welfare payment level ceiling. DHEW has determined by regulation that the eligibility standard for families of three or more should be at least at the level of the welfare eligibility standard for AFDC, and that the eligibility level for one- or two-person families must be the higher of the level of the AFDC standard or the highest income standard of the SSI program. Resources (real and personal property) must be at least as high as those under the SSI program in the state.

Families with dependent children and aged, blind, and disabled people whose incomes or resources are above the state's medically needy income or resource eligibility levels may become eligible for Medicaid by applying all of their excess income (i.e., the income above the income eligibility level) or resources first for medical insurance premiums (including any enrollment fee, copayment or deductible required by the state Medicaid program) and then for necessary medical or remedial care recognized under state law but not provided under the state Medicaid program; finally, the excess income is applied to Medicaid-covered services. When the state plan does not provide for dental care, for example, a medically needy eligible individual can apply excess income first toward dental costs, and then toward the cost of services for which the state Medicaid agency will pay. Once all such excess income and resources are exhausted, the state must pay for all additional services covered by the plan that the medically needy family receives.

For example, a family of four in a state where the AFDC payment level is $270 for such a family has a medically needy income eligibility level of $360. If the family's monthly income is $400 the family must pay or incur $40 per month of medical costs before becoming eligible for Medicaid. Insurance premiums, Medicaid premiums, copayments, deductibles, and the costs of non-Medicaid services are deducted. The family is then eligible for its monthly Medicaid card. The state must pay for all Medicaid-covered services the family uses once it has incurred the $40 spend-down each month. However, the state will never pay for the expenses incurred and applied toward the spend-down. A state may choose any period between 1 and 6 months on which to calculate the availability of income. During this time the Medicaid applicant must satisfy the spend-down. In the example above, if the state uses a 3-month period, the family's liability is $120 ($1200, the quarterly income, less $1080, the quarterly eligibility level).

4. *Medicare eligibility.*

Since Medicare is entirely a federal program and there is no "means" test as a prerequisite, eligibility for Medicare is relatively simple. All people over

65 years of age who receive Social Security old-age benefits and all people receiving Social Security disability benefits for at least 24 months are automatically eligible for Medicare—without regard to their income, assets, or any other characteristic. There are some people who are not eligible for Social Security benefits, e.g., the self-employed and some governmental employees, but at least 95% of the population is eligible. In addition anyone who is either aged or disabled but not receiving Social Security benefits may pay a premium of $36 a month and essentially buy Medicare just like private health insurance. The vast majority of Medicare beneficiaries, however, are also receiving Social Security benefits.

Services covered by Medicaid and Medicare

At the outset it must be pointed out that neither Medicaid nor Medicare provides services for eligible recipients. Both programs assure that payments will be made for certain kinds of medical services rendered by providers of medical care. There is no assurance that these services will be available or accessible. Providers are not required to accept either Medicaid or Medicare patients. These programs only assure that if the recipient receives the services, they will be paid for.

The federal Medicaid statute imposes certain requirements on each state, but also offers the state a number of options. All states must pay for certain basic medical services. The variety of additional services for which states may pay is almost infinite. Basic Medicaid-required services for the categorically needy are: (1) inpatient hospital services; (2) outpatient hospital services; (3) physician services; (4) x-ray and laboratory services; (5) skilled nursing home services for persons over 21 years of age and home health services for persons who have left nursing homes; (6) health screening services for children under 21 years; and (7) family planning services. If a state's program includes the medically needy, it must pay for either the basic required services listed or 7 out of a list of sixteen services described in the federal law for which Medicaid will pay (including such items as drugs, dental care, optometry services, medical equipment, and prosthetic devices).

An additional benefit that DHEW requires all states to pay on behalf of both the categorically and medically needy is transportation to medical care. While transportation is not a specific service defined in the federal law, DHEW considers it necessary to implement other provisions of the law, such as the requirement that services be available uniformly throughout the state and that persons have a free choice of providers. However, states have been notorious in failing to pay for medical transportation, probably because of its high costs.

The federal Medicaid law did not define the amount and duration of the services for which it required the states to pay. The frequent references to the "amount, scope and duration" in the Medicaid law indicate that Congress intended to give the states considerable discretion in limiting not only the number of services they cover but also to limit the amount and/or duration of each service. For instance, physician services might be limited to four visits per month or hospital stays to 15 days per admission. As the costs of the Medicaid program have become increasingly burdensome to the states, several states have chosen to drastically limit the amount of each of the services for which they will pay.

Medicare Part A (which is automatically available to social security beneficiaries who are over 65 years of age or disabled) covers 90 days of inpatient hospital care "per spell of illness," 100 days of skilled nursing home services after a period of hospitalization, and 100 days of home nursing care services after a hospital or nursing home stay. Persons eligible for Part A may also subscribe to Part B, the Supplementary Medical Insurance Program, which pays for physician's services, physical therapy, home nursing care, equipment, prostheses, and ambulance services. The monthly premium of approximately $7 is usually paid by the state Medicaid agencies for people eligible for both Medicaid and Medicare. The Medicare benefit package, designed more like a commercial insurance policy, is somewhat more limited than the benefits required by Medicaid law and considerably more limited than the services covered by the more liberal state Medicaid programs.

Cost sharing, utilization control, and quality assurance

In spite of the obvious hardship of imposing any cost sharing on Medicaid recipients, who are by definition without adequate financial resources, the Medicaid law permits states to impose premiums, deductibles, and copayments upon Medicaid recipients. States may impose deductibles and copayments on the categorically needy for nonmandatory services and may require the medically needy to pay monthly premiums related to income and impose deductibles and copayments upon the medically needy for all services.

In addition to the durational limitations explained above and the premium that must be paid by the recipient to receive Part B, Medicare recipients also are subject to substantiial cost-sharing requirements. As of 1975 there is a $92 deductible for hospital coverage and coinsurance of $23 per day on the sixtieth through ninetieth day, as well as a deductible for the cost of the first three pints of blood. There are coinsurance charges of $11.50 per day for the twentieth through the one-hundredth day of nursing home care. There is a $60 annual deductible for using Part B services and a 20% coinsurance fee for all services under Part B except home health care. Mental health services reimbursed are limited to $300 per year.

Both the Medicaid and the Medicare federal statutes require that providers be certified before they participate in these programs (see Chapter 8, *infra,* for a description of certification). Under both programs there are also required procedures for assuring that institutions participating in these programs have internal medical review of the quality of, and need for, institutional care. Under Medicaid, each state agency must establish a program of "utilization control" in order "to safeguard against unnecessary utilization of such care and services and to assure that payments . . . are not in excess of reasonable charges consistent with efficiency, economy and quality of care."

The Social Security amendments of 1972 contained several provisions requiring that these utilization controls be strengthened and become more functional. From these amendments DHEW adopted regulations that require that all hospitals participating in Medicaid and Medicare establish internal utilization review committees, which decide within 1 day of each Medicaid or Medicare patient's admission whether the admission is medically necessary and periodically review that decision. However, these regulations were the subject of a lawsuit challenging their validity in 1975, and prior to a final judicial determination they were withdrawn by DHEW for modification. In May 1976 modified regulations were proposed, but whether they will ever be finalized and put into operation is difficult to determine.

These utilization review regulations were obviously designed to prepare institutions for the eventual implementation of Professional Standards Review Organizations (PSRO's). Among the many provisions of the Social Security amendments of 1972 were provisions establishing a program of federally funded PSRO's and requiring peer review of all providers participating in the Medicare and Medicaid programs (and the Maternal and Child Health program). This system of peer review is to be first developed for institutionally based medical care, but will eventually review the care delivered in both institutional and noninstitutional settings.

The PSRO legislation establishes some ambitious goals. Through a variety of peer review activities, PSRO's are supposed to evaluate all medical services for which Medicaid or Medicare reimbursement is sought to determine if (1) the services provided were necessary, (2) the services provided were of adequate quality, and (3) whether, in the case of institutional care, those services could be provided more economically in a different type of facility.

In light of the obviously controversial nature of the PSRO program and the traditional resistance of the medical profession to any kind of outside review or control, the PSRO legislation delegated much of the responsibility for and control of the program to the profession itself. At least until 1976, in order to qualify as a PSRO an organization had to be open to all physicians practicing in the PSRO area and include in its membership at least a substantial proportion of those physicians. This local organization not only has the primary responsibility for conducting the review activities required under the PSRO program, but also is responsible for setting the standards to be applied in those activities.

While the PSRO law requires that, eventually, review be made of the necessity and quality of care provided under all three of these federal health programs, it is important to bear in mind that the PSRO program as a whole is still at an early developmental stage. Few existing PSRO's are operational, and those that are operating have a very limited scope of work. In fact, the PSRO program may never be fully developed, for at least two reasons: despite its intentions to save money, the PSRO program is a very costly one to administer; it could prove too costly to continue. Even if cost-effectiveness is not a problem, the intended PSRO functions may prove to be politically or technologically impossible.

Nonetheless, DHEW has outlined a work program for PSRO's that has three basic decision-making processes: admissions certification, continued stay review, and medical care evaluation studies.

Admission certification is a process by which a determination is made of the "necessity" and "appropriateness" of a patient's admission to a hospital. It occurs either prior to or immediately following a patient's admission. If the admission is unnecessary, or inappropriate, no payment will be made for any services rendered or costs incurred. At the time that an admission is certified, it is certified for a fixed period of time based on PSRO length-of-stay norms.

Continued stay review is virtually the same process as admissions certification, except that it is an evaluation of the necessity of further hospitalization and the quality of care being received and is made periodically during hospitalization. The first continued stay review is at the expiration of the initially assigned certification period. Each subsequent certification prescribes another fixed period of certification.

Medical care review is a retrospective in-depth study of some aspect of the health care delivered in a facility. Each PRSO (or each hospital delegated PSRO review function) must be conducting at least one medical care review study at any time. DHEW apparently intends that this review process be primarily informational and not focus on determinations regarding the specific performance of any one medical care provider. The PSRO Program Manual describes medical care reviews with the cryptic statement: "For the most part they do not deal with the individual patient or practitioner, but will require information related to the care provided by a number of practitioners to a number of patients." However, to the extent that medical care evaluation studies do evaluate the care delivered by specific providers, the determination could be the basis for sanctions against that provider, as described below.

PSRO's may be primarily concerned with discharging the responsibilities outlined above, at least in their first years of operation, but PSRO's will also be involved in other activities and in making other determinations.

The PSRO statute requires that PSRO's develop and maintain patient profiles. Depending upon how this heretofore undefined concept is actually defined, this might involve rather important determinations regarding the care given specific patients. The PSRO Program Manual indicates that PSRO's may also have to conduct retrospective claims review, although it is not clear exactly what is meant by this, nor is there specific statutory authority for it. The manual describes this review as not initially required of PSRO's, but it may be when other forms of review, i.e., the basic three processes described above, are not implemented, or if implemented, are not effective. The manual also requires discharge planning. This is a requirement that a determination be made that patients who are to be discharged from a hospital to another, less intensive, level of care actually have these alternative resources available to them. Although the manual lists this in conjunction with continued stay review, it is described as a process that begins immediately after admission, and it does include a quite different type of determination than that required in continued stay review. Another critical PSRO function will be the development of norms, criteria, and standards. These will be the basis for all PSRO determinations.

PSRO's must make reports and recommendations to DHEW when they identify providers in violation of the obligations imposed by the PSRO statute.

These obligations are simply a reversal of the responsibilities of the PSRO. Providers have an obligation not to deliver unnecessary or poor quality care and not to order hospitalization when a less intensive level of care would be appropriate. In addition to the PSRO authority to deny reimbursement for violations of these obligations through the admissions certification or continued stay review processes, the PSRO can, when appropriate, recommend to DHEW that one of the sanctions available to DHEW under the PSRO statute be imposed. DHEW may either exclude the provider from participation in Medicaid or Medicare (or the Maternal and Child Health program), or it may order the provider to reimburse the government for unnecessary services provided and/or to pay a fine. These sanctions are to be imposed when the provider fails to comply with PSRO obligations in a substantial number of cases, or grossly or flagrantly violates these obligations in one or more cases.

Provider participation in Medicaid and Medicare

One of the greatest problems facing Medicaid, and, to a lesser extent, Medicare, recipients is the unwillingness of providers to participate in these programs. This is particularly true of physicians. (This will only be compounded when the PSRO's become operational.) It is clear that neither Congress nor DHEW intends to require participation of any provider who is unwilling to take patients under either program; in fact the preamble to the Medicare statute states explicitly that there shall be no control over the practice of medicine or interference with the administration of health care facilities. (This is a product of the medical profession's political influence on the enactment of that program.) Yet such a policy is almost absurd if taken literally, and, despite this policy, the ensuing years since the enactment of Medicaid and Medicare have, in fact, resulted in some fundamental changes in the practice of medicine.

Physician enthusiasm for both Medicare and Medicaid has certainly diminished in the last 10 years. Yet physicians prefer to participate in Medicare rather than Medicaid because Medicare's payment levels and administrative requirements are less onerous. While Medicare does set up a rather limiting schedule that restricts the amount physicians may collect from the Social Security Administration for treating Medicare patients, the physicians are permitted to bill the patient for the remainder of the fee that they would have charged private patients. Thus physicians are not really disadvantaged by the lower Medicare fee schedule. Furthermore, the Medicare schedules are annually updated, and they better approximate the physician's actual charges. On the other hand, the Medicaid program specifically forbids physicians participating in Medicaid from charging additional sums to patients except copayments that the state expressly permits them to collect. Also, Medicaid fee levels in most states are much lower than those under Medicare. These financial limitations combined with many burdensome bureaucratic requirements such as requiring authorization before performing services, complex billing procedures, slow payment, and frequent changes in program services have turned many physicians away from Medicaid.

Access to hospitals is not as great a problem for the Medicaid recipient, since hospitals are reimbursed on a cost basis and have little to lose by participating in the program, although they may discriminate against the poor and minorities for other than financial reasons.

While the federal law does not mandate provider participation in Medicaid, it does require that the program be administered by the state "in the best interests of the recipients" and that it must provide medical assistance "promptly to all eligible recipients." These provisions can form the basis of a legal challenge to a state's Medicaid administrative system that is so complex as to discourage providers from participating in the program. However, proving that the administrative burdens themselves are the sole obstacle to provider participation is a very difficult legal proposition; it would require vast amounts of evidence and some frank admissions from Medicaid providers. Therefore, although a legal right to have services available may arguably exist, it would be very difficult to enforce.

Low fees are generally singled out as the main reason for providers refusing to participate in Medicaid. DHEW regulations require states to establish Medicaid reimbursement levels sufficient to encourage at least as many providers of medical services to enter the Medicaid program as are available to the general community. The regulations do, however, impose ceilings on what states may pay participating providers. In the case of hospitals the ceiling is "reasonable costs," and in the case of physicians and other noninstitutional providers it is "reasonable charges." Because of the breadth of that standard it is possible to argue that states must set their fee levels high enough to encourage physicians to participate in the program. Once again, however, it would be a difficult legal argument to prove, requiring a tremendous amount of evidence of appropriate reimbursement levels and the effect that they would have on physician participation. DHEW has never enforced these fee regulations, nor has it ever exercised sanctions against a state for having an inadequate number of Medicaid providers available to recipients.

Complexity of the legal structure

Much of the preceding summary of eligibility, coverage of services, and the cost-sharing, utilization controls, and quality assurance provisions of the Medicaid and Medicare programs have been simplified, perhaps oversimplified, into a rather general sketch of two extremely complicated programs. These summaries should be taken as general descriptions and with the awareness that the administrative policies, specific regulations, and, to a lesser extent, the statutory basis are constantly changing. The Medicaid program, since it is a joint federal-state program, is particularly complex and subject to almost daily changes. To understand all of the details of the Medicaid program from a legal perspective, one would have to start with the very long federal statute, 42 U.S.C. section 1396 *et seq.*, Title XIX of the Social Security Act. One would also have to have a working knowledge of the series of regulations issued periodically by DHEW, codified as 45 C.F.R. section 246 *et seq.*, which make more specific and detailed the express congressional requirements of the statute. Additionally, DHEW publishes a manual that interprets the regulations and describes program requirements in greater detail. That agency also issues policy information statements to state Medicaid agencies on topics of current interest, which require immediate distribution or are otherwise inappropriate subject matter for regulations. Then one would have to understand the program at a particular state's level. There must be a state statute authorizing the state Medicaid program and regulations interpreting and implementing that statute. There would probably be a state handbook and various policy statements. In addition there would be the state plan, the contract between DHEW and the state describing the program and the financial arrangements between the two levels of government. Of course, all of these legal documents would have to be read in light of the judicial opinions that have interpreted these various state and federal laws (as well as the various requirements imposed by the applicable provisions of the state and federal constitutions).

Given the nature of this legal structure where the governmental authority is shared between various levels of government, part of this complexity is inevitable. But it is also a reflection of the sheer size of these programs and the enormity of their intended undertaking: providing medical assistance to the great portions of a society of 220 million people who cannot afford it. Neither the Medicaid nor the Medicare program could be enacted in full detail in one comprehensive statute. Not only would it be cumbersome to draft, but it would be technically impossible within the legislative process. Legislators do not have the time, expertise, and, perhaps, the willingness to undertake such a task. It is in this context that the principle has developed of delegating what is in effect legislative law-making authority to admistrative agencies. As a consequence, however, the decision making at this administrative level becomes as important in determining the actual character and make up of these programs as is the legislation that establishes the general framework. The power and discretion vested in admistrative officials from DHEW to single state agencies to local welfare offices is tremendous. This may be necessary in order that these programs function, but it does give them a peculiar character; governmental accountability for its decisions is not focused but diffused throughout a number of agencies and among hundreds of people. As mentioned in Chapter 1, it is the wisdom of this delegation of authority, the validity of the assumption that some policy decisions can better be made at the agency level than in the legislatures, that is tested by these programs. Similarly, it is a test of the wisdom of a system wherein the responsibility for providing public services is shared by several levels of government. In light of the proposals now being considered, such as comprehensive national health insurance for all Americans, these considerations are particularly crucial.

Entitlements as legal rights

There are a number of obvious shortcomings in the Medicaid and Medicare programs. The most obvious is that they do not provide coverage for all people who cannot afford medical care. Under the Medicaid program, states are only required to cover welfare recipients and, after the 1972 amendments, need not even cover all recipients of federal welfare programs. The welfare programs are themselves limited to four arbitrary categories (the aged, the disabled, the blind, and dependent children), which eliminate from welfare and Medicaid many large groups of poor people such as adults between 21 and 65 years of age who are not blind and disabled and intact families that do not qualify for the AFDC program. (Such persons usually must receive charity medical care—or go without. A few states cover such persons in their Medicaid programs but receive *no* federal money for that part of the program.)

Another serious problem with the Medicaid program is that it varies significantly from state to state and the scope of benefits that each state is to provide is fairly limited. Services as basic as drugs are not required, and several states do not provide them. As mentioned earlier, Medicare is even more limited in terms of the benefits offered to recipients, and this is compounded by the significant cost-sharing required under that program.

On the other hand, one must also note that these two programs have provided medical care to millions of people who might not have otherwise received it. For the people who are eligible for benefits, Medicaid and Medicare are important legal rights, best described as statutory entitlements. That is, the government chose to enact these programs; it was not required to do so by any constitutional mandate. Likewise, the government through proper legislative action could repeal the statutory basis for either program. Yet while these programs exist, they establish important legal rights, relationships between individual people and the government, defined and enforced through the legal system.

The traditional interpretation was that when the government provided such a program, those benefits constituted a "privilege." A privilege, as opposed to a right, could be given to or taken away from a beneficiary rather arbitrarily, meaning without the usual requirements of due process. In the last decade, however, courts have reexamined the various public entitlement programs, particularly the welfare programs. Because of their subsistance nature and their beneficiaries' total dependence upon them, the modern approach has been that benefits under these programs are not strictly a privilege. Therefore, they cannot be terminated at the whim of the government that provides them. Thus courts have abolished the previous distinction between rights and privileges and have determined that public entitlements are more in the nature of property rights. The requirements of due process in the Federal Constitution, which prohibit the state and federal government from depriving people of *property* without due process of law, also apply to statutory entitlement like the welfare programs.

The general requirements of due process have already been explored in Chapter 3. Basically, due process requires that the government use fundamentally fair procedures. The specific requirements of due process differ depending upon the circumstances under consideration. In the context of welfare programs the issue has not been whether beneficiaries are entitled to such basic requirements as notice and hearing. By statute and regulation, people seeking welfare benefits and people having their benefits terminated are given notice of whatever decision is made, and eventually they are entitled to a hearing. The federal Medicaid statute requires that all states have a hearing system to resolve disputes about eligibility and payment for services. Similar provisions exist in the Medicare statute. However, the important issue in the welfare context has been the nature and timing of the available hearing. Is the available hearing constitutional, i.e., fundamentally fair? Particularly, does the requirement that the government use fundamentally fair procedures mean that this hearing has to occur before benefits are terminated? In the late 1960's a series of cases involving recipients under the AFDC program challenged the adequacy of the hearings available to a terminated recipient. The Supreme Court eventually held that before a state or federal government agency can terminate a recipient from eligibilty for a welfare program the government must provide for (1) notice to the recipient of the reason for the proposed action and (2) a *prior* hearing at which the recipient can testify, present witnesses, and confront adverse witnesses. Presumably such a recipient can also be represented by counsel, although it has never been held that the government must appoint counsel for people who cannot afford one (which would be most recipients).

Presumably, these requirements concerning a pretermination hearing would apply to anyone being terminated from eligibility for Medicaid or Medicare. The same kind of eligibility for an entitlement is involved as in a termination from AFDC or other welfare program. The recipient of Medicaid and Medicare may be as dependent on these benefits (it may be a matter of life or death) as on financial assistance under welfare. A tougher question arises when the Medicaid or Medicare recipient is denied coverage for a particular medical service. The government surely must conform to the general requirements of due process, but what does that require under these circumstances? For example, if an individual is in a nursing home or a hospital paid for by Medicaid, the state government might decide that they will no longer reimburse that nursing home for services, based on the decision of that institution's utilization review committee that care is no longer necessary. This is not a question of eligibility for Medicaid per se; however, it effectively terminates services to the individual. The few courts that have considered the issue have interpreted this to mean that a pretermination hearing is also required by due process in this situation. Although the state agency will eventually provide a hearing to that beneficiary, it might not be fundamentally fair to provide a hearing unless it is before the benefits are effectively terminated.

Conversely, due process does not require that the equivalent of a pretermination hearing be provided to an applicant for a welfare program. An individual applying for benefits under a welfare program whose application has been rejected cannot claim that he or she must receive benefits while pursuing a hearing challenging the denial of the application. Due process requires that the denied applicant is eventually entitled to a hearing, but the right to a pretermination hearing only accrues to someone who is already eligible for an entitlement program. In the same way an individual who has requested prior authorization to be admitted to a hospital or a nursing home, as is required under some state Medicaid programs, is not entitled to receive those services while waiting for a hearing to challenge the denial of prior authorization.

To generalize, the law recognizes entitlements as important legal rights, much in the nature of the right to property. The government must conform to the general requirements of due process in providing benefits under these programs, but the specific requirements of due process are different in a situation involving a deprivation of an entitlement than in, for example, a situation involving a deprivation of liberty.

Another example of the application of this due process analysis and the Medicaid program involves nursing home transfers. When first enacted in 1965, Medicaid only paid for institutional care in hospitals and nursing homes, not in other institutional health related settings, such as convalescent homes not meeting the definition of a "skilled nursing facility." In 1967 the Medicaid law was amended to include a new category of facility as an optional service—intermediate care facilities that provide the services of nurses during the day shift. Skilled nursing facilities must provide 24-hour nursing services. Many states incorporated intermediate care facilities into their state Medicaid plans, because they saw both a legitimate need to provide lower levels of care to the Medicaid population and realized this was an opportunity to reduce institutional costs. In 1971 several states began to reclassify nursing home patients as requiring only intermediate care or nonmedical boarding home care. The reclassifications took place without personal medical examinations and in many cases without consulting the attending physician. While some of the reclassifications and transfers were justified, many were not. Many people suffered from the inadequate care available at the institution to which they were transferred or the traumatic experience of the transfer itself. Medicaid recipients successfully enforced their right to a hearing on the question of the medical necessity of their continued stay in the institution before a threatened transfer could occur on the ground that their interest in remaining in the institution was an "entitlement," a legal right that the state agency could not take away without a prior hearing meeting the requirements of due process.

Conclusion—lessons for the future

It is important to return to the historical perspective on these programs of the introduction to this chapter. Medicaid and Medicare are not only important programs, but they are also an important stage in the development of social welfare programs in this country. It is impossible to review the experience under Medicaid and Medicare without looking ahead to future programs, particularly to some sort of national health insurance. Medicaid and Medicare are, after all, a kind of national health insurance for certain categories of people, at least under a broad definition of the term insurance. In addition, a large portion of these programs will probably be incorporated into any future national health insurance program. Given that reality, the experience under Medicaid and Medicare suggests certain questions that should be asked in evaluating any national health insurance proposal.

Is the program eligibility sufficiently broad to assure that medical care will be available to those who cannot afford it?

As this chapter has indicated, Medicaid eligibility is restricted by the categorical nature of the federal welfare programs. The gaps in coverage are obvious. Furthermore, income eligibility levels are unrealistically low for both welfare programs and the medically needy programs. These low-income levels leave a tremendous void between those people who are eligible for Medicaid and people who can actually afford to buy their own private health insurance. Obviously, Medicare also restricts eligibility to two categories of people, but it offers a better approach: there is no means test for eligibility. And, despite the fact that it is equally as expensive as Medicaid, it has remained a more politically popular program.

Are the eligibility and benefit requirements designed to assure uniformity of treatment without regard to geographic residence?

With the emphasis on state control, the Medicaid program has resulted in some rather drastic disparities in the eligibility requirements and benefits available in the various states. A national health insurance program should have basic national uniformity as does the Medicare program. The potential for state-by-state variations still exists, however, because it is unlikely that a new program would provide eligibility or benefits as comprehensive as those in states with the most progressive Medicaid programs. Poor residents of those states would suffer from a uniform system providing fewer benefits. Wealthier states might have an incentive to supplement the nationally financed medical assistance program for their residents. While this is desirable, since no individual should lose benefits under a new system, it would only perpetuate part of the geographic variations that now exist under Medicaid.

Are the medical benefits available reasonably comprehensive in scope?

The package of benefits that is required under the federal Medicaid law is rather limited. Many states have not chosen to offer any of the optional services or to expand their programs beyond the requirements of federal law. The benefits available under the Medicare program are even more limited than those required by Medicaid, particularly in light of the cost-sharing required of Medicare patients. Obviously a national health insurance scheme will be costly, and there are valid reasons for limiting coverage for some items or the amount and duration of covered services. But the program should be reasonably comprehensive. Important services such as outpatient care, prescription drugs, and preventive care should not be eliminated, and the program should try to encourage the rational use of services to control costs rather than to place arbitrary limitations on coverage. In any event the benefits available should exceed those available under the Medicare program or under Medicaid in many states.

Are there effective mechanisms to assure that necessary care will be of high quality?

In spite of some requirements to assure quality services in the Medicaid and Medicare programs, the programs have never emphasized quality care, and the administration of them has certainly not enforced it. The most dismal example of failure to enforce quality standards is with regard to nursing homes under Medicaid and Medicare. DHEW and state agencies have totally failed to enforce even standards that existed for such simple, yet critical, matters as fire safety. The result has been a national scandal. Mechanisms for ensuring that services are of high quality, such as an effective system of mandatory peer review, have to be developed and maintained.

Does the program contain effective mechanisms to contain costs?

Medicaid and Medicare have been charged with partial responsibility for the recent increases in the costs of medical care. Undeniably they have drastically increased the demand for services. However, the economic inflation of the past decade raised prices for all goods and services, not just medical care, although medical cost inflation has exceeded that of the total economy. If more attention had been paid to cost containment in the early stages of these federal programs, some of their inflationary impact might have been avoided. What is now needed is a rational, creative approach to cost containment. Such concepts as prepaid medical care, preventive programs, and streamlining the federal, state, and local bureaucracies might be effective without sacrificing the coverage available to beneficiaries. Instead, both Medicaid and Medicare have relied on the politically more feasible devices of reducing benefit coverage, lowering eligibility levels and raising the levels of cost sharing. Cost containment is an inevitable issue of a national health insurance program. Effective mechanisms must be built into the program or the issue will be solved retrospectively by more expedient but less equitable measures.

Is the financing mechanism equitable?

The federal share of the Medicaid program is paid out of federal general revenues. While nominally progressive in its impact, it is generally agreed that the federal tax structure is actually more proportional in its impact (i.e., all taxpayers pay an equal proportion of their incomes in taxes). State, county, and local taxes on the other hand, e.g., sales and property taxes, which make up 17% to 50% of the costs of Medicaid, are widely conceded to be regressive (i.e., people with lower incomes actually pay a larger proportion of their incomes for these taxes). Notwithstanding this regressive nature of the state share of Medicaid costs, the aggregate impact of Medicaid has been to favor the very poor. However, this tends to be regional in nature since beneficiaries in the western states and in the Northeast tend to benefit more than those in the South. One study has also shown that the total cost of Medicaid falls heaviest on middle-income people, rather than upper-income people, even though the program itself does not benefit the people with lower-middle incomes until they become very poor. Medicare is financed by a federal payroll deduction. The proportion paid by each wage earner is graduated (i.e., progressive) up to an income level of $15,000; but beyond that, all wage earners pay the same amount. Furthermore, since it is a tax on wages, not all forms of income, the total impact is regressive and falls heaviest on the middle- and lower middle-income people whose income is almost exclusively from wages.

The concept of national health insurance is really based on a notion of income redistribution. The government should assist those who cannot afford medical care by taxing those who can afford to pay. Obviously a federal and state tax system that more evenly distributes income from the wealthier to the poor and the very poor would provide the most equitable means of financing a national health insurance scheme. Given the realities of the legislative process, it is unlikely that federal income taxes will become substantially more progressive in the forseeable future. At the very least, any national health insurance proposal should at a minimum avoid regressive taxing mechanisms, whether in the form of state and local taxes, payroll deductions, or even employer-employee contributions, which are the equivalent of payroll deductions.

Will the administrative agencies be accountable to the program's beneficiaries?

State agencies have been notorious for their failure to fully implement Medicaid requirements. The federal government's enforcement of the Medicaid and Medicare program requirements has also left a great deal to be desired. The Social Security Administration's reputation is, relatively speaking, quite good. Of course, one must recognize that there are significant differences between Medicaid and Medicare: Medicare eligibility does not involve financial issues and is simpler to administer; the actual processing of provider billing is done by fiscal intermediaries; and, furthermore, the enforcement of portions of the quality standards has been delegated by SSA to the state health departments.

Whatever administrative structure is developed, there should be a single agency that is clearly responsible to Congress and accountable to the program's beneficiaries in order that the agency properly perform its role in the implementation of the law. The past experience with bifurcation of responsibility between levels of government has not been good. The mechanisms that ensure the accountablity of the single agency should be meaningful and creative. At the very least, beneficiaries should be provided with an effective means for filing complaints about the administration of the program and the care received under the program, as well as advocates or ombudsmen to ensure that those complaints are processed and acted upon.

Does the program assure availability and accessibility of medical care for its beneficiaries?

Medicaid recipients often find medical care inaccessible, particularly physician's services. This is especially true in the parts of the country with an insufficient number of physicans to serve all income levels, but it is also a problem where there is an adequate number of physicians, but they refuse to participate in the Medicaid program. A national health insurance scheme will have to include effective measures to assure an adequate supply of medical manpower and health care facilities. There are numerous options, ranging from more drastic measures to those that are more traditional: it might be necessary to mandate the participation of providers of medical care in the national health insurance scheme, to subsidize the training of more physicians and paraprofessional personnel who will then work in underserved areas, or to encourage the development of a better system of transportation. Whatever measure is taken, it must be effectively enforced—to a far greater extent than the governmental encouragement of participation of providers in the Medicaid and Medicare programs.

Does the program provide incentives for basic changes in the delivery of medical care?

The central concern of a national health insurance program is to assist people who cannot afford adequate care. The cost of medical care is, however, only the major problem. A number of related problems exist. The medical care delivery system in this country has been described as fragmented, impersonal, inefficient, episodic, and lacking in continuity. These and other problems affect not just the poor, but all consumers. The implementation of a national health insurance program is one of the few opportunities for any major change in the delivery system; once enacted, that opportunity might nor recur for some time, and many of the current problems may be further institutionalized if they are allowed to continue. While a proposal that solves all problems for all people is unrealistic, a proposal that would readjust the financial structure of the medical care delivery system without attempting to adjust other parts of that system would be unforturnate. At the least, the impact on these other problems should be taken into account in the overall evaluation of any national health insurance scheme.

References

Butler, P.: An advocate's guide to the Medicare program, Clearinghouse Rev. **8**: 831, 1975.

Butler, P.: The Medicaid program: current statutory requirements and judicial interpretations, Clearinghouse Rev. **7**:7, 1974.

Davis, K.: Medicaid—its impact on the poor, 1974.

Davis, K.: Lessons of Medicare and Medicaid for national health insurance, 1974.

Foltz, A.: The development of ambiguous federal policy: early and periodic screening, diagnosis, and treatment (EPSDT), Milbank Memorial Fund Quarterly: Health and Society **55**:35, 1975.

Harris, R.: A sacred trust, rev. ed., 1969.

Law, S.: Blue Cross: what went wrong? 1974.

Peckman, J., and Ochner, B.: Who bears the tax burden? 1974.

Spiegel, A.: Medicaid lessons for national health insurance, 1975.

Stevens, R., and Stevens, R.: Welfare medicine in America: a case study of Medicaid, 1974.

CHAPTER 6 Malpractice: liability of providers for poor quality medical care

The preceding chapters have been concerned with one set of legal rights relevant to public health: the legal rights that exist between the government and the individual. In this chapter and the following one, the focus will be on a different set of legal rights: those that exist between an individual patient and a private provider of medical care. Basically, this involves the rights between two private individuals. But, as will be demonstrated, when one of those individuals is a provider of medical care and the other is a patient, the legal rights of each are somewhat different and reflect the special nature of the provider/patient relationship.

The subject of this chapter is one of the most important and most controversial legal issues relating to the public's health. The law allows a patient who has been the subject of poor quality medical care to sue the provider of that care and to hold that provider liable for any damage the patient has suffered. This is known as the provider's malpractice liability.

Malpractice liability is a very interesting legal problem. For one thing, by holding a provider liable for malpractice, the law is attempting to control the quality of medical care. The threat of liability is supposed to act as an incentive to the provider to deliver care of sufficient quality. In theory the patient who does not receive a sufficient quality of care is at least compensated for any resulting damage. However, these objectives are probably not achieved, at least to an extent that should be considered satisfactory. The unfortunate truth is that given the practical realities of the existing legal system, malpractice liability is too unpredictable. Its effectiveness as either an incentive to the provider or a means of compensation for an injured patient is doubtful at best.

Malpractice liability is also a problem because of the costs involved. After a 2-year study, the Department of Health, Education, and Welfare published in 1973 the *Report of the Secretary's Commission on Medical Malpractice.* In that report it was estimated that providers paid over $350 million for professional liability insurance in 1970; in that same year over 14,500 new claims were reported to professional liability insurance companies and 16,000 claims files were closed—with the claimant receiving some amount of payment in only 25% of those claims. Yet 6% of the claims paid were in excess of $40,000 and 3% were in excess of $100,000. In other words there were many claims (and probably many more incidents of malpractice that went undetected), but few people recovered any compensation. On the other hand, a very few that did recover received very large settlements.

Recent estimates have predicted that the cost of professional liability insurance and, presumably, the total amount of payment to claimants will skyrocket during the 1970s. In states that have the highest frequency of malpractice suits, the average yearly premium for a physician's malpractice insurance policy may be as high as $10,000 by 1976 with premiums for some specialties as high as $50,000 to $60,000. In other states insurance companies have threatened to stop selling medical malpractice insurance altogether. Congress and the state legislatures have been debating proposals to solve this aspect of the malpractice problem ranging from federally funded malpractice insurance to complicated systems of compulsory arbitration for malpractice claims. No clear or immediate solution is in sight.

From a legal point of view, the most interesting aspect of malpractice liability is not its cost or its effect on the quality of medical care, but the fact that the legal basis for determining malpractice liability is so frequently misunderstood. Few people really understand that malpractice suits are supposed to compensate patients when the provider is negligent, but not when the provider makes an honest mistake. Even among providers, there is a general misunderstanding—and a great deal of misinformation—concerning the circumstances under which a hospital is liable for the negligence of a physician practicing in that hospital. Similarly, many people miscalculate the differences that can exist between the actual occurence of medical malpractice and the proof of that event in the courtroom according to admissible evidence.

If malpractice liability is to be one determinant of the quality of medical care and one component of the cost, it would seem to be important that both providers and consumers understand its legal basis. It is not surprising that a system of liability that is not well understood does not function very effectively. More importantly, if substantial changes in the basis for malpractice liability or the system for determining liability are to be considered intelligently, a general understanding of the existing legal principles would seem to be a necessary prerequisite. Therefore, the purpose of this chapter will be to explain the basic legal principles of malpractice liability and to establish a foundation whereby its function as a quality control and a compensation mechanism can be better understood.

The legal rights that exist between private individuals: property, contracts, and torts

What is the legal basis for malpractice liability? What sorts of legal rights are involved? To begin with, malpractice liability can only be understood against the background of the whole spectrum of legal rights that exist between private individuals.

One broad category of legal rights that establish relationships between private individuals consists of property rights. The law recognizes and provides for the protection of ownership of certain tangible and intangible things. Ownership generally includes the right to possess and the right to control the property. The owner of property can seek judicial enforcement of his or her right to possess and control property or can receive compensation for damage caused to the property by any third party.

Another major category of legal rights that establish relationships between private individuals involves contractual rights. The law has recognized that certain kinds of agreements between private individuals should be legally binding contracts and enforceable through the courts. Contracts are established by a variety of human activities. They can be written or oral agreements; they can be explicit agreements or implied by individual conduct. In order for a contract to exist, there need be little more than two individuals that intend to be legally bound by their agreement. Usually this involves some sort of mutual exchange: one individual exchanges something of value or a promise for something of value—or another promise—in return. Contracts are enforceable by the courts, either by requiring that the agreement be carried out or by requiring the individual who broke the agreement to compensate the other for any resulting damages.

In addition to property rights and contractual rights, the law also recognizes a category of legal rights between private individuals known as torts. Unlike property or contracts, torts cannot be easily summarized. A tort is usually defined in legal literature as any civil wrong, but that is hardly a useful description. A working definition might be that the law of torts refers to a variety of circumstances under which the law provides for the compensation of an individual damaged by another person. However, torts can only really be explained by referring to the range of specific activities that are considered to be torts.

Some torts involve intentional misconduct. When one person puts another in the fear of bodily harm, he or she has committed the tort of civil assault and can be held liable for any resulting damage. If that person does actual bodily harm to the other, the tort of civil battery has been committed and the "tortfeasor" can be, again, liable for any resulting damage. The tort of false imprisonment results when one person intentionally restrains or confines another individual. Slander (spoken) or libel (written) are torts committed by defamation, one person relating untrue statements about another. Other examples of intentional torts recognized in some but not all jurisdictions include the infliction of mental cruelty and the invasion of personal privacy.

Some torts, however, are committed by unintentional misconduct, meaning acts that are not intended to be harmful but that are in fact unreasonable or, in legal terms, negligent. A rough layman's translation would be that negligent conduct is the legal equivalent of "foolishness," acts for which the individual should have known better than to do.

The fact that an individual can be liable for negligence does not mean that an individual is simply liable for all damage he or she causes to another; for example, a driver of a car that hits a pedestrian by accident is not liable to that pedestrian unless the driver was acting negligently, e.g., driving too fast or with a lack of caution.

Understandably, negligence has proven to be a very complicated legal issue. There have been literally thousands of cases involving the allegation of negligence, and the concept has been applied in an endless number of situations. Whatever the situation, however, a negligence case involves the same basic issues. The law imposes on each individual a duty that must be observed in any activities that affect other people. For most people and most activities, that duty is simply to be reasonable. The most critical issue in a negligence suit is how that duty is measured. In theory this involves a statement of a standard of conduct to which the allegedly negligent conduct is compared. In practice this measurement is divided between a judge and, usually, a jury. The judge will state and explain the legal defintion of the standard of conduct. The jury is then supposed to base its verdict on its perception of whether the individual conduct involved in the case violated this standard of conduct. If so, the jury then determines how much damage was caused by this negligence.

The duty to be reasonable is measured by a standard of conduct based on the concept of a "reasonable man." That is, the judge would instruct the jury: "You are to find the defendant liable for negligence if you decide that a reasonable man under the same circumstances would not have done what the defendant did." Obviously this is a vague standard and leaves the jury with a great deal of discretion—as well as room for abuse.

These same basic issues frame a suit in negligence regardless of whether the case involves a car hitting a pedestrian or a lawyer neglecting a client, or any other unintentional misconduct. It is still a matter of establishing a standard of conduct, comparing that standard to what happened, and assessing whether there was any damage caused.

Malpractice

A malpractice suit is simply a special kind of negligence case. It involves establishing the negligence of a provider of medical care. The issues are basically the same as those outlined above: determining the standard of conduct to which the provider will be held, comparing what the provider did (or did not do) to that standard, and determining the extent of damage suffered by the patient as a result of that negligence.

There are, however, several differences between an ordinary negligence suit and a suit for malpractice.

The role of expert testimony in determining the standard of conduct

First of all, in applying the standard of conduct in a malpractice suit, the decision is not left entirely to the discretion of the jury. The law has traditionally required that the application of the standard of conduct for a provider of medical care be based on the testimony of other providers. The theory is that only a physician or other provider of medical care has the expertise and experience to decide what is a reasonable medical decision under a given set of circumstances; in most other situations, it is assumed that the jury can decide this question. In fact, opinions as to what is reasonable or negligent under the circumstances are inadmissible in most ordinary negligence suits. However, in malpractice suits it is required that such opinions be given to the jury. If, for example, a physician is sued for malpractice, there would have to be testimony by other physicians as to what a reasonable physican would have done under similar circumstances. Except in extreme circumstances, the jury in such a case can only base its verdict on the opinions of the physicians that do testify. The jury can only exercise discretion if the opinions given are conflicting. In that event the jury can choose to rely on one physician's opinion over any other. Otherwise, they must accept the opinions given, and, if they do not, the verdict may be reversed. As a practical matter, this would require that the plaintiff, in order to be successful, must find a physician willing to testify that what was done was negligence by another physician. This is not always easy to do. Physicians and other providers are under a great deal of social pressure not to testify against their peers and colleagues. In fact the medical community has been often accused of resorting to a "conspiracy of silence" in order to protect themselves from malpractice claims. Obviously, this conspiracy has not been overwhelmingly successful if it does exist, given the increasing number of malpractice actions during the past few years. Actually, in some areas individual providers are available that are so willing to testify that they become the equivalent of professional witnesses.

The community practice rule

Another difference between malpractice suits and other negligence suits is that the standard of conduct applied in malpractice actions is slightly different from that applied in ordinary negligence suits—or, at least, malpractice involves the consideration of several additional factors. The standard of conduct applied is not just what the mythical "reasonable man" would have done, but what a reasonable provider would have done under the circumstances. In making this decision the jury is usually instructed by the judge to take into account the experience, training, and continuing education of the provider. Many jurisdictions also instruct the jury to consider what is known as the community practice rule. This is in recognition of the fact that providers in some communities cannot be expected to have the same training, experience, or available resources as those in other communites. Thus one court expressed the standard of conduct for a physician in a malpractice suit in this way:

> The undertaking of a physician as implied by the law is that he possesses and will use the reasonable degree of learning, skill and experience which is ordinarily possessed by others of his profession *in the community where he practices,* having regard to the current state of advance of the profession . . . [italics added for emphasis]

The community practice rule historically developed as an allowance for the realities facing a physician or other provider of medical care in small rural communities. Obviously, the opportunities to learn the latest procedures and techniques are not always available to a provider in an isolated setting. The facilities and resources of a community might also prevent the use of a procedure that might be considered standard in many other places. While there is logic to this rule, and, until recently, it certainly had relevance, the differences between various medical communities have diminished as modern transportation and communication have increased. In response a few jurisdictions have abandoned the rule altogether and many have modified its application. Massachusetts is a typical example.

In a very early case, *Small v. Howard,* 128 Mass. 131, (1880), Massachusetts recognized the need for the community practice rule. Nearly a century later, that jurisdiction found it necessary to reevaluate its position. In the case of *Brune v. Belinkoff,* 354 Mass. 102, 235 N.E.2d. 733 (1968), the plaintiff was a woman who had given birth to a child in a New Bedford, Massachusetts hospital. During the delivery, the defendant, an anesthesiologist, administered a spinal anesthetic containing 8 milligrams of tetracaine (Pontocaine) in one cubic centimeter of 10% glucose. As a result of the injection the plaintiff developed a permanent numbness and a weakness in her left leg.

At the trial, several physicians testified that in their opinion the dosage of Pontocaine was excessive and that good medical practice required an injection of 5 milligrams or less. Other physicians testified that 8 milligrams was proper and customary practice in New Bedford for the kind of delivery involved. The judge instructed the jury as to the application of the standard of conduct and included an explanation of the community practice rule. The jury's verdict was in favor of the defendant. The plaintiff appealed claiming error in the judge's instructions.

The Supreme Judicial Court of Massachusetts reversed the verdict and remanded the case for a new trial based on the following opinion:

> Because of the importance of the subject, and the fact that we have been asked to abandon the "locality" rule we have reviewed the relevant decisions at some length. We are of opinion that the "locality" rule of *Small v. Howard* which measures a physician's conduct by the standards of other doctors in similar communites is unsuited to present day conditions. The time has come when the medical profession should no longer be Balkanized by the application of varying geographic standards in malpractice cases. Accordingly, *Small v. Howard* is hereby overruled. The present case affords a good illustration of the inappropriateness of the "locality" rule to existing conditions. The defendant was a specialist practising in New Bedford, a city of 100,000 which is slightly more than fifty miles from Boston, one of the medical centers of the nation, if not the world. This is a far cry from the country doctor in *Small v. Howard,* who ninety years ago was called upon to perform difficult surgery. Yet the trial judge told the jury that if the skill and ability of New Bedford physicians were "fifty percent inferior" to those obtaining in Boston the defendant should be judged by New Bedford standards, "having regard to the current state of advance of the profession." This may well be carrying the rule of *Small v. Howard* to its logical conclusion, but it is, we submit, a reductio ad absurdum of the rule.
>
> The proper standard is whether the physician, if a general practitioner, has exercised the degree of care and skill of the average qualified practitioner, taking into account the advances in the profession. In applying this standard it is permissible to consider the medical resources available to the physcian as *one* circumstance in determining the skill and care required. Under this standard some allowance is thus made for the type of community in which the physician carries on his practice.

Thus in Massachusetts the standard of conduct was what the average physician (an interesting departure from the concept of a reasonable physician) would have done under the circumstances; the fact that this particular physician was in a small town does not lower the standard to which the law holds that physician, but is only one of many circumstances that the jury can consider. While this may amount to little more than a semantic difference in many situations, this case is a good example of one in which the traditional community practice rule would exonerate the physician's conduct, but the general rule as stated by the opinion in *Brune* probably would not.

The duty of continuing care

The standard of conduct is also applied differently to providers of medical care in that providers are required to continue to provide medical care once a provider-patient relationship has been established. This is unusual. The law rarely requires a private individual to take affirmative action to help anyone. Without incurring liability for negligence or any other tort, one can actually ignore someone else in need or fail to go to their aid. In fact this is also true for providers of medical care, unless the person in need is their patient. However, for a provider who has accepted someone as a patient, quite the opposite is true; he or she is then obligated to take whatever steps are reasonably necessary including taking affirmative action to meet the patient's needs. To discontinue medical care could well result in malpractice liability.

One important situation in which this concept of the provider's affirmative obligations to act has been extended involves the provision of emergency medical care. As stated above, the general rule of tort law is that no one is required to render aid to anyone else. Consequently, no one is generally liable for failing to provide emergency medical care, unless, of course, they are responsible for or caused the emergency situation. The only exceptions to this rule are in a few states that by statute have imposed a special duty on all people to render emergency aid. Thus, except in those states, even a physician can usually refuse to render emergency medical care without incurring legal liability. It is only after a provider has entered into a provider-patient relationship with a patient that the provider must take affirmative action and continue to meet the needs of the patient. However, in some jurisdictions, the legal duties of providers who are holding themselves out as available for emergencies have been extended beyond this general rule. The leading case in this area is the decision in *Manlove v. Wilmington General Hospital,* 54 Del. 15, 174 A.2d 135 (1961).

In that case, the parents of a 4-month-old infant brought the infant to the emergency room of a private hospital. The infant had not slept in 2 nights and had been suffering from a high fever, a sore throat, and diarrhea. The parents had tried to reach their family physician, but it was his day off. At the emergency room they explained the symptoms to the nurse on duty. The nurse explained that it was hospital policy not to treat a patient under the care of a physician without the permission of that physician. The nurse tried to reach the family's physician, but took no other action and did not examine the infant. That afternoon the infant died of bronchial pneumonia.

The parents sued the hospital claiming that the hospital staff was negligent in refusing to render emergency care. The hospital in its defense relied on the general rule that no one is required to render aid. They argued that a private hospital is not required by law to accept all people who present themselves for treatment.

The Supreme Court of Delaware disagreed and felt that there should be an exception to the general rule in some situations:

> . . . we are of the opinion that liability on the part of a hospital may be predicated of the refusal of service to a patient in case of an unmistakable emergency, if the patient has relied upon a well-established custom of the hospital to render aid in such a case.

The court went on to conclude that if the plaintiff could prove that there were actually an unmistakable emergency in this case, then the hospital could be liable for the resulting damage, the death of the infant.

The decision in *Manlove* did little more than carve out a narrow exception to the general rule. The court specifically stated that a private hospital is not required to have an emergency room; only when it has one or customarily holds itself out as available for emergencies, need a hospital accept all patients presenting themselves, and then only those that are unmistakable emergencies. Nonetheless, as the decision has been followed by courts in a number of jurisdictions, it has required many hospitals to alter their admission practices in light of this basis for legal liability.

A discussion of provider liability in the emergency situation could hardly be complete without some mention of "good Samaritan laws." A typical good Samaritan law provides that a licensed physician who renders aid at the scene of an accident or other emergency cannot be held liable as a result of his or her actions as long as the physician acted in good faith, i.e., did not intentionally cause harm to the injured person. Although these laws vary slightly from state to state, statutes of this type have been passed in at least thirty states.

These statutes were passed because of the mistaken belief of many physicians that if they render emergency care at the scene of an accident that they will run a high risk of being sued for malpractice. In some states, legislation was prompted by publicized "horror stories" about physicians who ignored people who were seriously injured because of the physician's perceived threat of potential liability.

Theoretically, liability for negligence is possible in an emergency situation. It would be a logical extension of the standard of conduct that requires providers to care for accepted patients. A physician who renders emergency aid but subsequently leaves the scene could be accused of abandoning a "patient." Several courts have said that such liability is possible, but the interesting fact is that no reported case has ever found a physician liable for actions arising out of the rendering of emergency aid. Though liability is possible, it is extremely unlikely, as common sense would dictate. Yet the high risk of liability for the good Samaritan physician is still a persistent myth and one that has made it necessary for many states to pass protective (?) good Samaritan laws.

Malpractice liability in a hospital setting

Up to this point in this chapter the discussion of the basic principles of malpractice liability has referred generally to the liability of individual providers of medical care. However, in a hospital there are very often several providers involved in the care of the patient, and the liability that extends to each provider varies according to the situation. The underlying principles of liability are not particularly complex, but they are easily confused because of the intertwining professional relationships that exist between the different providers in a hospital. Once these relationships are sorted out, however, the liability of the various providers is fairly easy to understand.

Vicarious liability

In order to understand malpractice liability in a hospital setting it is first necessary to refer again to the general principles of tort law and to an additional principle for establishing liability.

The principle of vicarious liability is applied in a variety of situations in which one person is held liable for the torts of another because of the nature of the relationship between them. The most common situation in which vicarious liability exists involves the liability of an employer for the torts of his or her employees. An employer is generally liable for all torts of an employee committted within the scope of the employment. This requires no finding of fault or negligence on the part of the employer. It requires only that an employer-employee relationship or its equivalent exist. This principle is often given the Latin name "respondeat superior" or "let the master answer."

This principle derives from the reasoning that (1) the employee is acting on the employer's behalf, (2) the employer is usually exercising control and supervision over the employee's conduct, and (3) the employer is in the better position to accept financial responsiblity—or to insure against it.

The law does draw a distinction between employees and independent contractors. If the person employed is considered to be an independent contractor, the employer is usually not liable for the torts committed. The reasoning behind this distinction is tied to the lack of control exercised by an employer over certain kinds of employed people. Someone considered a contractor usually is not supervised and operates relatively independently; hence, part of the rationale for holding the employer liable breaks down. Obviously this distinction is a question of fact that is often disputed; the labels chosen by the parties involved to describe themselves, e.g., staff, consultants, or contractors, are not determinative. What is crucial is their actual working relationship.

The principle of vicarious liability or respondeat superior is an important one to understand in determining the malpractice liability of the various providers involved in a patient's care in a hospital. Probably the most important application of this principle has been in determining the liability of a hospital for the negligence of a physician practicing in that hospital. With the several exceptions explained below, the law has generally not held a hospital liable for the negligence of a physician on the attending staff. The attending staff of a hospital, those physicians who can admit their patients to that hospital, are not employees of that hospital. They generally receive no direct reimbursement from the hospital, only from their patients. Moreover, they practice relatively independently of any hospital control and supervision. Many courts have buttressed this by the claim that a hospital cannot control a physician's conduct even if it wanted to; interference with a physician's conduct toward his or her patient would be tantamount to the practice of medicine by the hospital and, by law, only a licensed physician can practice medicine. Therefore, these courts have reasoned, it would be unfair to hold the hospital vicariously liable for a physician's conduct. (See the argument expressed in the *Darling* case *infra*.)

A hospital is, however, vicariously liable for the negligence of its house staff and physicians who are actually employed by the hospital. The interns and residents in a teaching hospital are salaried employees and directly supervised in their conduct. Many hospitals have several salaried specialists, not merely members of the attending staff, and the hospital is vicariously liable for their negligence. Hospitals are also vicariously liable for the negligence of nurses, attendants, and other hospital employees.

There are some situations where the liability of the hospital is not as clear cut as the generalizations above might suggest. As is a hospital, a physician is generally liable vicariously for the negligence of a nurse or assistant in his or her private office. This would also be true of a nurse or attendant in a hospital who is under the exclusive control of a physician. A clear example is where a physician employs a private duty nurse to care for the physician's patient while in the hospital. More complex situations arise when the negligent individual is acting under the orders of the physician, but actually employed by the hospital. The issue then becomes whether the relationship between the physician and the negligent individual is such that the individual is the physician's "employee." A difficult example is the case where the hospital's salaried specialist is assisting an attending staff physician in surgery. If the assisting physician is negligent, the hospital might argue that it was not supervising the employee in that situation, that he or she was acting under the orders of another physician. The outcome could go either way and would depend upon the specific facts of the case.

It is important to point out that holding a hospital or a physician vicariously liable for the torts of an employee does not relieve the employee of liability. The negligent individual is jointly liable, and a malpractice suit can be brought against either the negligent employee or the vicariously liable employer or against both. The injured party can collect the full amount of the damages awarded from either. Theoretically, if only one jointly liable party has to pay a claim, he or she can legally require the others to pay their proportionate share; if all parties are insured, this usually happens. If one cannot pay, the other(s) have to pay the full amount of the claim, not their proportionate share.

Hospital's liability for negligence

In addition to a hospital's vicarious liability as an employer, a hospital through its governing body and its administrative staff can also be liable for its "own" negligence. Actually this is just another case of vicarious liability; the legal entity called a hospital is liable for the torts of its employees, the administrative staff, and its governing body. Conceptually it is easier to think of this as the hospital's conduct being negligent.

A hospital can be liable for negligence in hiring and supervising its own staff. Depending upon the circumstances, hiring an incompetent employee might be an act of negligence. Permitting an unlicensed person such as an orderly to perform an act that requires greater qualifications might result in liability for negligence on the part of the hospital. In some cases hospitals have been held liable for negligence in extending attending staff privileges to incompetent or inadequately trained physicians.

Hospitals can also be liable for negligence in their maintenance of the physical structure of the hospital or in the provision of supplies, drugs, and equipment for patient care. However, until recently, a hospital was rarely held liable for the quality of medical care practiced in the hospital. Unless there were grounds for vicarious liability, the notion persisted that hospitals only provide the equipment, facilities, and supporting staff for the physician, but could not interfere with the practice of medical care. The law required that the hospital be reasonable under the circumstances, but the interpretation of the standard of conduct usually exempted a hospital from any responsibility for the quality of medical care provided.

Historically it is understandable that such a principle would develop. Until recently hospitals were not actively involved in patient care, and certainly the medical profession has demanded a great deal of autonomy in treating patients. While once logical, times have changed, and it is now appropriate to call this principle somewhat of a fiction. The simple truth is that a hospital through its employees is directly involved in the medical care of hospitalized patients. Certainly there is wide discretion given to the individual patient's physician, but even the distinction between the administrative staff and the attending staff is becoming blurred. The hospital administration sets guidelines within which attending staff must practice and, conversely, the attending staff is very much involved in the policy decisions of the hospital. In particular, hospital bylaws, licencing standards, and the standards of hospital professional associations make it clear that the hospital is at least partially responsible for the quality of care a patient receives. With these changes in actual hospital practice, the law regarding the hospital's liability for patient care has also changed.

No malpractice case is better known, at least by name, to both physicians and hospital administrators than *Darling v. Charleston Community Memorial Hospital,* 33 Ill. 2d 326, 211 N.E.2d 253 (1965). *Darling* was the first case to directly confront the traditional rule limiting the liability of hospitals for the quality of patient care.

The case involved the following set of facts:

On November 5, 1960, the plaintiff, who was 18 years old, broke his leg while playing in a college football game. He was taken to the emergency room at the defendant hospital where Dr. Alexander, who was on emergency call that day, treated him. Dr. Alexander, with the assistance of hospital personnel, applied traction and placed the leg in a plaster cast. A heat cradle was applied to dry the cast. Not long after the application of the cast plaintiff was in great pain and his toes, which protruded from the cast, became swollen and dark in color. They eventually became cold and insensitive. On the evening of November 6, Dr. Alexander "notched" the cast around the toes, and on the afternoon of the next day he cut the cast approximately three inches up from the foot. On November 8 he split the sides of the cast with a Stryker saw; in the course of cutting the cast the plaintiff's leg was cut on both sides. Blood and other seepage were observed by the nurses and others, and there was a stench in the room, which one witness said was the worst he had smelled since World War II. The plaintiff remained in Charleston Hospital until November 19, when he was transferred to Barnes Hospital in St. Louis and placed under the care of Dr. Fred Reynolds, head of orthopedic surgery at Washington University School of Medicine and Barnes Hospital. Dr. Reynolds found that the fractured leg contained a considerable amount of dead tissue which in his opinion resulted from interference with the circulation of blood in the limb caused by swelling or hemorrhaging of the leg against the constriction of the cast. Dr. Reynolds performed several operations in a futile attempt to save the leg but it had to be amputated eight inches below the knee.

The plaintiff sued both Dr. Alexander and the hospital. The physician settled before the trial for $50,000; but the hospital, relying on the traditional legal principles of liability, contested the claim against the hospital. The arguments of both sides were summarized in the opinion:

> The plaintiff contends that it established that the defendant was negligent in permitting Dr. Alexander to do orthopedic work of the kind required in this case, and not requiring him to review his operative procedures to bring them up to date; in failing, through its medical staff, to exercise adequate supervision over the case, especially since Dr. Alexander had been placed on emergency duty by the hospital; and in not requiring consultation, particularly after complications had developed. Plaintiff contends also that in a case which developed as this one did, it was the duty of the nurses to watch the protruding toes constantly for changes of color, temperature and movement, and to check circulation every ten to twenty minutes, whereas the proof showed that these things were done only a few times a day. Plaintiff argues that it was the duty of the hospital staff to see that these procedures were followed, and that either the nurses were derelict in failing to report developments in the case to the hospital administrator, he was derelict in bringing them to the attention of the medical staff, or the staff was negligent in failing to take action. Defendant is a licensed and accredited hospital, and the plaintiff contends that the licensing regulations, accreditation standards, and its own bylaws define the hospital's duty, and that an infraction of them imposes liability for the resulting injury.

> The defendant's position is stated in the following excerpts from its brief: "It is a fundamental rule of law that only an individual properly educated and licensed, and not a corporation, may practice medicine. . . . Accordingly, a hospital is powerless under the law to forbid or command any act by a physician or surgeon in the practice of his profession. . . . A hospital is not an insurer of the patient's recovery, but only owes the patient the duty to exercise such reasonable care as his known condition requires and that degree of care, skill and diligence used by hospitals generally in that community. . . . Where the evidence shows that the hospital care was in accordance with standard practice obtaining in similar hospitals, and Plaintiff produces no evidence to the contrary, the jury cannot conclude that the opposite is true even if they disbelieve the hospital witnesses. . . . A hospital is not liable for the torts of its nurse committed while the nurse was but executing the orders of the patient's physician, unless such order is so obviously negligent as to lead any reasonable person to anticipate that substantial injury would result to the patient from the execution of such order. . . . The extent of the duty of a hospital with respect to actual medical care of a professional nature such as is furnished by a physician is to use reasonable care in selecting medical doctors. When such care in the selection of the staff is accomplished, and nothing indicates that a physician so selected is incompetent or that such incompetence should have been discovered, more cannot be expected from the hospital administration." [citations omitted]

In its various arguments the plaintiff was asking the Illinois courts to do that which all previous courts had been very hesitant to do: interpret the standard of conduct for a hospital to include a responsibility for the quality of medical care practiced by attending staff physicians. The plaintiff argued that the hospital should supervise an attending staff physician's conduct in various ways, including the requirement that in certain cases consultation with a specialist be sought. The plaintiff also contended that the nursing staff, the hospital's employees, should have acted on the hospital's behalf and reported to the hospital the developments of the case once it was clear that something was wrong. While unprecedented in malpractice cases, these arguments had some support. These sorts of requirements were incorporated into the accreditation standards of the Joint Commission on Accreditation of Hospitals, state licensing standards, and even the hospital's own bylaws. What the plaintiff was asking was that these standards applied in other situations be applied in determining a hospital's malpractice liability.

In its defense the hospital did not directly argue that the plaintiff's position was without merit, but emphasized that previous courts had rejected similar arguments. The hospital's argument as summarized above was a good summary of the traditional interpretation of the principles of malpractice liability as applied to a hospital before the *Darling* decision. This is usually an effective defensive position, but unfortunately for the hospital, the time was ripe for a revision of those traditional principles. The realities of medical care in a hospital were inconsistent with a literal application of the generalization that "only a physician can practice medicine."

After a lengthy trial, the jury awarded the plaintiff $110,000 in damages. (The original figure was $150,000, reduced by the settlement with the physician involved.) The defendant appealed to the state appellate court and then to the Illinois Supreme Court. However, that court held in its decision that the liability of the hospital could be established on the facts of the case:

> "The conception that the hospital does not undertake to treat the patient, does not undertake to act through its doctors and nurses, but undertakes instead simply to procure them to act upon their own responsibility, no longer reflects the fact. Present-day hospitals, as their manner of operation plainly demonstrates, do far more than furnish facilities for treatment. They regularly employ on a salary basis a large staff of physicians, nurses and interns, as well as administrative and manual workers, and they charge patients for medical care and treatment, collecting for such services, if necessary, by legal action. Certainly, the person who avails himself of 'hospital facilities' expects that the hospital will attempt to cure him, not that its nurses or other employees will act on their own responsibility." [citation omitted] The Standards for Hospital Accreditation, the state licensing regulations and the defendant's bylaws demonstrate that the medical profession and other responsible authorities regard it as both desirable and feasible that a hospital assume certain responsibilities for the care of the patient.

> We now turn to an application of these considerations to this case. The defendant did not object to the instruction of the issues, which followed Illinois Pattern Jury Instruction 20.01. Nor did it move to withdraw any issues from the jury. Under section 68 of the Civl Practice Act, an entire verdict is not to be set aside because one asserted ground of recovery was defective or inadequately proven, if one or more of the grounds is sufficient, unless a motion to withdraw the issue in question was made. (Ill. Rev. Stat. 1963, chap. 110, par. 68 (4).) Therefore we need not analyze all of the issues submitted to the jury. Two of them were that the defendant had negligently: "5. Failed to have a sufficient number of trained nurses for bedside care of all patients at all times capable of recognizing the progressive gangrenous condition of the plaintiff's right leg, and of bringing the same to the attention of the hospital admistration and to the medical staff so that adequate consultation could have been secured and such conditions rectified; . . . 7. Failed to require consultation with or examination by members of the hospital surgical staff skilled in such treatment; or to review the treatment rendered in the plaintiff and to require consultants to be called in as needed."

> We believe that the jury verdict is supportable on either of these grounds. On the basis of the evidence before it the jury could reasonably have concluded that the nurses did not test for circulation in the leg as frequently as necessary, that skilled nurses would have promptly recognized the conditions that signalled a dangerous impairment of circu-

lation in the plaintiff's leg, and would have known that the condition would become irreversible in a matter of hours. At that point it became the nurses' duty to inform the attending physician, and if he failed to act, to advise the hospital authorities so that appropriate action might be taken. As to consultation, there is no dispute that the hospital failed to review Dr. Alexander's work or require a consultation; the only issue is whether its failure to do so was negligence. On the evidence before it the jury could reasonably have found that it was.

As indicated earlier, the impact of the *Darling* decision was dramatic and widespread throughout the country. Within the next few years following the decision, decisions in several other jurisdictions agreed with the *Darling* interpretation of a hospital's malpractice liability; although not every state jurisdiction has had the opportunity to explicitly recognize the *Darling* principle, it is clearly the modern approach to the issue and the one that all courts can be expected to follow in the future. Understandably, within the medical community *"Darling"* has become a well-used, although somewhat unpopular, term.

Was the decision totally unprecedented? In some respects it was not. The basic principles of malpractice liability and the underlying concept of negligence were not revised. A provider of medical care, before or after *Darling,* is basically required to be reasonable under the circumstances or to be liable for the resulting damages. The only real change instituted by *Darling* was in the interpretation of the standard of conduct to which hospital providers are to be held. The traditional assumption that hospitals are not directly involved in patient care can no longer be made in determining a hospital's liability.

Even given the new approach to hospital liability, *Darling* cannot be accurately described as requiring drastic changes in hospital practice. With other intents and for other purposes, e.g., accreditation and licensure, hospitals should already have been exercising the kind of responsibility for a physician's conduct that is required by the *Darling* decision. More importantly, the *Darling* principle does not require rigorous supervision of each patient's care. It requires only a reasonable amount of general supervision. Requiring consultations in certain categories of cases or requiring that nurses report cases they believe to be mismanaged are fairly minimal requirements. They are—both legally and literally—reasonable. In fact common sense would have been offended if the preexisting principles of malpractice liability had been applied in the *Darling* case to exonerate the hospital's conduct under the circumstances.

Practical aspects of malpractice litigation

To put the theoretical principles of malpractice liability in a more useful perspective, there are a number of practical aspects of malpractice litigation that should be considered.

Some aspects of malpractice litigation have been alluded to already. The plaintiff in a malpractice suit must rely heavily on expert witnesses to prove his or her case. Yet provider-witnesses are often unavailable, expensive, or simply uncooperative. Even with experts to testify and, just as importantly, to assist in the preparation of a malpractice case, a fully contested malpractice trial can take a year or more to prepare and schedule, months to try, and years to complete appeals. The time and money involved can be extraordinary. In some jurisdictions it is not uncommon for a malpractice suit to take 5 to 7 years to complete.

Due to the expenses of litigation, smaller claims are often impractical to pursue. Even when a large claim is at stake, some plaintiffs cannot afford to wait several years for a final award and may be forced to negotiate a settlement for less than they deserve. On the other hand, providers find that defending against even a baseless suit can be costly. Consequently, there is a "hassle" value: the provider or the provider's insurance company may decide it is worth settling for a small amount in some situations even when the provider is confident that the plaintiff's claim is without merit.

The practical finances of malpractice suits are also skewed by the practice of most attorneys of representing clients in malpractice suits on a contingency fee basis. Under a contingency fee, the attorney does not charge on an hourly basis or for services rendered, but agrees to take a percentage of the amount that the client wins. In a malpractice suit, some attorneys charge as much as 30% to 50%. For providers who think in terms of million dollar awards, that always sounds like a rip-off for the attorney. In some cases, it is. In theory, however, the contingency fee is supposed to act as a mechanism to discourage unmeritorious lawsuits. Fifty percent of nothing is nothing. On the other hand, if even a suit that has no basis at all can have a hassle value to the provider, that mechanism is not always an effective disincentive to the plaintiff or his or her attorney.

A full list of the practical considerations in malpractice litigation would be nearly endless. The problems in financing and preparing a malpractice suit listed above are only several important examples of those considerations. The point is that between the theoretical liability of a provider for malpractice and the actual proof of that liability lies the American legal system. It is more than occasionally cumbersome and sometimes ineffective; even at its best it is predictably expensive and surprisingly time-consuming.

The malpractice problem

Given the foregoing brief introduction to the principles of malpractice liability, and some of the practical aspects of litigation, it is appropriate to consider again the characterization of malpractice as a major legal problem relevant to the public's health. Certainly the principles underlying malpractice liability are not problems necessitating immediate changes in the law. Some of the aspects of liability, e.g., the policy implications of increasing the liability of hospitals for patient care, are debatable, but overall the basic principles are at least logical. While not ideal, a system of liability based on the concept of negligence represents in theory a fair system for allocating responsibility for poor quality medical care. If anything seems appropriate for change, it is not the underlying principles of malpractice liability, but the way in which those principles are enforced.

Many state legislatures are, in fact, considering proposals directed at the practical aspects of malpractice litigation. Some states are considering legislation that would limit the contingency fee to a certain fixed maximum. Other states have already tried to reduce the delays inherent in malpractice litigation by requiring that the parties to a malpractice suit go through an arbitration process and try to settle the claim before a trial. It has been proposed that this concept be expanded to require that all malpractice claims be settled through a compulsory arbitration process and not by the courts at all. Other changes in the traditional legal process that are under consideration include eliminating the role of the jury or prohibiting juries from awarding damages for "pain and suffering."

Changes in the current system for insuring against malpractice liability have also been proposed as solutions to the malpractice "problem." A state could require that all insurance companies offering malpractice insurance in that state accept a proportionate share of all providers or a share of the bad risks. Alternatively, in states where malpractice insurance is not available, the federal or state government could finance an insurance program, either by preempting the field altogether or as an alternative competitor to private insurance. It has even been proposed that a system of "no-fault" insurance be developed for providers of medical care. Under such a scheme, anyone injured as a result of medical practice could recover from the provider's insurance company regardless of any finding of fault or negligence. The cost of this insurance might be reduced by restricting the amount a patient could recover, and by reductions in the cost of the litigation and the administration now required for the determination of liability.

Whatever the nature of the proposal for change to be considered, from drastic revisions of malpractice liability to slight adjustments in the legal process, the same question must first be asked: What exactly is this problem that everyone is trying to solve?

In much of the recent public debate over the malpractice "problem," the focal issue has been the astronomically high cost of malpractice insurance coverage for providers. This is an important part of the problem for the consumer, since sooner or later the cost of the provider's insurance will be shifted to the patient. For the provider, the cost by itself is not the only problem; there is also the accompanying threat that malpractice insurance will not only be expensive to some providers but unavailable. Even in areas where insurance companies continue to write policies, they may not offer coverage to all providers. Some categories of providers, e.g., cosmetic surgeons, and some individual providers are predictably bad insurance risks and are finding it increasingly difficult to buy insurance at any price.

The high cost and unavailability of malpractice insurance are matters that deserve attention, but they cannot be seen as the central issues. The primary problem is that the legal determination of malpractice liability does not adequately achieve its dual purposes: it is not an effective quality control and it is not a good means for compensation of injured patients. The high cost and unavailability of malpractice insurance are only indications of that larger problem. Therefore, any solution to the malpractice problem ought to be measured in terms of the fulfillment of these purposes for imposing liability in the first place, not solely in terms of the costs of insuring against it.

Unlike some of the critical issues in public health outlined in previous chapters, this particular problem is one that will be likely dealt with in the legislative arena, not in the courtroom. Accordingly, just as the flaws and eccentricities of the judicial process have to be taken into account when predicting future responses to some legal problems, the realities of the legislative process must be taken into account in predicting the likely response to the malpractice problem. For example, one must remember that legislators may represent their constituents' interests, but some constituents are more influential than others. The organized bar will certainly lobby heavily and effectively against any attempt to prohibit the use of contingency fees or to limit the amount that can be recovered in malpractice suits. Likewise, the medical profession will instruct its traditionally powerful lobbyists to work for legislation that fosters reasonably priced and easily obtained malpractice insurance, even if the result is to unfairly restrict the compensation of deserving claimants. In general terms well-organized, well-financed interest groups will always have a great deal of influence on legislative change while the general public— the consumer, the individual, the average patient—usually will not. Within these political constraints it is likely that certain aspects of the malpractice problem will be effectively resolved. Undoubtedly some means of providing malpractice insurance to most providers of medical care at a reasonable cost will be found. It is possible that these changes, whatever they are, will also have positive effects on the quality of available medical care or will assure that injured patients are adequately reimbursed. Yet while possible, given the current realities of the legislative process, such an outcome would be somewhat serendipitous.

References

California Department of Public Health: A report to the California Legislature: 1972 health facilities malpractice actions, 1973.

Cullen, C.: Hospital duty to provide emergency medical care for the indigent and the medically indigent, Clearinghouse Rev. 4:297, 1970.

Curran, W., and Shapiro, E.: Law, medicine, and forensic science, ed. 2, 1970, Chapters 5 and 6.

Hayt, E., Hayt, L., and Groeschel, A.: Law of hospital, physician, and patient, Part III, ed. 3, 1972.

Institute for Interdisciplinary Studies of the American Rehabilitation Foundation: Arbitration of malpractice disputes, 1972.

McDonald, D.: Medical malpractice: a discussion of alternative compensation and quality control systems (Center for the Study of Democratic Institutions, 1971).

Medical malpractice: a study of defensive medicine, Duke L.J. 39:957, 1971.

U.S. Department of Health, Education and Welfare: Report of the secretary's commission on medical malpractice, 1973 (the appendix to this report compiles thirty related articles on various aspects of the malpractice problem).

CHAPTER 7

Patients' legal rights

It has become stylish lately to speak of patients' rights. In the Fall of 1972 the American Hospital Association published the following "Patient's Bill of Rights," purporting to affirm certain rights to which a patient is entitled in a hospital setting.

1. The patient has the right to considerate and respectful care.
2. The patient has the right to obtain from his physician complete current information concerning his diagnosis, treatment, and prognosis in terms the patient can be reasonably expected to understand. When it is not medically advisable to give such information to the patient, the information should be made available to an appropriate person in his behalf. He has the right to know by name, the physician responsible for coordinating his care.
3. The patient has the right to receive from his physician information necessary to give informed consent prior to the start of any procedure and/or treatment. Except in emergencies, such information for informed consent, should include but not necessarily be limited to the specific procedure and/or treatment, the medically significant risks involved, and the probable duration of incapacitation. Where medically significant alternatives for care or treatment exist, or when the patient requests information concerning medical alternatives, the patient has the right to know the name of the person responsible for the procedures and/or treatment.
4. The patient has the right to refuse treatment to the extent permitted by law, and to be informed of the medical consequences of his action.
5. The patient has the right to every consideration of his privacy concerning his own medical care program. Case discussion, consultation, examination, and treatment are confidential and should be conducted discreetly. Those not directly involved in his care must have the permission of the patient to be present.
6. The patient has the right to expect that all communications and records pertaining to his care should be treated as confidential.
7. The patient has the right to expect that within its capacity a hospital must make reasonable response to the request of a patient for services. The hospital must provide evaluation, service, and/or referral as indicated by the urgency of the case. When medically permissible a patient may be transferred to another facility only after he has received complete information and explanation concerning the needs for and alternatives to such a transfer. The institution to which the patient is to be transferred must first have accepted the patient for transfer.
8. The patient has the right to obtain information as to any relationship of his hospital to other health care and educational institutions insofar as his care is concerned. The patient has the right to obtain information as to the existence of any professional relationships among individuals, by name, who are treating him.
9. The patient has the right to be advised if the hospital proposes to engage in or perform human experimentation affecting his care or treatment. The patient has the right to refuse to participate in such research projects.
10. The patient has the right to expect reasonable continuity of care. He has the right to know in advance what appointment times and physicians are available and where. The patient has the right to expect that the hospital will provide a mechanism whereby he is informed by his physician or a delegate of the physician of the patient's continuing health care requirements following discharge.

11. The patient has the right to examine and receive an explanation of his bill regardless of source of payment.
12. The patient has the right to know what hospital rules and regulations apply to his conduct as a patient.

The AHA list of rights is similar in form and concept to the statement of patients' rights included in the Preamble to the Accreditation Manual of the Joint Commission on Accreditation of Hospitals. Some individual providers, consumer organizations, and legal services agencies have also published similar statements concerning patients' rights and explanations of "your rights as a patient." In addition to the rights enumerated by the AHA, the other statements of rights have included such diverse things as the right to be called by your proper name, the right to expect the best medical care, and the right to be helped.

With most of these statements, it is not clear what is meant by the term right. Does this mean a legal right according to the definition that has been adopted in this book, a relationship that is defined and enforced through the legal system? Or is a patients' bill of rights only a statement of human or moral rights? Most critically, are these statements reflecting the status quo or statements of rights that ought to exist?

The AHA bill cryptically states that the rights listed are "recognized as affirmed." The JCAH preamble intimates that a failure to observe these rights will be considered as a factor by the JCAH in determining the accreditation status of a hospital. Most of the other statements of patients' rights have either stated or strongly implied that there will be direct legal consequences for a violation of any of the patients' rights. The most interesting approach to patients' rights is in the *Report of the Secretary's Commission on Medical Malpractice* (see Chapter 6, *supra*), which states that a failure to observe patients' rights in a hospital setting "is both to betray humanity and to invite dissatisfaction that may lead to malpractice suits."

Although many of the patients' rights listed in the AHA bill and other patients' rights statements are legally enforceable, some of the rights listed in these various statements are not what could be considered legal rights. For example, consider the patient's right to be called by his or her proper name. This may be a right by some definitions of that term, but it is certainly not a legal right. There is no provision of any constitution or any statute or any legal principle that establishes such a relationship between patients and providers of medical care. There is no existing legal process that would enforce such a right. Similarly, the right to considerate and respectful care and many of the other rights listed in these statements are not directly enforceable through the law. That does not mean, however, that things like consideration and personal kindness are not important aspects of medical care. Obviously they are. These "rights" or interests or whatever they are labeled should be advocated, demanded in their absence, and recognized as critical parts of the provider-patient relationship. This may require political action, consumer organization, or simply interpersonal pressure. But to treat these types of rights as legally enforceable would only lead to unjustified expectations and inappropriate action to protect or enforce them. These rights may be recognized in current society as moral or human rights, but if they are enforceable at all, it is with the force of personal pressure or moral suasion, not through the legal system. To state that a patient has a right to be called by his or her proper name is probably best translated as the statement that a patient *ought to be* called by his or her proper name. It is not a statement of the law as it stands today. Perhaps these recently published statements of patients' rights are the beginnings of a process that will lead to their recognition in the law. At the moment, it would be inaccurate and misleading to consider some of these rights as legally enforceable.

On the other hand, many of these patients' rights are enforceable through the legal system. This chapter will be an explanation of the legal bases of some of the more fundamental patients' rights. It will not be an attempt to define a complete list of the legal rights of a patient. Instead it will discuss several fundamental rights, explain how they are recognized and enforced by the law, and try to indicate what these rights mean in practical terms.

The right to consent to treatment

The most basic of a patient's legal rights is the right to consent to treatment. Medical treatment without valid consent of the patient is a violation of the law; no person can be forced against their will to submit to medical treatment or to continue to receive medical treatment. There are a few narrow exceptions to these rules. As discussed in Chapter 2, people previously found to be incompetent and minors may be treated involuntarily, but in both cases only with the consent of their legal guardian. In rare instances states will exercise their broad police powers to confine, examine, or treat people with certain communicable diseases that present hazards to the public's health. Other than in these exceptional situations, the general rule is that the patient is always entitled to refuse treatment or to leave the care of a physician or a health facility, even if leaving is expressly against medical advice.

This right to consent to treatment derives from the basic principles of tort liability between private individuals. The tort of battery is literally any unconsented to touching of one person by another. This is one of the several ways in which the law has recognized the freedom of each person with respect to their own body and their inherent right of self-determination. It makes no difference if the touching is for the purpose of medical treatment. If there is no valid consent, any touching will technically constitute a battery.

Any unconsented to touching makes the person who touched liable to be sued for damages. There is no need for the plaintiff in a battery suit to show that the touching resulted in any harm. Legally the harm is the touching itself. A patient who is treated without consent or beyond the limits of the consent can sue the provider for battery and recover any actual damages suffered or, if none, nominal damages and in some cases, punitive damages. The amount of the recovery by the offended patient has been quite extraordinary given the apparent circumstances of some battery cases.

Consent need not be expressed. The consent to be touched can either be explicit or implied. For example, in the medical setting very often a patient implies consent to an initial examination by his or her actions after entering a physician's office. The law also recognizes that consent is not a prerequisite to emergency medical care when the patient is unconscious. In that situation some courts create the fiction that the consent is implied by the situation; others consider that the requirement is waived altogether in an emergency. Consent can also be implied in the sense that a patient may agree to a particular kind of treatment or touching, and this will be interpreted to include anything reasonably necessary to accomplish that which is consented to. There are, however, some important limits on the extent to which consent can be implied, as will be discussed below.

Consent can either be in writing or verbal. The general practice of most providers of medical care to ask for consent in writing is for their own protection; it facilitates the proof that consent was obtained if there is later a dispute. The fact that a consent is once given or given in writing does not in any way affect the patient's ability to withdraw consent, expressly or implicitly. The basic issue is always whether at the time of the procedure the patient actually consents to that touching.

In order for the patient's consent to treatment to be considered legally valid, it must be voluntary, competent, and informed. Each of these elements involves slightly different considerations.

Voluntary consent

Basically, a voluntary consent is one where there is no misrepresentation or coercion. The fact that a patient actually communicated a consent to the provider may be invalidated if conditions exist that indicate that the consent was not really the free choice of the patient. A failure to tell the patient an important fact or a misstatement of the truth may mean that the law will consider that the consent was never obtained and thus that a battery occurred. Similarly, the use of vague terms may also be considered misleading to the patient and invalidate consent.

Experimental medical procedures often are performed—illegally—without voluntary consent. For the consent to the procedure to be valid, it must be made clear to the patient that the experimental procedure is not standard medical practice. There are also many situations where a provider's patients are coerced into participating in an experiment, e.g., the testing of a new drug, by the real or incorrectly perceived threat that if the patient fails to consent, the provider will discontinue giving medical care to the patient.

Competent consent

A consent that is legally voluntary must also be competent. That means that the person giving the consent is mentally competent and of proper legal age. A provider must decide prior to obtaining consent that the patient is mentally competent. If not, only the legal guardian can consent to the procedure. The provider must also ascertain that the patient is of the proper age to consent. In most states, people below a fixed age, usually 18 or 21 years of age, are considered minors and cannot make legally binding decisions for themselves, including the decision to accept medical care. Some states by statute have lowered that age for decisions involving medical care, for treatment of communicable diseases, or family-planning procedures. Almost all states recognize an exception for emancipated minors. Otherwise, the consent of a minor's legal guardian must be obtained prior to treatment. Even in an emergency, a reasonable attempt must be made to find the guardian, if there is any amount of time to do so. Consent that is not given competently is not valid and can result in the provider being sued for battery.

Informed consent

A consent that is legally voluntary and competent must also be informed. The precise definition of informed consent and its legal basis are conceptually rather difficult to understand.

Consent is obviously meaningless if the patient does not know the relevant implications of one treatment when compared to another course of action. The patient must have enough information to make an intelligent choice between alternative treatments or to choose no treatment at all. Because in many situations only the provider of medical care can supply that information, the law has recognized that the provider must bear the responsibility for providing the necessary information.

Unlike the requirements that consent be obtained and that the consent be voluntary and competent, the requirement of informed consent is not based on the concept of battery. Any touching, even for the purposes of medical treatment, without consent is a battery. Consent that is given but is not voluntary or competent is not valid, and any subsequent touching would be a battery. However, the principle that consent must be an informed choice is based on the concept of negligence. As discussed in Chapter 6, a provider of medical care has a duty of reasonable care toward his or her patient at all times during treatment. If the provider violates the standard of conduct that defines that duty under the circumstances and the patient is damaged, the patient may have grounds for a malpractice suit. Entirely independent of any malpractice claim, a patient who is damaged by a provider of medical care may also sue on the grounds that the provider was negligent not in the treatment itself but in the process of obtaining the patient's consent to treatment. To be specific, it would be unreasonable conduct under the circumstances to allow a patient to make the consent decision without sufficient information upon which to make that decision.

There is no clear demarcation between when the consent is truly informed and when it is not. Obviously any legal determination based on the concept of negligence or reasonableness is not an exact one. It is clear, however, that such a requirement imposes some duty of disclosure on the provider and that some amount of information must be communicated to the patient to allow the patient to be the ultimate decision maker. It is one way in which the law has recognized a patient's right to make decisions regarding his or her own body. Basically this requires that the patient be told enough information about the treatment, the alternatives, and the inherent risks of the treatment to make an intelligent choice. These are the essential elements of an informed consent.

The leading case interpreting these general principles of informed consent is the California Supreme Court decision in *Cobbs v. Grant,* 8 C.3d 229, 502

P.2d 1 (1972). The *Cobbs* decision did not recognize the patient's right to informed consent for the first time; previous decisions in California and other jurisdictions had recognized that right in principle. The *Cobbs* decision is important because the court took the opportunity to analyze the right to informed consent in some detail and depth; the express purpose of the opinion was to provide guidance to the lower court to which the case was remanded. The practical effect was to provide a rather complete explanation of how the right to informed consent should be applied.

The opinion reads as follows:

> Plaintiff was admitted to the hospital in August 1964 for treatment of a duodenal ulcer. He was given a series of tests to ascertain the severity of his condition and, though administered medication to ease his discomfort, he continued to complain of lower abdominal pain and nausea. His family physician, Dr. Jerome Sands, concluding that surgery was indicated, discussed prospective surgery with plaintiff and advised him in general terms of the risks of undergoing a general anesthetic. Dr. Sands called in defendant, Dr. Dudley F. P. Grant, a surgeon, who after examining plaintiff, agreed with Dr. Sands that plaintiff had an intractable peptic duodenal ulcer and that surgery was indicated. Although Dr. Grant explained the nature of the operation to plaintiff, he did not discuss any of the inherent risks of the surgery.
>
> A two-hour operation was performed the next day, in the course of which the presence of a small ulcer was confirmed. Following the surgery the ulcer disappeared. Plaintiff's recovery appeared to be uneventful, and he was permitted to go home eight days later. However, the day after he returned home, plaintiff began to experience intense pain in his abdomen. He immediately called Dr. Sands who advised him to return to the hospital. Two hours after his readmission plaintiff went into shock and emergency surgery was performed. It was discovered plaintiff was bleeding internally as a result of a severed artery at the hilum of his spleen. Because of the seriousness of the hemorrhaging and since the spleen of an adult may be removed without adverse effects, defendant decided to remove the spleen. Injuries to the spleen that compel a subsequent operation are a risk inherent in the type of surgery performed on plaintiff and occur in approximately 5 percent of such operations.
>
> After removal of his spleen, plaintiff recuperated for two weeks in the hospital. A month after discharge he was readmitted because of sharp pains in his stomach. X-rays disclosed plaintiff was developing a gastric ulcer. The evolution of a new ulcer is another risk inherent in surgery performed to relieve a duodenal ulcer. Dr. Sands initially decided to attempt to treat this nascent gastric ulcer with antacids and a strict diet. However, some four months later plaintiff was again hospitalized when the gastric ulcer continued to deteriorate and he experienced severe pain. When plaintiff began to vomit blood the defendant and Dr. Sands concluded that a third operation was indicated: a gastrectomy with removal of 50 percent of plaintiff's stomach to reduce its acid-producing capacity. Some time after surgery, plaintiff was discharged, but subsequently had to be hospitalized yet again when he began to bleed internally due to the premature absorption of a suture, another inherent risk of surgery. After plaintiff was hospitalized, the bleeding began to abate and a week later he was finally discharged.
>
> Plaintiff brought this malpractice suit against his surgeon, Dr. Grant. The action was consolidated for trial with a similar action against the hospital. The jury returned a general verdict against the hospital in the amount of $45,000. This judgment has been satisfied. The jury also returned a general verdict against defendant Grant in the amount of $23,880. He appeals.
>
> The jury could have found for plaintiff either by determining that defendant negligently performed the operation, or on the theory that defendant's failure to disclose the inherent risks of the initial surgery vitiated plaintiff's consent to operate. Defendant attacks both

possible grounds of the verdict. He contends, first, there was insufficient evidence to sustain a verdict of negligence, and, second, the court committed prejudicial error in its instruction to the jury on the issue of informed consent.

NOTE: In Part I of the opinion (omitted here) the court concluded that there was insufficient evidence to support a verdict for the plaintiff on the ground that the defendant had been negligent in the performance of the operation. In Part II, the court examined the question of whether the failure to obtain informed consent is negligence or a battery and concluded that it is negligence.

III

Since this is an appropriate case for the application of a negligence theory, it remains for us to determine if the standard of care described in the jury instruction on this subject properly delineates defendant's duty to inform plaintiff of the inherent risks of the surgery. In pertinent part, the court gave the following instruction: "A physician's duty to disclose is not governed by the standard practice in the community; rather it is a duty imposed by law. A physician violates his duty to his patient and subjects himself to liability if he withholds any facts which are necessary to form the basis of an intelligent consent by the patient to the proposed treatment."

Defendant raises two objections to the foregoing instruction. First, he points out that the majority of the California cases have measured the duty to disclose not in terms of an absolute, but as a duty to reveal such information as would be disclosed by a doctor in good standing within the medical community. (*Carmichael v. Reitz* (1971) *supra,* 17 Cal. App. 3d 958, 976 95 Cal. Rptr. 381; *Dunlap v. Marine* (1966) *supra,* 242 Cal. App. 2d 162, 51 Cal. Rptr. 158; *Tangora v. Matanky* (1964) *supra,* 231 Cal. App. 2d 468, 42 Cal. Rptr. 348; contra, *Berkey v. Anderson* (1969) *supra,* 1 Cal. App. 3d 790, 82 Cal. Rptr. 67.) One commentator has imperiously declared that "good medical practice is good law." (Hagman, *"The Medical Patient's Right to Know"* (1970) 17 *U.C.L.A.L. Rev.* 758, 764.) Moreover, with one state and one federal exception every jurisdiction that has considered this question has adopted the community standard as the applicable test. Defendant's second contention is that this near unanimity reflects strong policy reasons for vesting in the medical community the unquestioned discretion to determine if the withholding of information by a doctor from his patient is justified at the time the patient weighs the risks of treatment against the risks of refusing treatment.

The thesis that medical doctors are invested with discretion to withhold information from their patients has been frequently ventilated in both legal and medical literature. (See, e.g., *Salgo v. Leland Stanford etc. Bd. Trustees* (1957) *supra,* 154 Cal. App. 2d 560, 578, 317 P.2d 170; *Mitchell v. Robinson* (Mo. 1960) *supra,* 334 S.W. 2d 11 (even though patient was upset, agitated, depressed, crying, had marital problems and had been drinking, the court found that since no emergency existed and he was legally competent he should have been advised of the risks of shock therapy); Mosely, *Textbook of Surgery* (3d ed. 1959) pp. 93-95; Laufman, *"Surgical Judgment,"* in *Christopher's Textbook of Surgery* (Davis ed. 1968) pp. 1459, 1461; Louisell & Williams, *Medical Malpractice* (1970) §22.02; McCoid, *"A Reappraisal of Liability for Unauthorized Medical Treatment"* (1957) 41 *Minn. L. Rev.* 381; Plante, *"An Analysis of 'Informed Consent'"* (1968) 36 *Fordham L. Rev.* 639.) Despite what defendant characterizes as the prevailing rule, it has never been unequivocally adopted by an authoritative source. Therefore, we probe anew into the rationale which purportedly justifies, in accordance with medical rather than legal standards, the withholding of information from a patient.

Preliminarily we employ several postulates. The first is that patients are generally persons unlearned in the medical sciences and therefore, except in rare cases, courts may safely assume the knowledge of patient and physician are not in parity. The second is that a person of adult years and in sound mind has the right, in the exercise of control over his own body, to determine whether or not to submit to lawful medical treatment. The third is that the patient's consent to treatment, to be effective, must be an informed consent. And the fourth is that the patient, being unlearned in medical sciences, has an abject dependence upon and trust in his physician for the information upon which he relies during the decisional process, thus raising an obligation in the physician that transcends arms-length transactions.

From the foregoing axiomatic ingredients emerges a necessity, and a resultant requirement, for divulgence by the physician to his patient of all information relevant to a meaningful decisional process. In many instances, to the physician, whose training and experience enable a self-satisfying evaluation, the particular treatment which should be undertaken may seem evident, but it is the prerogative of the patient, not the physician, to determine for himself the direction in which he believes his interests lie. To enable the patient to chart his course knowledgeably, reasonable familiarity with the therapeutic alternatives and their hazards becomes essential.

Therefore, we hold, as an integral part of the physician's overall obligation to the patient there is a duty of reasonable disclosure of the available choices with respect to proposed therapy and of the dangers inherently and potentially involved in each.

A concomitant issue is the yardstick to be applied in determining reasonableness of disclosure. This defendant and the majority of courts have related the duty to the custom of physicians practicing in the community. (*Aiken v. Clary* [Mo. 1965] 396 S. W. 2d 668, 675; *Roberts v. Young* (1963) 369 Mich. 133, 119 N.W.2d 627, 630; *Haggerty v. McCarthy* (1962) 344 Mass. 136; 181 N.E.2d 562, 565, 92 A.L.R.2d 998; *DiFilippo v. Preston* (1961) 53 Del. 539, 173 A.2d 333, 339.) The majority rule is needlessly overbroad. Even if there can be said to be a medical community standard as to the disclosure requirement for any prescribed treatment, it appears so nebulous that doctors become, in effect, vested with virtual absolute discretion. (See Note, *"Physicians and Surgeons"* (1962) 75 *Harv. L. Rev.* 1445; Waltz and Scheuneman, *"Informed Consent to Therapy"* (1970) 64 *Nw. U. L. Rev.* 628.) The court in *Canterbury v. Spence, supra,* 464 F.2d 772, 784, bluntly observed: "Nor can we ignore the fact that to bind the disclosure obligation to medical usage is to arrogate the decision on revelation to the physician alone. Respect for the patient's right of self-determination on particular therapy demands a standard set by law for physicians rather than one which physicians may or may not impose upon themselves." Unlimited discretion in the physician is irreconcilable with the basic right of the patient to make the ultimate informed decision regarding the course of treatment to which he knowledgeably consents to be subjected.

A medical doctor, being the expert, appreciates the risks inherent in the procedure he is prescribing, the risks of a decision not to undergo the treatment, and the probability of a successful outcome of the treatment. But once this information has been disclosed, that aspect of the doctor's expert function has been performed. The weighing of these risks against the individual subjective fears and hopes of the patient is not an expert skill. Such evaluation and decision is a nonmedical judgment reserved to the patient alone. A patient should be denied the opportunity to weigh the risks only where it is evident he cannot evaluate the data, as for example, where there is an emergency or the patient is a child or incompetent. For this reason the law provides that in an emergency consent is implied (*Wheeler v. Barker* (1949) 92 Cal. App. 2d 776, 785, 208 P.2d 68; *Preston v. Hubbell* (1948) 87 Cal. App. 2d 53, 57-58, 196 P.2d 113, and if the patient is a minor or incompetent, the authority to consent is transferred to the patient's legal guardian or closest available relative (*Ballard v. Anderson* (1971) 4 Cal. 3d 873, 883, 95 Cal. Rptr. 1, 484 P.2d 1345, 42 A.L.R.3d 1392; *Doyle v. Giuliucci* (1965) 62 Cal. 2d 606, 43 Cal. Rptr. 697, 401 P.2d 1; *Bonner v. Moran* (1941) 126 F.2d 121, (75 App. D.C. 156), 139 A.L.R. 1356. In all cases other than the foregoing, the decision whether or not to undertake treatment is vested in the party most directly affected: the patient.

The scope of the disclosure required of physicians defies simple definition. Some courts have spoken of "full disclosure" (e.g., *Berkey v. Anderson, supra,* 1 Cal. App. 3d 790,

804; *Salgo v. Leland Stanford etc. Bd. Trustees, supra,* 154 Cal. App. 2d 560, 578) and others refer to "full and complete" disclosure (*Stafford v. Shultz* (1954) 42 Cal. 2d 767, 777, 270 P.2d 1; *Pashley v. Pacific Elec. Ry. Co.* (1944) 25 Cal. 2d 226, 235, 153 P.2d 325, but such facile expressions obscure common practicalities. Two qualifications to a requirement of "full disclosure" need little explication. First, the patient's interest in information does not extend to a lengthy polysyllabic discourse on all possible complications. A minicourse in medical science is not required; the patient is concerned with the risk of death or bodily harm, and problems of recuperation. Second, there is no physician's duty to discuss the relatively minor risks inherent in common procedures, when it is common knowledge that such risks inherent in the procedure are of very low incidence. When there is a common procedure a doctor must, of course, make such inquiries as are required to determine if for the particular patient the treatment under consideration is contraindicated—for example, to detemine if the patient has had adverse reactions to antibiotics; but no warning beyond such inquiries is required as to the remote possibility of death or serious bodily harm.

However, when there is a more complicated procedure, as the surgery in the case before us, the jury should be instructed that when a given procedure inherently involves a known risk of death or serious bodily harm, a medical doctor has a duty to disclose to his patient the potential of death or serious harm, and to explain in lay terms the complications that might possibly occur. Beyond the foregoing minimal disclosure, a doctor must also reveal to his patient such additional information as a skilled practitioner of good standing would provide under similar circumstances.

In sum, the patient's right of self-decision is the measure of the physician's duty to reveal. That right can be effectively exercised only if the patient possesses adequate information to enable an intelligent choice. The scope of the physician's communications to the patient, then, must be measured by the patient's need, and that need is whatever information is material to the decision. Thus the test for determining whether a potential peril must be divulged is its materiality to the patient's decision. (*Canterbury v. Spence, supra,* 464 F.2d 772, 786.)

We point out, for guidance on retrial, an additional problem which suggests itself. There must be a causal relationship between the physician's failure to inform and the injury to the plaintiff. Such causal connection arises only if it is established that had revelation been made consent to treatment would not have been given. Here the record discloses no testimony that had plaintiff been informed of the risks of surgery he would not have consented to the operation. (*Shetter v. Rochelle* (1965) 2 Ariz. App. 358, 409 P.2d 74; *Sharpe v. Pugh* (1967) 270 N.C. 598, 155 S.E.2d 108; cf. *Aiken v. Clary* (Mo. 1965) *supra,* 396 S.W.2d 668.)

The patient-plaintiff may testify on this subject but the issue extends beyond his credibility. Since at the time of trial the uncommunicated hazard has materialized, it would be surprising if the patient-plaintiff did not claim that had he been informed of the dangers he would have declined treatment. Subjectively he may believe so, with the 20/20 vision of hindsight, but we doubt that justice will be served by placing the physician in jeopardy of the patient's bitterness and disillusionment. Thus an objective test is preferable: i.e., what would a prudent person in the patient's position have decided if adequately informed of all significant perils. (*Canterbury v. Spence, supra,* 464 F.2d 772, 791.)

The burden of going forward with evidence of nondisclosure rests on the plaintiff. Once such evidence has been produced, then the burden of going forward with evidence pertaining to justification for failure to disclose shifts to the physician.

Whenever appropriate, the court should instruct the jury on the defenses available to a doctor who has failed to make the disclosure required by law. Thus, a medical doctor need not make disclosure of risks when the patient requests that he not be so informed. (See discussion of waiver: Hagman, *"The Medical Patient's Right to Know," supra,* 17 *U.C.L.A.L. Rev.* 758, 785.) Such a disclosure need not be made if the procedure is simple and the danger remote and commonly appreciated to be remote. A disclosure need not be made beyond that required within the medical community when a doctor can prove by a preponderance of the evidence he relied upon facts which would demonstrate to a reasonable man the disclosure would have so seriously upset the patient that the patient would not have been able to dispassionately weigh the risks of refusing to undergo the recommended treatment. (E.g., see discussion of informing the dying patient: Hagman, *"The Medical Patient's Right to Know," supra,* 17 *U.C.L.A.L. Rev.* 758, 778.) Any defense, of course, must be consistent with what has been termed the "fiducial qualities" of the physician-patient relationship. (*Emmett v. Eastern Dispensary and Casualty Hospital* (1967) 396 F.2d 931, 935, 130 App. D.C. 50.

The judgment is reversed.

The *Cobbs* case was remanded by the California Supreme Court to the lower state court for a new trial. (At the time of this publication, that trial had not yet taken place.) At that trial the basic issue would be whether Dr. Grant was negligent in performing his duty to disclose information to his patient, Mr. Cobbs. The measure of that duty, the standard of conduct, is that the disclosure must provide the patient with adequate information with which to make an intelligent choice of treatment. This is what the law considers reasonable under the circumstances. In applying this standard of conduct in the *Cobbs* case or any subsequent case, a jury will be given the facts and circumstances of the case and an explanation of the legal standard of conduct; the final decision as to whether the standard of conduct was violated will be a question for the jury to decide.

The *Cobbs* opinion specifically rejected an application of a form of the community practice rule. The measure of reasonableness is not what other physicians disclose to their patients in Dr. Grant's community; nor must it be based on professional testimony as to what is reasonable. What is reasonable is not to be defined by the medical profession, but by a layperson jury. As the court put it, "Respect for the patient's right of self-determination on particular therapy demands a standard set by law for physicians rather than one which physicians may or may not impose on themselves."

The decision in *Cobbs* did allow that under certain circumstances informed consent need not be obtained. There are obviously exceptions for emergency medical treatment when the patient is unconscious and for treatment of minors and incompetents (with the informed consent of their guardians). The decision also allowed that a patient could ask not to be informed. Presumably, even this decision would require some explanation by the provider of the decision that the patient was waiving. There is also an exception allowed where the provider can prove that making an informed decision would seriously upset the patient. Otherwise, the patient must be given adequate information and be the final decision maker, or the provider of medical care risks liability for violating the right of the patient to informed consent.

Cobbs v. Grant met with an uproar from the medical professions. Representatives of organized medicine throughout the country and particularly in California protested that the opinion would open a Pandora's box of new litigation. Yet such an interpretation of the *Cobbs* decision and the principles that it interpreted is rather simplistic and to a large extent inaccurate.

There is little doubt that the principles of law outlined in the *Cobbs* opinion require a change in the standard behavior of many providers of medical care. More communication between the provider and the patient must take place. The ultimate decision concerning choice of treatment must be made by the patient; prior to *Cobbs,* many providers would have argued that ultimately the decision is to be made by the provider. Notwithstanding the fact that provider behavior will have to change, it is not clear that more lawsuits will be filed claiming that there has been a violation of informed consent. *Cobbs v. Grant* defined a violation of the right to informed consent as negligence. Had it defined a violation of that right as battery, any violation of that right could result in liability; under the legal principles defining battery discussed earlier in this chapter, the touching without consent itself is the harm. Consequently, under a battery theory, if a provider fails to get informed consent, the provider might be liable for nominal or punitive damages even if the resulting treatment were successful and without complicaton.

A suit based on negligence, however, requires not only a violation of the standard of conduct, but proof that the violation resulted in some damage to the offended person. In a case alleging negligence in obtaining informed consent, a plaintiff will have to show that the provider failed to provide adequate information and that some harm resulted, e.g., the procedure was not successful or some complication resulted. Furthermore, to show that the violation and the damage were causally related, the plaintiff will have to show that had he or she known of the undisclosed risk of damage or undisclosed treatment alternative, he or she would have chosen some other alternative choice. In the *Cobbs* case that will require Mr. Cobbs to convince the jury that had Dr. Grant explained the risk of complications to the spleen and the development of a subsequent ulcer, Mr. Cobbs would have chosen not to consent to the operation. He may or may not be successful.

The resulting effect is that only violations of informed consent that cause actual damage to a patient will result in provider liability—a result that seems to be both logical and fair.

The right to confidentiality

Another of the basic legal rights of a patient is the right to confidentiality. Confidentiality, however, is a term that is not always clearly defined.

Generally confidentiality means that a promise has been made not to divulge information. A receiver of information implies or expresses a promise not to reveal that information to other people. The term is frequently used in everyday relationships, e.g., conversations are often "in confidence," and most people are extremely offended by any act that constitutes a breach of their notion of confidentiality. Confidentiality in the context of medical treatment is basically the promise by the provider of medical care made to the patient not to divulge to others any informaton obtained during the period of the provider-patient relationship.

The medical profession has always recognized confidentiality as an extremely important part of medical practice. Hippocrates' self-imposed oath included the provision that:

Whatsoever things I see or hear concerning the life of man, in any attendance on the sick or even apart therefrom which ought not to be noised abroad, I will keep silent thereon, counting such things to be professional secrets.

Hippocrates' oath has more than historical value; it has had a continuing influence on the medical profession and it is one consideration in determining current interpretations of ethical behavior. Unfortunately, the oath does little more than beg the important question: what exactly "ought not to be noised abroad?"

A more recent formulation of the ethical standards of the medical profession in the Principles of Medical Ethics of the American Medical Association included a prohibition paraphrasing the Hippocratic oath and establishing the importance of confidentiality:

A physician may not reveal the confidence entrusted to him in the course of medical attendance, or the deficiencies that he may observe in the character of patients, unless he is required to do so by law or unless it becomes necessary in order to protect the welfare of the individual or of the community.

At least in theory, the organized medical profession has recognized confidentiality as an ethical right, one that is enforceable by the sanctions available to a provider's professional associations, e.g., a physician could lose membership in his or her local medical society—with all the social and economic consequences that would result—for violating a patient's confidentiality.

Most physicians and other providers of medical care not only believe that they are ethically required to respect the confidentiality of their patients, but also they generally believe that they are legally bound to do so. Unfortunately and surprisingly, there is no general legal right to confidentiality that applies to all medical treatment situations. Rather, there are a number of ways in which the law protects the confidentiality of patients under some, but not all, circumstances.

One way in which the law has recognized that the patient has a right to confidentiality is through the evidentiary principle known as the physician-patient privilege. In many states statutes have been passed that prohibit a physician or other categories of provider from testifying in court concerning any information acquired during the course of a patient's medical treatment. It is not that the testimony is considered inaccurate or misleading. It is that those states have a policy of protecting confidentiality, even to the extent of prohibiting certain kinds of evidence from being admitted in court.

The privilege is the right of the patient, not the physician; the patient can evoke the privilege to prevent the physician from testifying or the physician can claim it on behalf of the patient in the patient's absence. It cannot be claimed by the physician against the patient's wishes.

The privilege is only relevant to judicial proceedings. Some states recognize the privilege only in criminal cases; others recognize it only in civil cases. All states recognize that the privilege is not applicable when the patient is suing the physician. In fact there are so many exceptions to the rule in some states that it is hard to imagine a situation where a physician would be testifying and the privilege would not be excepted. Furthermore, some states do not recognize the physician-patient privilege at all.

The patient's confidentiality is not protected by privilege statutes from violations outside of the courtroom; indeed the extent to which the patient has a legal right to confidentiality outside of the courtroom is somewhat limited.

It is possible that a provider will be civilly liable to the patient for a breach of confidentiality. Some courts that have considered the issue have denied that there is any possible ground upon which a breach of confidentiality could be considered the basis for civil liability. Other courts have, however, awarded damages to the patient based on a variety of legal theories. Accordingly, liability is possible, but not certain. But it is the possibility of liability—perhaps better phrased "the threat"—that makes a legal right potentially enforceable and the right to confidentiality a legitimate expectation.

One possibility is that a breach of confidentiality may be interpreted to be an invasion of the patient's privacy. As mentioned in an earlier chapter, some states have recognized invasions of privacy as a tort.

Invasions of privacy that result in liability are usually (1) unwarranted or unreasonable interference with a person's personal life, or (2) unauthorized publicity about the person, usually for financial gain, although financial gain is not necessary. The tort of invasion of privacy has been summarized in the *Restatement of Torts,* section 867 as:

. . . a person who unreasonably or seriously interferes with another's interest in not having his affairs known to others or his likeness exhibited to the public is liable to the other.

The type of damage that must be shown by the plaintiff is very subjective; invasions of privacy are determined by the injury to the person's feelings, not to property or pecuniary interest or even reputation. Liability can exist where the only harm is embarrassment or humiliation.

Consequently, a patient could sue a provider who breaches the confidentiality of the provider-patient relationship for an invasion of privacy, at least in those states that recognize this particular basis for tort liability. In one case a physician was held liable for damages for a breach of a patient's privacy for publication of pictures and documentaries about the patient's medical history. In another it was held to be a breach of privacy to allow a lay person to be present during the delivery of the patient's child; under less drastic circumstances, a suit for an invasion of privacy was dismissed where there was an unauthorized disclosure, but it was very limited, i.e., the disclosure was to the patient's spouse.

An invasion of privacy does have to be unreasonable, and courts have looked at a variety of factors in making this determination. In a case involving a physician's disclosure of the fact that a patient's bill was overdue, the court held that this was a *reasonable* invasion of privacy since the physician was legitimately trying to collect his compensation.

In *Schwartz v. Thiele,* 242 Cal. App. 2d 799, 51 Cal. Rptr. 767 (Ct. App. 1966), the California Court of Appeals upheld a dismissal of a complaint alleging an invasion of privacy where a physician apparently contacted the plaintiff briefly in a parking lot and, based on a short period of observation, requested that the appropriate state agency have the patient committed. The court held that even if an invasion of privacy occurred, it was not unreasonable in light of the public's interest in restraint of the mentally ill.

In general for an invasion of privacy to constitute a tort, the invasion must be serious, i.e., unreasonable, and a variety of factors will be considered in this determination, including the public interest.

Although most of the cases that have found a provider liable to a patient for a breach of confidentiality have held it to be an invasion of privacy, there are a number of other possible legal bases for civil liability.

A few courts have treated a violation of confidentiality as a special category of tort, although the reasoning and bases of these conclusions have not always been clear. One case found the basis for tort liability implied in the state physician-patient privilege statute; another argued that tort liability was implied by the provisions of the state physician licensing statute that allowed license revocation for a breach of confidentiality (see discussion below); other arguments have been that professionally recognized duties should be legally recognized as bases for civil liability, that a breach of confidentiality is a breach of the physician's duty of "total care," and simply that good public policy requires that a breach of confidentiality be the basis for civil liability.

It should also be added, somewhat parenthetically, that civil liability of a provider for a breach of confidentiality could also be based on the tort of defamation, but only if the disclosure involves misleading or inaccurate information.

Tort liability is not the only possible basis for provider liability. In at least one jurisdiction, it has been held that a breach of confidentiality is a violation of the contract between the provider and the patient. As described in an earlier chapter, a contract is a promise between two individuals that is legally binding. Generally a contract exists when two individuals have actually exchanged something of value. Usually it involves a commercial situation, but contracts are not limited to sales and business transactions.

The provider-patient relationship involves a contract. Obviously there is a promise to pay by the patient and a promise to render services by the provider, but rarely are all of the other terms of the contract discussed in any detail; in fact most of the terms are implied by the situation or by custom. Is it understood that part of the contract that the provider and the patient make is a promise by the provider to respect the patient's confidentiality? The law of contracts very often turns on what can be reasonably expected under the circumstances; the patient would have to argue that confidentiality was a reasonable expectation. In theory it is possible. At least one court has accepted that argument. The provider's contract with the patient could be the basis for awarding civil damages to the patient whose confidentiality is violated by the provider.

It should also be mentioned that in many states there are statutes imposing either civil liability or even criminal penalties for violations of the right to confidentiality of certain categories of patients, e.g., mental patients in public hospitals. Also, under both state and federal law, recipients of public assistance are usually granted a limited right to confidentiality when receiving services paid for by public funds.

Put together, these various bases for civil liability for violations of the patient's confidentiality establish sufficient legal protection of confidentiality to consider it a legal right. None of these legal bases is universally accepted in all jurisdictions or applicable to all situations, but any serious violation of a patient's confidentiality could well lead to a successful suit for civil damages against the provider.

It is also possible that a physician or other provider of medical care that breaches the right of a patient to confidentiality will be subject to license revocation.

In order to gain the privilege of being able to practice their professional skills, physicians and other categories of providers must qualify for and hold an occupational license. In addition to setting standards and requirements for new entrants into the profession, occupational licensing statutes also provide for a means by which licenses can be revoked or suspended for a variety of reasons, including unprofessional or unethical conduct. These statutes do not always explicitly define the nature of the unprofessional or unethical conduct required. Some statutes explicitly state that a license can be revoked for a breach of confidentiality or for wilfully betraying a professional secret. Even where the occupational licensure statute is vague and merely allows license revocation for unprofessional or unethical conduct, it is safe to assume that a violation of the established ethics of such groups as the American Medical Association will be sufficient grounds.

To a provider of medical care, loss of license is loss of livelihood and a serious threat. However, providers of medical care, particularly physicians, rarely have their licenses revoked, and it is doubtful that a provider's license has ever been revoked solely for a breach of patient confidentiality. Even though license revocations are a function of state government agencies, the agency is usually dominated by members of the medical profession; predictably, providers of medical care have a more conservative view of patients' rights, even the right to confidentiality, especially when recognition of that right requires the revocation of the license to practice of one of their peers. Hence, this is another way in which the law has recognized the right of the patient to confidentiality, but one that must be understood in terms of the realities of its enforcement.

The right to medical records

Another set of basic legal rights of patients concerns the ownership of and access to medical records.

On the most primary level, a medical record is a file of papers documenting a patient's treatment. It can contain notes, reports, photographs, and x-rays of the patient. Increasingly, the medical record is being converted into other forms of recorded information. Information taken from the medical record may be compiled with that from other records for various purposes. Third-party payers or quality-control committees may want duplicate copies of all or part of the record. Medical records are also being fed into computers and other information retrieval systems where the nature of the record is changed completely.

From a patient's point of view, the medical record is a collection of personal facts, professional opinions about the patient, and clinical information. These data may be seen as embarrassing, harmful, or nobody else's business.

The medical record belongs to both the patient and the provider who keeps the record. The provider owns the record, meaning the property rights to the actual physical document. The law will enforce a physician's or a hospital's right to possess a medical record in much the same way that it will enforce the right of ownership to other kinds of private property. However, the provider is restricted in the use of the medical record since the patient has certain legal rights in the information contained in the record.

One legal right, or set of legal rights, of the patient relating to the information in a medical record has already been discussed earlier in this chapter. The patient's right(s) to confidentiality prohibits a provider from disclosing the information in a medical record to many third parties. There are, however, a number of qualifications to this general rule.

Obviously by divulging personal information to a physician a patient is implying that a nurse or other assistant to the physician involved in the patient's medical treatment will have access to that information. Similarly, in a hospital setting, it is generally assumed that a patient is implying consent that all hospital personnel directly involved in the medical treatment of the patient can have access to the information in the record. Although many people are not aware of it, most health insurance policies include a provision giving the insurance company's representative permission to examine the medical record in matters relating to reimbursement of the provider.

Even without the patient's permission, in each state there are certain kinds of information that must be released by the provider to the police or a public agency. For example, most states have statutes requiring that evidence of child abuse, gunshot wounds, or cases of dangerous or communicable diseases be reported to the police or to the state health department. In some states there is statutory authorization for agents of the state or federal government to gain access to medical records for the purposes of collecting statistical data and related research. Medical records can also be inspected as part of the inspection of a health facility for purposes of determining its licensure status.

The medical records of recipients of public assistance can also be monitored for control of cost or quality by an authorized governmental agency.

In each of these situations the release of information should be no more than is required to fulfill the intended purpose. In some cases the third party seeking information in a patient's medical record needs only part of the record and does not need the patient's identity. The record can be released in part and/or the identity of the patient can be withheld or coded. Unless the release of information by the provider is no more than that required by some authorizing statute or than that allowed by the expressed or implied permission of the patient, a release of information from the medical record could be a violation of the confidentiality of the patient with all of the possible legal consequences discussed earlier in this chapter.

Most providers of medical care not only protect medical records from unauthorized disclosures, but many deny patients access to their own records. Even though it is standard practice to release a copy of a patient's record on the patient's request to another provider, many providers will not release a copy directly to the patient. The reasons for this common practice are not clear. Some providers will argue that a patient can easily misunderstand a medical record if it is examined without expert assistance. This may be true in some cases, but it does not explain the blanket prohibition against release of records imposed by many providers. Another reason often cited is that providers withhold medical records in an attempt to shield themselves from possible malpractice suits.

Patients have the legal right of access to their medical records under many circumstances. All states allow patients to subpoena their medical records for evidentiary purposes when suing the provider of medical care. Thus the policy of withholding medical records practiced by some providers may actually increase the number of malpractice suits, rather than discourage them.

In addition at least nine states have passed legislation allowing any patient or the patient's attorney to inspect the patient's hospital medical records. (None of these statutes allow access to medical records kept in physicians' private offices.) In California the patient's access statute also provides that the patient must be reimbursed by the provider for all legal expenses incurred in the enforcement of the provisions of the statute.

When there is no special statute allowing access or no suit pending against the provider, the patients' right of access to their own medical records is not clearly settled.

In an Illinois case a physician was required to allow a patient access to the medical record where the patient wanted the record to prepare a workman's compensation claim against his employer. Even though the physician had been hired by the employer to treat the patient, the court held that it was part of the physician's duty of disclosure to the patient to allow the patient access to his medical record. In a similarly reasoned opinion, *Emmett v. Eastern Dispensary & Casualty Hospital*, 396 F.2d 931 (1967), the U.S. Court of Appeals for the District of Columbia ordered the medical records of a deceased person released by the hospital to the patient's son, who was investigating the death of the patient. The court said that it found "in the fiducial qualities of that relationship the physician's duty to reveal to the patient that which in his best interests it is important that he should know . . ."

Another court allowed that a patient generally has a legal right of access to medical records, but that the right may be denied if the patient's physician testifies in good faith that the release of information in the record to the patient will be harmful to the patient's health.

Most of the cases that have decided the issue of the patient's access to medical records have held that a nonlitigant patient does have access to copy and inspect his or her own records as long as some legitimate reason for wanting access can be cited by the patient. Only where some countervailing reason exists to deny access or where the patient claims only mere curiosity have courts denied that such a right exists.

Conclusions

Patients' rights to consent, to confidentiality, and to access to their medical records only sketch the outline of the principles that define the legal relationship between patients and providers of medical care. Obviously the various situations in which these rights must be applied are virtually unlimited, and the principles themselves have not been fully developed. Many important questions remain to be answered and will be undoubtedly raised in the next few years.

Why is it that at this point in time the nature of the provider-patient relationship is becoming a legal issue of such importance? The answer is related to many of the factors that were discussed in the introductory chapter. The physician/family friend/confidant has all but disappeared. The provider is more often a stranger or one of several agents of an institutional provider. At the same time, the patient is demanding more and expecting more. In addition there are a number of pressures on providers, e.g., third-party payers, quality controls, and governmental agencies, that potentially compete with the providers' obligations to their patients. As a consequence, the provider-patient relationship is taking on more often an adversarial character. It is in this context that the legal rights that define that relationship become increasingly important. Perhaps it is an inevitable growing pain of a transition toward a better health care delivery system, or maybe it is an inherent attribute of any organized human endeavor in a large, industrialized society. Whatever the reason, patients and providers often find themselves to be adversaries. It is therefore important that both providers and patients understand their legal rights. Those rights are one important determinant of their behavior toward one another. For the patient it is also important to understand that his or her legal rights are only realities to the extent that they are enforced through a legal system that has not often been able to enforce the rights of individual people with the same dispatch that the system enforces the rights of well-financed institutions and organizations.

References

Annas, G.: The rights of hospital patients, 1975.

Annas, G., and Healey, J.: The patient rights advocate: redefining the doctor-patient relationship in the hospital context, Vand. L. Rev. **27**:243, 1974.

Cantor, N.: A patient's decision to decline life-saving medical treatment: bodily integrity versus the preservation of life, Rutgers L. Rev. **26**:228, 1973.

Curran, W., Stearn, B., and Kaplan, H.: Privacy, confidentiality, and other legal considerations in the establishment of a centralized health-data system, N. Engl. J. Med. **281**:241, 1969.

Ethical aspects of experimentation with human subjects, Daedalus **98**:219, 1969.

Hayt, E., Hayt, L., and Groeschel, A.: Law of hospital physician, and patient, Part VI, ed. 3, 1972.

Note: Action for breach of medical secrecy outside of the courtroom, U. Cin. L. Rev. **36**:103, 1967.

Plante, J.: An analysis of informed consent, Fordham L. Rev. **36**:639, 1969.

Schack, R., and Ng, J.: Non-litigant patients' access to medical records and medical reports: a survey of the medical literature, the law, and the practice (unpublished student paper filed with the Health Law Project, University of Pennsylvania Law School, 1974).

U.S. Department of Health, Education and Welfare: Report of the Secretary's Commission on Medical Malpractice, Chapter 6; app. at 177 and 758, 1973.

CHAPTER 8   Governmental control of health facilities

Given the important role played by the hospital in the modern American health care delivery system, it is not surprising that governmental control of hospitals and other health facilities has become one of the most debated issues in public health. If anything is surprising, it is that governmental control of health facilities in any form is such a recent phenomenon: as late as the 1940's, many states did not even require that hospitals be licensed, and it has only been in the last decade that licensing has been extended to many other kinds of health facilities. Furthermore, more stringent controls over health facilities and control over the distribution or "quantity" of facilities are even more recent phenomena.

Governmental control or regulation of health facilities has been discussed as a matter of public policy by various authors in some detail. The purpose of this chapter is not to summarize or synthesize those other works, but to discuss this issue from a legal perspective. This will involve a description of the way that the law has been involved in the control and regulation (or lack thereof) of health facilities and an examination of some of the governmental programs that are currently developing. Although it is necessary to understand the specific programs now evolving in order to appreciate the issue, it is most important to concentrate on the general legal principles underlying these programs, particularly since this is an issue that is undergoing very rapid evolution. The future nature of governmental control and regulation of health facilities will be related to their current predecessors, but the programs of the future will be predictably somewhat different in their specific nature and function; nonetheless, whatever their nature, they will be formed around the same legal principles.

This chapter will focus on those principles. Many of these principles will be based on the same concepts discussed in earlier chapters relating to the rights that exist between the individual and the government. However, as will be demonstrated, when the "individual" is both a provider of medical care and an institution (rather than a person), the rights of that "individual" with respect to the government are in some important ways different and unique.

The emergence of the issue

Until relatively recently, the delivery of medical care primarily involved a relationship between an individual patient and an individual physician. To most patients, and in the eyes of the law, hospitals were little more than facilities where physicians treated seriously ill patients. In fact one need only consider the etiology of the word "hospital" to recall some of the early history of those institutions.

All that has changed as medicine has changed. In many medical encounters the relationship is not between a physician and a patient, but between a patient and an institution; often that institution is a hospital. The physician is still very much involved in the hospitalized patient's care. The physician's decisions dictate admission and release from the hospital and the treatment received there, but, undeniably, hospitals now play a larger role in those processes. Hospitals can no longer shield themselves from responsibility with the fiction that they do not practice medicine. In many ways hospitals can and do affect the utilization of hospital services and the care received by hospitalized patients. The modern hospital does not just provide bed space, ancillary equipment, and support personnel. It now provides equipment, services, and personnel directly responsible for the patient's care. In terms of the patient's perspective, the patient is "in the hospital," not just "in the care of a physician."

Modern health care delivery encompasses not just hospitals but also an array of other health facilities expanding our ability to provide for patients, but expanding as well the role played by institutional providers. Whether or not this is a necessary trend—or even a desirable one—it is likely that the future health care delivery system in this country will find that institutional providers are playing an even bigger role in the delivery of medical care, particularly large medical centers surrounded by networks of hospitals and other health facilities. One response that the public, and consequently the government, will probably have to this trend is to favor the increase in the amount and kind of governmental control and regulation over these facilities.

This is a peculiarly American problem. In almost all other industrialized countries health facilities are owned or controlled by the government. But consistent with our traditional American value system, the operation of health facilities has remained in large part a private enterprise—with some important exceptions. The government does own some hospitals in this country. Of the over 7000 hospitals approximately 2000 are state, county, or district hospitals. (District hospitals are operated by a hybrid governmental unit created by state law and existing with the power to tax and sell bonds for the sole purpose of supporting the hospital.) The federal government operates about 500 hospitals including the Public Health Service hospitals and the hospitals for veterans and the military service. The remaining 4500 hospitals are privately owned. Furthermore, even those owned by the government can not really be described as controlled or regulated. They often offer the worst quality of care and are in no way coordinated, even within a level of government, let alone between the various state, local, and federal levels.

On the other hand, even though our system of health facilities is largely privately owned, many of these health facilities have been built or maintained with public funds. The federal government has been very heavily involved in the financing of private health facility construction through the Hill-Burton program and several other federal programs. In addition both the state and federal governments indirectly subsidize the over 3500 voluntary or "nonprofit" hospitals by exempting their income from state and federal taxes.

Notwithstanding the fact that the government has often provided funds for the construction or maintenance of health facilities—and often provided the funds for the consumer of health facility services—there is still the tradition that medical care be maintained, at least in appearance, as a private enterprise. Until recently, the government has been very hesitant to break this tradition and to impose controls or to regulate hospitals and other health facilities.

Like many other things relating to health, this too is changing. In many ways the government is now showing less hesitation to impose direct controls on the health care delivery system. On clear direction of that changed attitude is toward greater control and regulation of health care facilities, particularly hospitals.

Thus the debated issue: to what extent can and should the government control health care facilities? Should the government regulate the quality of care that is available? Should the government regulate the distribution of facilities? What about rate setting? The range and combination of alternatives is almost endless. At one extreme, some advocates scream for a return to a more competitive health care delivery system regulated only by the "invisible guiding hand" of the profit motive; others would go to the opposite extreme, and would regulate health facilities in the manner of a public utility as power, water, or telephone services are controlled. Indeed, both state and federal government have already taken the first steps in that latter direction.

The future direction of this trend, however, is not settled, nor are a number of alternatives precluded as possibilities.

Licensing, certification, and accreditation

To trace the evolution of this important issue in public health and to begin to outline some of the underlying legal principles, one must first look at the existing legal relationship between the government and health facilities and the programs of regulation and control that have been implemented.

Licensing

In various ways state and federal governments have attempted to regulate the quality of health facilities.

Although many states only enacted state health facility licensing laws after hospital licensing became a prerequisite to the receipt of federal Hill-Burton funds (see *infra*), every state now requires that some categories of health facilities be licensed. Virtually all states require that at least hospitals and nursing homes be licensed. However, licensing laws vary from state to state in terms of the categories of facilities that must be licensed and the requirements that facilities must meet.

Licensing is an attempt to regulate quality, but licensing at its best ensures only that a state's facilities meet a minimum level of quality; the standards enforced through licensing are not intended to set norms for health facilities but only to prohibit the operation of facilities that are below an acceptable minimum. Furthermore, until the last few years, most licensing standards were directed primarily at such things as maintenance of the physical plant, building safety, and record keeping, although many states are now developing standards that include requirements directly relating to patient care (e.g., requirements for staff skills, qualifications, and duties).

The legal justification for licensing is obvious and well-settled in the law: the operation of a hospital or other health facility affects the health, welfare, and safety of the public; consequently, an attempt to regulate the quality of that operation fulfills a proper state purpose. Courts have consistently recognized that health facility licensing is a proper exercise of the state's police powers.

Although clearly within the authority of the state, licensing must be authorized by statute. A licensing statute will usually define as a crime the operation of a health facility or hospital without a license and then set out requirements and standards that must be complied with before a license is issued. Typically, the statutory standards will be rather vague and the statute will delegate to an administrative agency the authority to develop and promulgate by regulation more specific standards. This agency will also be delegated the authority to review new facilities, issue licenses to complying facilities, periodically inspect licensed facilities, and renew, suspend, or revoke facilities licenses. There is generally an administrative process outlined in the statute that must be followed in making these decisions, and the process must also conform to the general requirements of due process.

In deciding to allow or refuse a license state licensing agencies are generally required by statute to find that a facility is in "substantial compliance" with the state's standards. This is a somewhat subjective decision to make, and this tends to give the agency some discretion in the enforcement of licensing standards. State licensing agencies are also given a great deal of discretion in the development of standards. Courts have generally upheld as valid a variety of health facilities standards developed by state agencies, even where those standards are rather vague or only indirectly related to the health, welfare, and safety of the public.

Despite their considerable authority and discretion, state licensing agencies are often extremely lax in the enforcement of licensing laws and are seldom funded or structured so as to provide for a meaningful review of the quality of a state's health facilities. It is doubtful that state health facilities licensing has done any more than eliminate the very worst facilities from operation.

Accreditation

In addition to state health facilities licensing, hospitals may be subject to accreditation by a voluntary accreditation body. Many different accreditation organizations exist for a variety of purposes, but by far the most important for health facilities is the Joint Commission on Accreditation of Hospitals (JCAH). Organized during the 1950's and sponsored by a coalition of the American Medical Association, the American Hospital Association, the American College of Physicians, and the American College of Surgeons, the JCAH has developed its own standards for evaluating hospitals similar to state hospital licensing standards. Accreditation of a hospital by the JCAH is for much the same purpose as state health facility licensing, but there are a number of important differences between licensing and accreditation.

First and most obviously, accreditation is a voluntary process conducted by a privately sponsored organization, not an agency of the government. The JCAH is, literally, hired as a private consultant by the hospital to inspect the hospital and evaluate the facility and its services. Second, the standards developed (and periodically revised) by the JCAH are also minimum standards for hospitals, but deal more directly with patient care and services than most state licensing standards. The JCAH standards are also more complete in their form: they are stated in terms of general principles, specific standards, and textual interpretations of each standard. Although JCAH standards tend to avoid specific requirements for hospitals and have several serious omissions, they are on the whole an improvement on the licensing standards that exist in most states.

From a legal point of view, accreditation is an entirely voluntary, nongovernmental process; in fact accreditation meant little more than added prestige for a hospital until the passage of Medicare in 1965. Accreditation then took on new significance based on its role in the Medicare certification process.

Certification

In order for any of the health facilities eligible to participate as a provider in the Medicare program to receive reimbursement, the facility must be certified by DHEW. No facility is required to be certified unless it wants to participate in Medicare. Since Medicare is a major source of business for many facilities, few facilities can afford not to submit to this form of governmental regulation.

There is no federal certification or conditions of participation for health facilities that participate in the Medicaid program. Since Medicaid is administered by each state and not directly by the federal government, except for the utilization review requirements (see Chapter 5), the only requirement of federal law is that the state plan implementing the state's Medicaid program include "standards" for eligible providers. Most states only require that participating facilities be licensed or, in some cases, qualify as a provider under Medicare.

Certification to participate as a provider in the Medicare program imposes a number of requirements on health facilities, including (1) the requirement that a health facility be licensed under its own state licensing law and (2) the requirement that the facility meet certain standards of quality outlined in the Medicare statute and in regulations developed by DHEW; collectively these standards are known as the Conditions of Participation. There are separate sets of Conditions of Participation for each category of health facility eligible as a provider under Medicare.

Certification and accreditation are interrelated. The original Medicare statute required that participating hospitals meet the requirements outlined in

the statute and authorized DHEW to set "such other requirements . . . necessary in the interest of health and safety . . . except that such other standards
may not be higher than the comparable requirements prescribed for the accreditation of hospitals by the Joint Commission on Accreditation of Hospitals
. . ." The only independent finding that DHEW was required to make was
to assure that the hospital was complying with the statute's requirements for
utilization review. DHEW interpreted this provision to mean that (1) the
standards in the Conditions of Participation for hospitals should be based
on the JCAH standards, but also that (2) hospitals that are accredited by the
JCAH will be accepted as certified for Medicare purposes.

It is not often that a nongovernmental private agency is mentioned explicitly in a statute and given the authority to carry out part of a governmental
program. In fact both the wisdom and the legality of this delegation of authority can be questioned. Given the number and kind of hospitals that have
been accredited, it is doubtful that accreditation provides for a rigorous evaluation of quality. A number of hospitals notorious for their inadequate status
have received accreditation, and rarely is accreditation denied or revoked.
This is probably inherent in a process of evaluation by an organization that
must rely on the cooperation of the facilities it evaluates and that must maintain the sponsorship of the various elements of organized medicine. The second problem is related to the first: Can a governmental function, i.e., certification for Medicare, be constitutionally delegated to a nongovernmental
agency?

Generally, the legislative branch of the government can delegate fact-finding
authority to a nongovernmental organization or individual or employ them in
administrative capacities. Similarly, the executive can hire private agents to
perform such tasks on behalf of the government. However, either branch of
government must retain overall control and supervision. Among other things,
the authority to be exercised by the private organization or individual must be
clearly delineated and the standards for decision making must be explicitly
defined. Neither branch of the government can abdicate its responsibilities.
In the case of the Medicare statute's delegation of authority for certification
to the JCAH, Congress arguably did just that. The JCAH was given virtually un-
conditional authority to make decisions for a governmental program.

The 1972 Social Security amendments altered the statutory basis for Medicare certification requirements in an attempt to mitigate these problems. The
Medicare statute now allows DHEW to impose higher standards for certification of participating facilities (if it so chooses) and to have the option of
relying on JCAH accreditation or making its own determinations. The JCAH
still plays a major role in certifying hospitals, but the ultimate authority is
more clearly consistent with constitutional principles.

Health facility planning

In addition to the governmental programs that have attempted to ensure
that the quality of health facilities is minimally adequate, both state and federal governments have shown a recent willingness to impose more direct and
more controversial controls over health facilities.

Control, of course, can take many forms. One form of control is to impose rate setting or price control over an industry; an industry can also be controlled by regulating new entrants into the market—or in some cases by eliminating some existing competitors from the market. An industry can also become a public utility with almost every aspect of its operation controlled by a government agency. All forms of control have at least one unifying element: they make economic decisions, e.g., who-gets-what-and where, not on the basis of economic competition or the profit motive but on the basis of certain planned objectives. The concept of planned economic decisions, however, always waves a red flag in the face of the traditional American value system and is often politically unpopular. Actually, on reflection, the government already in some ways plans and regulates a number of industries, e.g., airlines, television and radio, the water and power supplies, and even taxicabs. More importantly, the government has been attempting to plan, at least indirectly, the American health care delivery system for some time.

The billions of dollars that have been invested by the government in various health care programs, services, and facilities are financial incentives designed to bring about changes in the existing system; this could be characterized as a "carrot and stick" approach to planning and a form of indirect control. In addition various governmental programs (the most relevant of which will be discussed later in this chapter) have been planning the distribution of health care resources and have been attempting to enforce their plans through a variety of incentives and, in some cases, through mandatory enforcement authority. Hospital rate regulation has even been attempted in several states, and health facility construction is now directly regulated in over half of the states.

The most direct forms of controls and regulation have been directed at health facilities and particularly at hospitals. Through a series of programs over the past 20 years, both state and federal governments have become increasingly willing to regulate not only the quality of these facilities, but to regulate their distribution. This is not a point in time where hospitals or health facilities in general can be considered a regulated industry in the sense of a public utility, but it is clear that the government has been moving for the last decade in that direction, albeit in a series of slow, hesitant steps.

The Hill-Burton program

The first governmental attempt at planning for any part of the health care delivery system was directed at hospitals and was basically a voluntary planning effort. In 1946 in response to the shortage of hospital beds in this country that was recognized during World War II, Congress enacted the Hill-Burton program, codified as 42 U.S.C. section 291 *et seq.* The Hill-Burton program provided federal funds for each state government to survey the need for hospital construction in that state. It also provided funds and loans for publicly owned and privately owned nonprofit hospitals to assist in construction projects to meet these needs. In order to receive Hill-Burton funds, a state was required to have a state agency and an advisory council that would prepare a yearly plan. This plan had to include a survey of the need for hospital construction and a method for determining the priority of proposed projects. Individual hospitals receiving funds under Hill-Burton had to comply with the plan and a number of requirements, including those relating to community service and a reasonable volume of care for indigent people (see Chapter 9).

The Hill-Burton program provided no small portion of the existing health facilities. It has been estimated that in its first 20 years the Hill-Burton program provided funds for more than 30% of the hospital beds in this country. But as a planning program, Hill-Burton was entirely voluntary. No state was required to plan for hospital construction, and hospitals were not required to comply with the plans that were developed. There were only the financial incentives: the states received money if they did develop a planning program, and facilities received money if they built according to the plans' determinations of need. Thus Hill-Burton could be called "carrot and stick" planning. The planning that was developed was, therefore, not always determinative of the distribution of hospitals, and in many cases the plans were more influenced by politics than by any rational basis for the distribution of health facilities. In fact the program resulted in some areas in a substantial oversupply of hospital beds, a situation that contributed to the inflation of health care costs that later planning efforts would have to try to correct.

The Regional Medical program

A similar sort of carrot and stick approach to planning led to the enactment of the Regional Medical program legislation (RMP), 42 U.S.C. section 299 *et seq.* The original legislation was labeled the Heart Disease, Cancer, and Stroke Amendments of 1965. However, the program was never really limited to projects concerning exclusively those disease categories.

RMP did not involve direct financial assistance to health facilities, but was intended to finance the coordination of research efforts and to finance the distribution of information from research institutions to the whole health care delivery system. In theory each RMP was to facilitate on a regional basis the cooperation between medical schools and other research institutions, on the one hand, and the practitioners of medicine.

Although not as ambitious as the Hill-Burton program, RMP was still a major financial investment. Over one billion dollars was spent in the first 10 years of the program to fund both the local RMP agencies and the projects they sponsored. Administrated directly by DHEW, the program provided "planning" grants to public and nonprofit private institutions that wanted to be designated as the regional agency for a geographic region within a state or several states. These regional agencies received funds with which to finance, with the approval of a statutorially required advisory council, projects within their area. Projects could include research, training, data exchange, direct patient care on a demonstration basis, or the construction of equipment and facilities relating to these activities. In short, RMP was federal funding for "needed" changes in the existing health care delivery system. RMP did not develop actual plans, but was, in effect, planning based on financial incentives for private providers to change the existing health care delivery system. Like Hill-Burton, it was entirely voluntary.

It is generally agreed that RMP has failed to achieve its purposes and in many cases even to stay within its statutory authority. Regional agencies usually have become deeply involved in the medical politics of the communities in which they operate, and though a great deal of money has changed hands, there is little evidence that it has been well spent.

Comprehensive Health Planning

The first governmental program that attempted to institute a national system of health planning for all health services was enacted through the Comprehensive Health Planning and Public Health Services Amendments of 1966, also known as the "Partnership for Health,"42 U.S.C. section 246 *et seq.* The Comprehensive Health Planning (CHP) legislation set up five new programs, all of which were related to health planning. However, only two of the CHP programs are really germane to a basic understanding of the CHP system.

The first of these programs became the new section 314(a) of the original Public Health Services Act and unfortunately (since it tends to confuse outsiders) led to the widespread use of the terms "314(a) program" and CHP "A" agency. This program provided funds to state governments to maintain a state health planning agency and a consumer-dominated advisory council to that agency and to establish a state plan for health planning activities. (For some reason, there was no requirement that the CHP state agency be coordinated with the state Hill-Burton program, and in many states separate CHP health planning and Hill-Burton agencies were formed, each with its separate plan.)

The second program, "314(b) program" or CHP "B" agency, provided funds to locally based nonprofit private or publicly owned agencies designated by the state CHP agency as the approved areawide planning agency for a geographic region within a state.

In addition to meeting the requirements established by the state agency, the areawide agency also had to meet the requirements of the federal law. This meant that there had to be an appropriately staffed areawide agency and properly designated consumer-dominated governing council to conduct comprehensive health planning activities within the designated area, including the development of an areawide plan.

With very few exceptions, the CHP program established a complete network of local and state health planning agencies for the whole country. However, these agencies were given very limited authority with which to enforce compliance with the plans they developed. The amount of money that CHP agencies were given to offer as incentives for compliance was insignificant. The only comprehensive authority was to "review and comment" on requests for federal funds coming from their areas. Anyone seeking federal funds under almost any one of the various federal health related programs was required (under a variety of legal authorities) to channel their application through the state and areawide agencies for their review and comment. Whatever the potential effect of this authority, most CHP agencies have been so ineffective, understaffed, and administratively inept that this review and comment process has been little more than added paperwork for the funding applicants. Federal agencies have generally not paid attention to these comments, and this authority has not really provided the CHP program with the power to enforce compliance with CHP plans. The real theory behind CHP seems to have been that provider participation would encourage voluntary compliance. The governing boards of areawide agencies and the advisory boards of state agencies were supposed to have consumer majorities, but the remaining seats were to be filled with representatives of providers of health services. Through their participation and input into the process of developing health plans, it was hoped that providers would voluntarily comply with the final planning product. Ideally, the final plans would fulfill the needs of both providers and consumers. Thus the CHP program was popularly entitled the "Partnership for Health."

Despite its intentions, the CHP program never developed this spirit of "voluntary wonderfulness," and CHP became just another attempt to indirectly control the health care delivery system that failed to achieve its goals and objectives.

Certificate of need laws

In addition to the federal programs above, in the late 1960's and in the 1970's a number of states passed legislation that imposed a form of direct regulation on health facilities. By 1974, over half of the states, and all of the larger population states, had passed what are known collectively as certificate of need statutes. Each state certificate of need law differs in the scope of its authority and the type of administrative structure that carries out the certificate of need functions, but all certificate of need laws provide some administrative agency (or agencies) with the power to determine the public's "need" and to approve or disapprove applications for construction or expansion of certain categories of health facilities.

Almost all certificate of need laws cover hospital construction or expansion. This may include the expansion of the number of beds and/or substantial capital improvements and/or additions of new services. Most certificate of need laws also cover nursing home construction, and some extend to other categories of health facilities. In a few states there is a requirement that facilities closing or reducing their services must receive certificate of need approval. Nowhere, however, is there the authority to declare unnecessary and to decertify existing health facilities.

Most states have integrated their certificate of need functions into either their CHP agencies or their Hill-Burton agency; this gives these voluntary planning efforts new "teeth" with which to enforce compliance with their plans. Not all states have integrated these various programs, and even where there is one coordinated program of health planning, the result has been a rather complex structure existing under several different sets of state and federal statutory authorities.

Whatever the administrative structure, certificate of need programs are clearly direct regulation of at least one part of the health care delivery system.

The sanction on denied applications is usually that a facility without certificate of need approval cannot proceed with construction or cannot get a license to operate.

Certificate of need programs tend to be run in one of two ways. Either a master plan is developed to which all new applications are compared, or each case is decided on a case-by-case basis comparing the proposed investment to a number of general principles and factors. In either situation the process tends to take on some of the aspects of traditional administrative decision making. Because of the mandatory authority being exercised by these decisions, the process has raised many of the legal questions often encountered in this type of regulatory context, ranging from the kind and nature of hearing required for applicants to the constitutionality of the entire exercise of power.

At least one court has declared its certificate of need statute unconstitutional. The Supreme Court of North Carolina in *In re Certificate of Need for Aston Park Hospital Inc.,* 282 N.C. 542, 193 S.E.2d 729 (1973), declared that (1) the state had not convinced the court that unregulated competition would not by itself eliminate "unnecessary" hospitals, and (2) the state did not show a reasonable purpose for the statutory program. Thus the court reasoned that the certificate of need program in that state was a violation of the due process clause and other provisions of the state constitution. Since it was based on several state constitutional grounds, not all of which are in the federal or other state constitutions, the case has limited authority in other jurisdictions. However, the court did outline several basic constitutional objections that can be at least raised, if not accepted, before other courts.

Certificate of need laws are of too recent origin to adequately assess their impact and effectiveness. There have been a few surveys of these laws and some preliminary evaluation, but no clear conclusions can be drawn. It is certain, however, that there are more states moving in the direction of adopting the certificate of need concept as their response to the need to regulate and plan the distribution of health care resources.

In 1972 Congress adopted the certificate of need concept and gave existing health planning agencies another potential source of authority. Under the Social Security amendments of 1972, reimbursement from the federal government to providers for services rendered under Medicaid, Medicare, or the Maternal and Child Health programs can be proportionally reduced by DHEW to the extent that the provider has engaged in capital expansion of a health facility that has been found to be "unnecessary" or out of conformity with state and local planning activities as determined by a designated state planning agency.

It is, in effect, a federal certificate of need law. It is not required that the CHP agencies be specified as the requisite decision-making body. The regulations promulgated under the statute state that the requisite agency may be the CHP state agency, the CHP areawide agency, or the Hill-Burton planning council. Furthermore, this authority is in effect in only those states where DHEW and the state governor have come to an agreement as outlined under the federal statute and regulations.

The process contemplated mirrors most state certificate of need programs. After receiving an application, the designated agency makes a decision based on a set of need criteria. The applicant is entitled to a hearing and, after the decision, an appeal to DHEW, which has final authority over the decision.

Unlike most certificate of need statutes, the sanction imposed is not denial of licensure, but a denial of a portion of the federal reimbursement, a portion equal to the percentage of the facility's cost that is determined to be "unnecessary."

This federal certificate of need law could be an effective planning tool. It applies to a wide range of health facilities, and it applies to all capital expenditures over $100,000, changes in the facility's bed capacity, or to other substantial changes in the facility's services. Other than the possibility that a state may opt not to participate, the only real limits are (1) the ability of health planning agencies to handle the rather legalistic approach to decision making mandated by the law and (2) the incentive value of the percentage reimbursement denial to a given hospital. The answers to both questions are at this point impossible to determine.

National Health Planning and Resources Development Act of 1974

After a 2-year legislative battle of unexpected intensity, Congress again moved to increase the amount and scope of governmental regulation of health facilities by the enactment of the National Health Planning and Resources Development Act of 1974, 42 U.S.C. 300K. Theoretically, this act was to set up a new system of state and local health planning agencies and to integrate into these agencies a program for the support of certain kinds of health facility construction. Actually, it is more accurately described as a reorganization and revitalization of the CHP, RMP, and Hill-Burton programs. Faced with the expiration of the statutory authorizations for these programs, Congress opted to merge most of their preexisting functions into one program and to institute a variety of programmatic changes intended to cure some of the more obvious shortcomings of these previous planning efforts. Among these changes are a general strengthening of the regulatory authority (the "teeth") of planning agencies and an attempt to ensure that this authority is vested in one coordinated program of health planning. The new act does not attempt to enact a complete system of government control over health facilities, although such a proposal was given serious consideration in the congressional debate, but the act is definitely a new phase in the evolution of health planning in this country and an intermediate step in a course whose direction is becoming increasingly clear and irreversible.

The federal role

As in all previous health planning efforts, most of the actual health planning activities funded under the new act will be performed at the local and state levels. However, the legislation mandates a more active role for the federal government to play. DHEW will have a greater responsibility in the various decision-making processes and in supervising the performance of the state and local agencies. DHEW will also be required to maintain a set of national health planning goals and objectives, the first attempt in this country to develop a national plan for health. In carrying out its responsibilities, DHEW will be assisted by a sixteen-member advisory council made up of government officials, representatives of state and local health planning agencies, and at least five "consumers."

Local health planning funded by the HSA legislation

The local or area level agencies funded under the new legislation will be known as Health Systems Agencies (HSA's). In many areas these agencies will be little more than preexisting CHP "B" agencies, operating under a new name, with slight adjustments in their organizational structure and possibly new geographical jurisdictions. In other areas other nonprofit or local government agencies may compete with the CHP "B" agencies for designation as HSA's. In theory, although it is unlikely given the practical problems of putting an organization together, an altogether new organization could be formed and designated as the area HSA.

The initial stage of the program's development will require DHEW to designate HSA areas according to a variety of criteria outlined in the legislation. Basically this will require a consideration of the population, the health resources, the preexisting planning boundaries, and other factors considered relevant to effective planning. The ultimate decsion is to be made by DHEW, but the statute clearly mandates substantial input from the area's state governor.

Within 18 months of the effective date of the legislation, DHEW is supposed to have designated HSA's. DHEW will first make a conditional designation, an agreement with an organization capable of performing the HSA functions and meeting the requirements summarized below relating to organizational structure. However, in making this designation, DHEW is required to give first priority to existing CHP or RMP agencies in the HSA areas. These conditional designations are renewable yearly thereafter. With designation, of course, comes a grant to cover the HSA's budget and the costs of performing the HSA functions—a grant that is separate and distinct from the grant for the Areawide Health Services Development Fund (see description below).

In order to qualify as an HSA, a designated organization must meet certain statutory standards and any additional requirements that DHEW may promulgate by regulation. From an organizational point of view, the statutory standards are very similar to those now required of the CHP "B" agencies, again leading to the presumption that in many areas the HSA will be a revitalized CHP agency.

In terms of the legal structure an HSA may be (1) a nonprofit private corporation that engages exclusively in health planning and development, (2) a public regional planning agency if the governing body is composed of elected governmental officials, but only if the regional planning agency has a jurisdiction identical to the HSA area, or (3) a unit of local government if the unit's jurisdiction is identical with the HSA area.

The governing body of an agency designated as an HSA must be composed of ten to thirty members; a majority of that body must be consumers who are "broadly representative" of the public. The remaining members are to be representative of the providers of the HSA's area. The governing body must also include representatives of local governmental authorities and a percentage of nonmetropolitan members equal to the percentage of the nonmetropolitan population of the area. The HSA statute defines the term consumer rather broadly, but is fairly specific in defining who must be considered a provider. Thus a consumer is almost anyone who is not defined by the statute (or the regulations) as a provider.

If the HSA is a regional planning body or a unit of local government, it still must meet these structural requirements and have a separate governing body for HSA purposes if the composition of its existing governing body does not meet HSA requirements, particularly the requirement of consumer participation.

The governing body is responsible for all of the business, health planning, and development activities of the HSA. Among these responsibilities are the approval of the area's health plans (see explanation below), the approval of grants and contracts, and the approval of all other HSA activities or policy decisions. Hence assuming that the HSA actually takes effective action and has some impact on the health care delivery system, the governing board and the consumers who in theory dominate it will have direct control over the agency's direction. On the other hand, one must remember that the predecessor organizations with similar structure and authority did little of any consequence and usually managed to emasculate the consumer control requirements of these various programs.

Once designated and operational, HSA's will perform a number of health planning functions intended to (1) improve the health of the residents of the area or (2) control the costs of health services. The statute defines the general responsibility of these agencies as:

> . . . the provision of effective health planning for its health service area and the promotion of the development within the area of health services, manpower, and facilities which meet identified needs, reduce documented deficiencies, and implement the health plans of the agency.

In specific terms these responsibilities translate into the following functions and activites:

HSA's will compile a great deal of data on the delivery of health care services in their areas. This includes surveys of the health status of the area residents and the utilization of health services, an inventory of health resources in the area, an evaluation of the effectiveness of the area's health services, and an evaluation of environmental and occupational health exposure factors.

HSA's will develop two separate health plans for their areas. The first plan, the Health Systems Plan (HSP), will state long-range objectives, based on the national guidelines and priorities to be developed by DHEW and the data collected in the various surveys and evaluations. The second plan, the Annual Implementation Plan (AIP), is supposed to state the short-run objectives for the area and list the projects that need to be implemented to achieve the long-term objectives expressed in the HSP.

HSA's will be given a fund with which to finance projects in their areas according to their AIP and to encourage/coerce compliance with the HSP and AIP. This fund, known as the Area Health Services Development Fund (AHSDF), will be a source of "carrots" for area agencies to wave in the face of the area's providers. Once operational, each HSA will receive an AHSDF grant—over and above its operational budget. From the list of objectives listed in the AIP, priorities are to be established and funded to the extent that funding is available. The size of each grant will vary according to a number of factors and, in any event, cannot exceed one dollar per resident in the area. The total amount available according to the statutory authorization is $25 million for 1975, $75 million for 1976, and $120 million for 1977. While this will be a source of power for those agencies and a sizable amount of money, it is doubtful that by itself it will give the HSA enough coercive economic force to bully an industry that frequently speaks in billions of dollars—or to have a significant impact on any aspect of the health care delivery system.

The new legislation also gives the HSA the authority to review and *approve* or *disapprove* applications from its area for federal funds under several of the federal health related programs. Again, this will probably not give enough real power to HSA's to coerce complete compliance with their planning efforts, but it is an additional source of "teeth" for these agencies. In addition the HSA's will probably by given by administrative decision within DHEW the authority to review and comment on all other federal health funding applications coming from their areas, notwithstanding the historical failure of most CHP agencies to exercise their review and comment authority in any meaningful way.

HSA's will also make recommendations to the state level agency on applications from their area for health facility development funds (the new program replacing the Hill-Burton program) and on certificate of need decisions, although final decisions will be made at the state level (see the explanation of this new program and the requirement for the certificate of need program *infra*).

The most intriguing of the powers that will be exercised by HSA's is their authority under the new legislation to review existing institutional health services and make recommendations on their "appropriateness." Presumably, this will be the equivalent of deciding whether or not an existing facility is "needed." Within 3 years of the effective date of the statute, HSA's are required to have completed a review of all health facilities in their area and to forward to the state agency and to DHEW their recommendations. There is no power, however, to eliminate the inappropriate services, and this may be little more than a useless exercise. Actually, the statutory provisions providing for this review are the emasculated skeleton of a previous version of the HSA legislation that would have also given the state health-planning agencies the authority to close facilities whose services were found to be inappropriate. That provision of the bill was amended out before the legislation passed.

As it stands, this review of appropriateness may be little more than a warning of things to come, of steps that might be taken in the future should more direct regulation of health facilities become appropriate.

State level health planning funded by HSA legislation

The National Health Planning and Resources Development Act of 1974 also provides for state level health planning agencies.

Under the new legislation, DHEW is to contract with each state's governor to establish a state agency that will carry out health planning and resources development activities. In order to be eligible and to receive federal funding, the state must comply with a series of requirements intended to ensure that the agency is properly staffed and administered and that it has the proper state statutory authorization to perform a number of health planning and regulatory functions within the state.

The state agency is required to have an advisory council, the Statewide Health Coordinating Council (SHCC). The SHCC must meet membership requirements similar to those imposed on the governing bodies of HSA's. The governor must appoint an equal number of members from a list of nominees submitted by each state HSA. Of these appointments, a majority must be consumers (i.e., not providers). The governor may appoint additional members on his or her own nomination, not to exceed 40% of the total membership; a majority of these appointments must also be consumers. (At the other end of the spectrum, of the providers on the council, at least one-third must be direct providers of medical care.)

Whereas the national advisory council is entirely advisory to DHEW, and the HSA governing body has full control over the local health planning agency, the state level council shares responsibility for the health planning activities with the state agency.

The SHCC's primary functions are to advise the state agency in carrying out the agency's functions to develop a state health plan, which will be a composite of all of the state's various HSP's revised by the council to achieve coordination, and to comment on applications to DHEW for HSA funding and funding under the new resources development fund (described below).

The agency itself will be performing a variety of functions. Under the new federal law, in addition to its supervisory powers over the state's HSA's, the agency must (1) have the authority to implement a state certificate of need program, (2) serve as the state agency for the federal "certificate of need" program (described *supra*), if the state opts to implement such a program, (3) review the recommendations of HSA's relating to appropriateness of existing facilities and make public their findings, and (4) prepare a state medical facilities plan—the fourth separate plan mandated by this legislation—for the purposes of allocating resource development funds, as discussed below.

Thus in return for federal funding (75% of the cost of running the state program), the state must have a coordinated system of health planning, a certificate of need program for new facilities construction, and a program for reviewing the appropriateness of existing health facilities. In addition six states will receive reimbursement from DHEW for maintaining a program of health services rate regulation. This is not mandatory nor available to all states; it provides for a series of demonstrations or experiments with this alternative form of regulation.

Also contingent on the performance of these functions is the state's eligibility to participate in the new federal program for health facility construction and modernization. Under the new act the Hill-Burton program is in effect replaced by a new program that will finance a variety of kinds of health facilities. Direct grants, loans, loan guarantees, and interest subsidies are available for: (1) the modernization of existing medical facilities, (2) the construction of new outpatient facilities, (3) the construction of new inpatient facilities in areas that have received rapid population growth, (4) conversion of existing facilities to provide new health services, and (5) upgrading substandard facilities.

In order to qualify for this funding, an applicant must be from a state that has a DHEW-approved state medical facilities plan. This plan must inventory the existing health facilities in the state, determine the need for new or improved facilities of various types, and determine the priority of various projects. Any public or nonprofit private entity can apply for financial assistance from this fund by applying through the state agency to DHEW. The final decision is made at the federal level on the basis of the priorities in the state plan and the comments of the SHCC and the HSA.

In the application for funds the applicant must make assurances that the project will comply with construction and performance standards outlined in the statute, including assurances that the constructed facility will be available to all people and to a reasonable volume of people who are unable to pay. The amount available under this program for each project is based on a complicated formula weighing the state population, financial need, and the need of the state for medical facilities. No state will receive less than one million dollars. In all, $125 million is authorized for 1975, to be expanded to $135 million by 1977.

Conclusion

In the last three decades the amount and nature of governmental control of health facilities has grown and changed considerably. An industry once free from any but the most minimal governmental control now finds itself subject to various kinds of governmental regulation. Large amounts of government funds are being spent to encourage a variety of changes. Various governmental agencies are planning for the future development of the entire health care delivery system, and, for most types of health facilities, compliance with these plans is becoming more often a necessity and less often voluntary. Although as yet not widespread, governmental rate regulation is now a reality in some states.

Is the current level of governmental involvement a proper balance of regulation and free market competition, i.e., will it help cure the acknowledged (but rarely satisfactorily defined) crisis in the delivery of health care in this country? For that matter, is this conglomerate of overlapping/interlocking plans, governmental and quasi-governmental agencies, consumer councils, intergovernmental agreements, statutes, and implementing regulations even a rational approach to the problem(s)?

The answer to the first question is probably no. The current level of governmental control is more of an experimental and a transitional phase than a point of equilibrium. New approaches and ideas are being tested, while at the same time much of the theory and practice of the preexisting system has yet to be abandoned. In fact there seems to be a preference for testing new approaches by grafting them on to preexisting structures and institutions, even where the combination seems glaringly inappropriate. As for the second question, if the current level of governmental control can be called rational at all, it can only be from a perspective cognizant of the history of governmental control, being mindful of its probable future.

The temptation is to describe this situation metaphorically. Any legislative change in our legal system is almost always incremental and frustratingly slow. Like a person wandering across a fresh sheet of new ice, each step is usually small and tested before any weight is shifted to it. But the metaphor fails to illustrate part of the explanation. It is not just the uncertainty of the outcome that makes any legislative decision unlikely to favor immediate major change; it is also because of the fact that our legislatures are not single units formulating policy or even two competing parties trying to establish different sets of policies. It is more accurate to think of Congress or the state legislatures as having many competing political forces at work at any one time. Successful legislation is more often backed by a loosely held together coalition of different interests than by a like-minded majority. This is a situation that lends itself to compromise and moderation, not radical departures from the status quo. Particularly when the proposal under consideration is potentially detrimental to powerful economic interests, any social change is likely to be brought about, if at all, in small steps, rather than in one single dramatic sweep in the public interest.

Relatedly, once laws are enacted mandating change, no government of 220 million people—or one where the power is shared by local, state, and federal levels—can implement major changes with easy dispatch. Existing programs simply do not disappear or rearrange easily. Bureaucracies give up their standard operating procedures and their self-interest reluctantly. Even when a new idea or approach is able to overcome institutional or structural barriers, the problem of implementation may be compounded by the fact that we do not have the capabilities or the expertise to carry out what the program is supposed to do. It is one thing to pass a law requiring the development of annual implementation plans, the determination of the health needs of a community, or the designation of medically underserved areas. It is another to find workable techniques for doing so, or even to find acceptable terminology for discussing the issues. These sorts of programs take time to develop; some are little more than test runs for an idea or an approach. Even the most successful are generally successful in the sense of showing progress toward their programmatic goals and objectives, not in achieving them.

For example, the proponents of the CHP legislation in 1966 undoubtedly did envision that someday there would be a nationwide system of state and local health planning agencies and did hope that these agencies would encourage compliance with their plans. Realistically, in the first 5 to 10 years of the program, it is doubtful that anyone really expected anything more than some progress toward those objectives and some important lessons concerning the practical problems of health planning. For that matter, had the CHP agencies been given the authority to enforce compliance with their decisions or the funding to build a comprehensive nationwide program, it is unlikely that at that point in time the legislation would have passed Congress.

By 1974, the political climate in Congress had changed somewhat, and Congress took a further step. Again it was an incremental step; it did not impose direct federal control over health facilities or require the state government to exercise much more regulatory authority than already existed in at least some states. It adjusted the system, revitalized existing functions, and shifted some authority for health planning activities to the federal level. The overall objectives of the new legislation are to develop a coordinated national system of health planning, to require the states to exercise rather strict controls over health facility construction, and to coordinate federal funding of health facilities with planning efforts. As indicated above, the most that can be hoped for in the short run is that the program is implemented within a reasonable amount of time and that there is some progress toward those objectives. Again, even if fully implemented, it is unlikely that this program is the hoped-for proper balance of governmental regulation and economic competition. Rather, it is a step in the direction of some future point of equilibrium.

What, then, is going to happen in the long run? As indicated throughout this chapter, unless there is a major change in the general direction of public policy, we are moving toward more governmental control of health facilities, particularly hospitals, perhaps to the extent that some public utilities are now controlled and regulated. Further, while there is a clear legal and political preference for having that authority exercised at the state level of government, it is likely that the impetus behind the increasing governmental control will continue to come from the federal level. Congress has discovered that, while avoiding direct federal control, it can coerce the states and even private providers of health care into compliance with its will by flexing its control over federal health dollars. With the spectre of national health insurance and massive federal financial involvement on the horizon, that promises to be a recurring and effective strategy.

The unsettled issue does not seem to be the direction of the future, but whether governmental control of health facilities will really be the answer, or even part of the answer, to the problems that led to its proposal as a solution. So far, none of the government programs has been particularly effective. The irony is that while change is slow and incremental, it also tends to be irreversible for the very same reasons.

References

Comments: Comprehensive health planning—federal, state, local: concepts and realities, Wis. L. Rev. 839, 1970.

Havighurst, C.: Regulating health facilities construction, 1974.

Havighurst, C.: Regulation of health facilities

and services by 'certificate of need', Va. L. Reg. **59:**1143, 1973.

Herzog, B.: The participation of the poor in federal health programs, Clearinghouse Rev. **3:**293, 1970.

O'Donoghue, P.: Evidence about the effects of health care regulation, 1974.

Somers, A.: Hospital regulation: the dilemma of public policy, 1969.

U.S. Department of Health Education and Welfare: State licensing of health facilities, 1968.

Worthington, W., and Silver, L.: Regulation of quality of care in hospitals: the need for change, Law and Contemp. Prob. **35:**305, 1970.

CHAPTER 9 Public obligations of nonprofit hospitals

Chapters 1 through 5 focused on the most important set of legal rights relating to the public's health, those that define the relationship between private individuals and the government. Chapters 6 and 7 concerned a conceptually different set of legal rights, those existing between two particular groups of private individuals, namely patients and providers of medical care. Chapter 8 examined government control of health facilities and explained the legal rights that define the relationship between the government and provider institutions. The subject of this chapter does not fall into any of these categories, but is, in effect, a hybrid topic: certain legal rights exist between private individual patients and private providers of health services because of the quasi-public nature of the provider. That is, because many health facilities, particularly hospitals, are somewhat involved with or subsidized by the government, the law has recognized certain obligations that the institution must observe that normally would not be required of private institutions. These obligations, which are legal rights defining a relationship between the consumer/patient/public and certain health care institutions have become increasingly important as the focus of health care delivery in this country has become directed toward institutional providers, as discussed in the introduction to Chapter 8.

This chapter will trace the development of the basis for these legal rights, particularly in regard to the various obligations of nonprofit hospitals to provide free care to indigent people.

The origin of the nonprofit concept: charitable trusts

From a legal point of view, hospitals can be described as either governmental, proprietary, or private nonprofit. This is basically a reflection of who owns the facility or makes decisions for the individual institution. A government hospital is operated directly by the federal, state, or local government (or other government body, as in the case of a district hospital) or it may be operated by a corporation set up by any of these units of government. A proprietary hospital is operated essentially as any other business enterprise, with the declared purpose of making a profit. Nonprofit hospitals, also known as community hospitals or voluntary hospitals, are a hybrid of the other two. They are public in the sense that no private individual has a direct financial interest in the income they produce. They are private in the sense that they are not operated by the government; they are, technically, operated by a board of directors made up of members of the public. Hence many courts have begun to refer to them as quasi-public. The designation nonprofit does not refer to the institutions' balance of expenses and income, but is related to the facts that they pay no taxes on their income and do not pay out their net profit (gross income minus operating expenses) to any private individual.

To understand the evolution of the concept of a nonprofit hospital and the legal obligations that apply to it, it is necessary to know a little legal history.

As mentioned in Chapter 8, the original purpose of hospitals was not to maintain a medical facility or to provide any kind of health services. They were primarily charitable institutions set up to provide shelter and the basic necessities of life to the sick, the poor, and the aged. These early hospitals were often financially supported by what is known as a charitable trust. As early as 1600, England allowed, first by common law and then under a special statute, charitable trusts to be formed that would serve a public function. Such things as services for the sick and the aged, education of orphans, the building of highways, and the redemption of prisoners were included in the definition of charitable. Among the advantages of the charitable trust to the donor of the money were that the donor (usually his or her estate after death) was not taxed when the money was given to the trust, and the trust assets and income from them were exempt from taxation while the trust existed. The idea behind the charitable trust was that the government was encouraging private individuals to contribute to organizations that were performing designated activities that the government might have had the burden of supporting. Because of this, the government, through the king's attorney general, had the duty to protect and preserve the assets of these charitable trusts should they be mismanaged or used improperly. (In the United States this is a duty that today falls upon the attorney general of each state.)

What exactly does it mean to establish a trust? Perhaps the best way to illustrate the concept is with this primitive example: Imagine that you have grown up on a South Sea island and have a family to raise: one day you decide to make an urgent visit to another island, which means that you will be away from your island for some time. You give your fishing pole and other valuable property to a respected citizen who promises to see that these things will be used to provide your family with food and shelter. You have created a trust. You have trusted the possession of the property to another person with the expectation that it will be used for the benefit of a third person. The respected citizen is the trustee of the property, and your family is the beneficiary of the trust. The trustee has the legal responsibility for protecting the property and carrying out the purpose for which the trust was established. The beneficiary can call the trustee to account by bringing a lawsuit if the trustee fails to meet his or her responsibilities with regard to management of the trust.

Because of the considerable amount of trust or reliance being placed in the trustee and the ease with which a trust can be abused, the law holds a trustee to a strict standard of care. Unlike the legal concept of negligence (see Chapter 6), which requires that each person act reasonably or "nonfoolishly," the actions of trustees are examined much more closely to see if the beneficiaries' interests are actually being served. This special relationship between the beneficiary of a trust and the trustee is called a fiduciary relationship and carries with it this strict basis for liability.

The only major difference between a simple trust and the slightly more complex concept of a charitable trust is that a charitable trust can only be formed for designated purposes that the law has defined as benefiting the general public. This would not be satisfied by providing food and shelter to one individual or even several people, but must benefit a sufficiently large group of persons to be serving the public interest. If a hospital were only open to persons whose last name began with "R," the public purpose would not be sufficient to qualify it under the law of charitable trusts. If the hospital's declared purpose was to provide for the care of the sick and the poor, however, it would qualify as a charitable trust even though wealthy persons could not qualify for admission to the hospital; it would be serving the entire public by assuming a governmental function of providing hospital care for poor people that otherwise might be paid for at the expense of every taxpayer. The specific beneficiaries of a charitable trust are usually not ascertainable in advance. For example, any indigent person might qualify for care in a charitable hospital, but not all of them may actually use the hospital. Since it is not thought practical to expect these unknown beneficiaries to adequately protect their interest in the charitable trust, the attorney general of each state is required to act on his own, as well as the public's, behalf.

Instead of a sole trustee, most charitable trusts are operated by a board of trustees, consisting of several members. The ultimate beneficiary is, of course, the public. Therefore, one could say that a fiduciary relationship exists between the members of the board of trustees of a charitable trust and the general public. The general public can enforce a breach of a fiduciary duty by the trustees through the public's lawyer, the attorney general.

The emergence of corporate hospitals and their legal obligations

The charitable trust is an obsolete legal form for operating a hospital in this country. Most nonprofit and proprietary (and some governmental) hospitals are organized as a complex entity known as a corporation. The corporate form of doing business, credited by some for the tremendous economic growth in the United States over the last 150 years, has many advantages that set it apart from other legal entities, such as the sole proprietorship or the partnership. When a business is organized as a corporation, no individual is personally liable for the business debts of the corporation, the corporation can continue to exist for an indefinite period of time, and there is great flexibility in terms of management and utilizing financial resources.

Most hospitals that were set up originally as charitable trusts have taken advantage of the corporate form of business. Many have organized under special statutes allowing for nonprofit or charitable corporations. As with charitable trusts, this allows donors to give to the corporation and deduct the gift from their federal and state income tax and also allows the corporation to be exempt from state and federal tax on the corporation's income. One important difference between charitable trusts and charitable or nonprofit hospitals is that charitable or nonprofit hospitals are allowed by law to serve the entire public, not just the poor or other "deserving" classes of people.

All corporate hospitals, like their ancestors, the charitable trusts, are operated by a board of trustees or, in the case of a proprietary hospital, a board of directors. Members of these boards do not own the hospital, nor are they allowed to operate it for their own personal profit. They must operate the hospital to accomplish the purposes for which it was incorporated. These purposes are usually spelled out in the articles of incorporation and the corporation's bylaws. Thus the members of the board of trustees or the board of directors of a corporate hospital are fiduciaries who must operate the hospital for the beneficiaries of the hospital and may be held liable for mismanagement (see discussion below).

The complex nature of a modern hospital makes it difficult to say who actually are its beneficiaries. In the case of a proprietary hospital the beneficiaries are the hospital itself and, ultimately, the corporation's stockholders. What about the nonprofit hospital? Are the beneficiaries the people whom it serves; the hospital, meaning the institution; or the public as a whole? Unfortunately, there has not been any clear and definite answer to these issues. However, some aspects of these fiduciary relationships have been established in the law as will be outlined below, and they give some guidance in determining other obligations of hospital boards.

1. *The duty to properly manage the corporate property.*

A member of a hospital board has a fiduciary duty to the hospital of care and loyalty in the management of hospital property. This apparently is governed by the negligence or reasonableness standard of care, rather than the higher standard of care that must be adhered to by the trustee of a simple trust or a charitable trust. This has been justified as caused by the increased complexity of operating a corporation, as compared with a simple trust or charitable trust, and the desire to create a legal entity of maximum flexibility. Since most nonprofit hospitals are merely charitable trusts that have reorganized by making use of the nonprofit corporate structure, the determination of which standard of care to apply is one that has given the courts some problems.

In a decision involving the nonprofit Sibley Hospital in Washington, D.C., *Stern v. Lucy Webb Hayes National Training School for Deaconesses and Missionaries,* 381 F. Supp. 1003 (D.D.C. 1974), the court was faced with precisely this issue. As the court said, "The charitable corporation is a relatively new legal entity which does not fit neatly into the established common law categories of corporation and trust." In deciding to apply the standards of care applicable to corporations, rather than the higher standard applicable to trusts, the court reasoned:

> This distinction may amount to little more than a recognition of the fact that corporate directors have many areas of responsibility, while the traditional trustee is often charged only with the management of the trust funds and can therefore be expected to devote more time and expertise to that task. Since the board members of most large charitable corporations fall within the corporate rather than the trust model, being charged with the operation of ongoing businesses, it has been said that they should only be held

to the less stringent corporate standard of care. More specifically, directors of charitable corporations are required to exercise ordinary and reasonable care in the performance of their duties, exhibiting honesty and good faith.

After determining the applicable standard of care, the court proceeded to apply it to the facts that were established with regard to Sibley Hospital. The court found that for a number of years the hospital had placed large amounts of money on deposit with several banks in accounts that were drawing inadequate or no interest. The defendants were members of the board of trustees of Sibley Hospital, and they had interlocking duties and interests in the financial institutions in which these funds had been placed. In several instances a hospital trustee was also chairman of the board of directors of the financial institution and its principal stockholder. The court found that the decision to invest in these financial institutions was made by two other trustees who had since died, and not by the defendant trustees. Nevertheless, the defendant trustees in many instances had knowledge that these decisions had been made. Furthermore, the defendant trustees were members of the hospital's investment committee, which had responsibility for investing these funds, and they failed to object when no meetings were called for more than 10 years.

The court found that, ". . . these men have in the past failed to exercise even the most cursory supervision over the handling of Hospital funds and failed to establish and carry out a defined policy." The court also found that the trustees had "affirmatively approved self-dealing transactions" with the financial institutions. Thus the trustees had violated even the less stringent duty of exercising "ordinary and reasonable care in the performance of their duties, exhibiting honesty and good faith." Although the court refused to require the trustees to pay damages to the hospital, they were ordered to take various measures to force all hospital trustees to disclose their ties with the banks and to take other measures to assure that the events would never be repeated.

The *Sibley Hospital* case establishes the authority of a court to intervene in the internal affairs of a hospital when the trustees are managing it in a manner that is detrimental to its own interests. The parameters of such judicial intervention will only be defined after other cases and other courts have further interpreted this authority. Would a court, for instance, be willing to prevent a hospital from undertaking a costly program expanding the hospital's facilities if the hospital presently was not able to fill more than half its beds and the new construction project was detrimental to the hospital's financial position and threatened to destroy its solvency? In any event the *Sibley* case indicates that the internal affairs of nonprofit hospitals may be subject to close judicial scrutiny.

2. *The duty to the public.*

Apart from the duty of the board of directors or trustees to properly manage the corporate property, which is really for the benefit of the hospital itself, there is a similar duty owed to the public as a whole. The board actions may have to be consistent with the public's interest, at least under some circumstances.

Most of the cases that discuss this issue concern a policy of the hospital that restricts physicians' privileges in a manner that is alleged to be contrary to the public interest, and are brought to court by the physicians themselves. In cases decided in California, Hawaii, and New Jersey, courts have held that hospitals have a fiduciary duty to the public and that such duty is violated by arbitrarily denying a physician hospital privileges because in doing so the hospital is also closing its doors to persons in the community who are under the care of that physician. These cases may have far-reaching implications in holding that the courts have inherent power under the common law to require hospitals to establish policy that is consistent with the public interest.

In *Greisman v. Newcomb Hospital,* 40 N.J. 389, 192 A.2d 817 (1963), Dr. Greisman was the only licensed physician who practiced in the city of Vineland, New Jersey, where the hospital was located. Dr. Greisman was an osteopathic physician and was denied physicians' privileges under a hospital bylaw that restricted application for staff privileges to physicians who had graduated from a medical school approved by the American Medical Association. The hospital was tax-exempt, solicited and received private donations, and was the only hospital in the area. In the course of its opinion the court said:

> Broad judicial expressions may, of course, be found to the effect that hospitals such as Newcomb are private in nature and that their staff admission policies are entirely discretionary . . . They are private in the sense that they are nongovernmental but they are hardly private in other senses. Newcomb is a nonprofit organization dedicated by its certificate of incorporation to the vital public use of serving the sick and injured, its funds are in good measure received from public sources and through public solicitation, and its tax benefits received because of its nonprofit and nonprivate aspects . . . It constitutes a virtual monopoly in the area in which it functions and it is in no position to claim immunity from public supervision and control because of its allegedly private nature. Indeed, in the development of the law, activities much less public than the hospital activities of Newcomb, have commonly been subjected to judicial (as well as legislative) supervision and control to the extent necessary to satisfy the felt needs of the time.

> During the course of history, judges have often applied the common law so as to regulate private businesses and professions for the common good; perhaps the most notable illustration is the duty of serving all comers on reasonable terms which was imposed by the common law on innkeepers, carriers, farriers, and the like.

In requiring Newcomb Hospital to consider Dr. Greisman's application for physicians' privileges, the court concluded:

> . . . while the managing officials may have discretionary powers in the selection of the medical staff, those powers are deeply imbedded in public aspects, and are rightly viewed . . . as fiduciary powers to be exercised reasonably and for the public good.

In other jurisdictions, courts have held that in granting, denying, or revoking physicians' privileges, hospitals are required (1) to use procedures that at least meet the minimum requirements of due process, e.g., hearing and notice, and (2) to have rules that are reasonable, particularly those that are the basis for excluding a physician from the medical staff.

While most of these cases involved physicians' privileges, one lower court in New Jersey applied this doctrine to another aspect of hospital activity.

In *Doe v. Bridgeton,* 130 N.J. Super. 416, 327 A.2d 448 (1974), the judge of the New Jersy Superior Court was faced with the argument that the policy of Newcomb Hospital and Salem County Memorial Hospital in not allowing physicians to perform nontherapeutic abortions was contrary to the public interest. The court stated:

> The fact that the policy under attack here is concerned directly with patient services is not sufficient to distinguish the holding in *Greisman* so as to render it inapplicable . . . Consequently, the policy challenged by plaintiffs is subject to review by this court for the purpose of determining whether it is consistent with the public good . . .

The court went on to decide, however, that under the totality of the circumstances the hospital's policy could not be said to be totally arbitrary or contrary to the public good. The court found that prior to implementation of these policies, the hospitals received input from the communities they served and that ". . . the consensus of the respective governing boards was that a majority of citizens in each of the communities favored the respective policy decisions." In fact emotional demonstration by members of the public took place, including pickets that were stationed outside the hospital entrances for both sides of the controversy, and many letters were received opposing as well as favoring the hospital policy. The court's opinion noted that the hospitals depend on private contributions and that to require a hospital to act contrary to the community conscience would be itself contrary to the public good. The court also found that women desiring an abortion could be accommodated in other hospitals, although such facilities were some distance away. (But see cases discussed below relating to the applicability of the *Roe* and *Doe* decisions.)

3. *Constitutionally based obligations of nonprofit hospitals.*

A similar approach has also been used to impose obligations on nonprofit hospitals. Rather than simply expanding the hospital's private fiduciary duties to include obligations to the public, a few courts have gone one step further and held that nonprofit hospitals can be so "involved" with the government that they are considered governmental for certain purposes. Thus under some circumstances they must operate within the various limitations on governmental action.

Government hospitals, of course, as any other extension of the government, are subject to all constitutional limitations imposed on the government (see Chapters 1 and 2). Several examples are particularly relevant in the hospital situation.

In a recent case, *Memorial Hospital v. Maricopa County,* 415 U.S. 250 (1974), the Supreme Court held unconstitutional an Arizona statute requiring a year's residence in a county as a condition to receiving nonemergency medical care at the county's expense. Henry Evaro was an indigent person suffering from a chronic asthmatic and bronchial illness who moved from New Mexico into Maricopa County in Arizona. He received treatment for a severe respiratory attack in Memorial Hospital, a nonprofit hospital that had an agreement with the county for reimbursement when providing medical care to indigent persons. The county refused to reimburse Memorial Hospital because of Henry Evaro's failure to qualify under the year's residency requirement. The county's hospital also refused to provide medical care to Henry Evaro because of the 1-year residency requirement. The Court held that the residency requirement was a violation of the equal protection clause of the fourteenth amendment, especially in view of the facts (1) that it interfered with the constitutional right of a citizen to travel from one state to another and (2) that medical care is a necessity of life.

Other cases have decided that a government hospital cannot refuse to perform abortions (based on the decisions in *Roe v. Wade* and *Doe v. Bolton,* cited in Chapter 4) and that government hospitals cannot discriminate on the basis of race, creed, or color.

Some courts have held, contrary to the implications of *Doe v. Bridgeton,* that a private hospital has been sufficiently involved with the government so that the private facility will be required to abide by these same constitutional constraints that ordinarily apply only to strictly governmental hospitals. The reason for this may be easier to understand by reference to several cases involving racial discrimination. In *Brown v. Board of Education,* 347 U.S. 483 (1954), the Supreme Court struck down the "separate but equal" doctrine and held that the due process clause is violated when the government establishes separate schools on the basis of race. The reaction in some areas of the United States was to build a private school system that was to be supported by funds provided indirectly by the county or other governmental subdivision. These plans were usually unsuccessful; federal courts held that the private schools had been sufficiently involved with the government to make the constitutional prohibition against racial discrimination applicable to them.

The federal Hill-Burton program, enacted prior to *Brown v. Board of Education,* forbade racial discrimination in the state plan, but embraced the separate but equal doctrine by permitting separate hospitals to be built as long as a sufficient number of beds were allocated to each race. In *Simkins v. Moses H. Cone Memorial Hospital,* 323 F.2d 959 (4th Cir. 1963), a federal court overturned this provision and held that a nonprofit hospital that received Hill-Burton construction funds was sufficiently involved with the government that it was bound by the same constitutional constraints that were applicable to government hospitals, i.e., discrimination was unconstitutional even if separate facilities were equal. (Subsequent to that decision, Congress amended the Hill-Burton Act, deleted the the separate but equal doctrine, and forbade all forms of racial discrimination in hospitals that received federal construction funds.)

The reasons given by the court in *Simkins* for its holding included that the Hill-Burton program subjected hospitals to an elaborate and intricate pattern of governmental regulations, both state and federal, including the duty to comply with minimum standards for maintenance and operation of the hospital to be set by the state; that the federal government had to approve the number of hospital beds and other facilities in each state; and that the hospital must provide services for persons unable to pay. The court concluded that the Hill-Burton program, of which the funded hospitals were integral parts, was a comprehensive intermeshing state and federal program designed to properly allocate existing medical and hospital resources for the best possible promotion and maintenance of public health. The court apparently concluded that an extensive federal program to provide hospital care such as Hill-Burton, is not exempt from constitutional constraints just because it utilizes private rather than government-operated hospitals.

At this point in time it is impossible to delineate with any specificity what comprises sufficient involvement with the government to impose these governmental obligations on nonprofit hospitals. Clearly the courts are prepared to look at a number of factors, but the several lower courts that have considered the problem have not been completely consistent with one another; perhaps the issue will only be clarified when there is a definitive decision by the Supreme Court. Nonetheless, the implications of these cases are potentially far-reaching.

The obligations of nonprofit hospitals to provide free care to indigent people

As the modern hospital has evolved from the simple institution that provided only food and shelter to the sick and the poor, and as it has evolved from the charitable trust to, in many cases, nonprofit corporate status, the question has been raised of whether today's nonprofit hospitals should continue to provide free care to those unable to pay for it. In many cases these hospitals have voluntarily continued this tradition; however, with the recent increases in the costs of medical care, some hospitals have been less willing to do so.

Some economists have persuasively argued that there is no such thing as "free care." The cost of free care is merely added to the bills of the paying patients in a nonprofit hospital, thus escalating further the already skyrocketing cost that the individual patient must pay. The logic of this position is that people who cannot afford to pay for hospital services ought to have their care paid for directly by the government.

Of course, the reality is that the various governmental programs, including Medicaid, Medicare, and the programs financed solely by the state or local governments, do not cover all people who cannot afford hospital care. Perhaps the best answer would be to urge the legislatures to expand these programs, but in the meantime the question remains as to whether nonprofit hospitals should provide free care to these people.

It can be argued that nonprofit hospitals are legally required to do so. The bases for these arguments are that (1) the government has provided support for many of these hospitals through programs such as Hill-Burton, and (2) the government has provided indirect support for these institutions by exempting them from state and federal taxation.

1. *The free care obligations of Hill-Burton hospitals.*

Before receiving construction funds under the Hill-Burton program, each of the over 6000 recipient health facilities gave assurances to DHEW that (1) the facility would be made available to all people residing in the territorial area of the recipient, and (2) a reasonable volume of free services would be made available to people unable to pay. These assurances, commonly referred to as the community service and free care requirements, are expressly required by the Hill-Burton statute. While assisting the private nonprofit hospital system to grow and expand to meet the nation's needs, rather than only building more public hospitals, Congress wanted to assure that certain public purposes would be achieved. Therefore, in return for the federal subsidies they received, Hill-Burton recipients were obligated to accept these requirements.

The Hill-Burton statute also required DHEW to promulgate regulations implementing these requirements and to assure their enforcement. Although the original Hill-Burton legislation was passed in 1946, it was not until July 1972 that the necessary regulations were actually promulgated by DHEW, and then only after a concerted effort by attorneys representing indigent people who brought lawsuits against both DHEW and several noncomplying hospitals.

The regulations that were finally issued required a relatively modest volume of free services from Hill-Burton hospitals. As the regulations currently stand, a hospital is able to satisfy the free services requirement by meeting one of three options: (1) a hospital must offer free services in an amount not less than 3% of operating costs, (2) a hospital must offer free services in an amount not less than 10% of all federal assistance provided to the hospital under the Hill-Burton program, or (3) a hospital must certify that it will not exclude any individual from admission on the ground that such individual is unable to pay for needed services.

The regulations relating to the community service requirement required that the hospital make its services available to all people in the community subject only to restrictions based on age, indigency, or type or kind of medical or mental disability. They also require that each Hill-Burton hospital accept Medicaid and Medicare patients (for which, of course, the hospital is reimbursed).

Even if fully enforced, these are not strict requirements. However, thus far the record of enforcement of these regulations leaves a great deal to be desired. The regulations delegate much of the responsibility for enforcement of these requirements to the various state agencies responsible for the Hill-Burton program. This appears to have resulted in widespread noncompliance with these requirements.

The unwillingness of DHEW to implement these statutory requirements and, after implementation, to enforce them is another lesson in the limitations of administrative agencies. Government agencies have been frequently accused of being "captured" by the very institutions that they are supposed to regulate or supervise. This may well be part of the explanation of DHEW and the state agencies' reluctance to enforce these requirements. The influence of private health institutions on these agencies is substantial. For example, the American Hospital Association, which represents the nation's hospitals, fought a hard campaign before DHEW to minimize the effect of the free service regulations. As a result, many of the provisions in the regulations contain what could be considered loopholes that can serve no purpose other than minimizing the real impact of the regulations. Among other things, the original regulations permitted Hill-Burton hospitals to bill patients and then write off any unpaid bill as free services to the indigent. This provision was later declared invalid in *Corum v. Beth Israel Hospital,* 373 F. Supp. 550

(S.D.N.Y. 1974). That case held that a Hill-Burton hospital must determine prior to admission that a patient is eligible for free services and is being admitted toward the fulfillment of the hospital's free service requirement, except in emergencies or in other situations where it is impractical to make this determination.

Too often under these regulations the requirement of providing free care to the indigent is fulfilled merely by engaging in some highly questionable accounting manipulations, rather than actually providing services to the persons.

The passage of the National Health Planning and Resources Development Act of 1974 effectively replaced the Hill-Burton program with a slightly different program for funding a variety of health facilities. However, the Hill-Burton statute was not repealed; the authority to spend funds for that program has merely expired. Consequently, the Hill-Burton hospitals must still comply with the requirements for free care and community service. In addition the new legislation contains similar provisions requiring facilities funded under the new program to make assurances for a reasonable volume of care to indigent people and community service. While the congressional policy of requiring federally funded hospitals to fulfill certain obligations to the public has been continued, the policy will only become meaningful if the new statutory provision is effectively implemented and enforced; the history of the Hill-Burton program casts some doubt on the likelihood of that happening.

2. *Free care: an obligation of charitable institutions?*

The government has indirectly encouraged the development of charitable trusts, nonprofit hospitals, and other nonprofit corporations by giving them the preferred status of tax-exempt institutions. The justification for this exemption is the public purpose that they serve. The tax exemption that is most significant to nonprofit hospitals is the exemption from federal income tax, although they are also exempted from state property and income tax.

Once a hospital establishes eligibility for exemption from federal income tax in accordance with section 501(c) (3) of the Internal Revenue Code (the federal tax statute), it is eligible to receive private donations, which the donor can then deduct from his or her own federal income tax obligation. The hospital is also exempt from a tax on the income it earns. In effect the government is permitting tax revenues to be distributed directly to the hospital: funds that would otherwise be paid into the federal treasury are paid to or kept by the hospital.

A recent decision, *Jackson v. Statler Foundation,* 496 F.2d 623 (2d Cir. 1974), gave the following justification for the tax exemption and accompanying deduction available to donors:

> The legislative history concerning the purpose of the Internal Revenue Code's charitable exemption and deduction sets forth this rationale:
>
> The [deduction] is based upon the theory that the Government is compensated for the loss of revenue by its relief from financial burden which would otherwise have to be met by appropriations from public funds, and by the benefits resulting from the promotion of the general welfare. [citation omitted]

According to the federal tax statute, in order for a hospital to qualify for federal tax exemption and for private tax-deductable contributions, it must be "operated exclusively for . . . charitable . . . purposes." This language had in years past been interpreted to permit hospitals to charge those able to pay for services rendered, in order to pay the expenses of the hospital, while not denying admission to others unable to pay. Until recently, hospitals failing to provide free services to the poor were denied the exemption. In 1969, however, the Internal Revenue Service reversed itself on this long-standing interpretation and issued a revenue ruling (an administrative regulation) that permitted hospitals to qualify for tax-exempt status if they "were operated for the care of all persons in the community able to pay the cost thereof either directly or through third party reimbursement."

In effect the new regulation allowed hospitals to provide care for poor people by accepting Medicaid and Medicare patients, for which they would be reimbursed by the government, but not to provide free care to other poor people who did not have some kind of third party coverage.

Shortly after it was issued, this regulation was challenged by a suit that claimed it was an invalid interpretation of the statutory term "charitable." A lower federal court agreed that it was invalid and held that a hospital must to the extent financially feasible provide services to those who are unable to pay, or lose its tax-exempt status. The court also required that tax-exempt hospitals post in accessible public areas of the hospital a notice that informs patients unable to pay of their right to receive free care.

On appeal, the lower court's rulings were reversed. In *Eastern Kentucky Welfare Rights Organization v. Simon,* 506 F.2d 1278 (1974), the court of appeals held that the Internal Revenue Service's interpretation of the term "charitable" was valid; this effectively means that hospitals are inherently charitable if they are providing services to everyone in the community who can afford to pay, even though they provide no care to indigent people. As of the date of this publication, the Supreme Court had heard argument on appeal, but no decision had been rendered.

Even if the court of appeal's decision is eventually upheld, nonprofit hospitals may still be required to provide free care to the poor under state tax laws. Many states have specifically exempted nonprofit hospitals operated for "hospital" purposes from tax exemption. Other states follow the federal approach of requiring hospitals to be operated exclusively for charitable services in order to qualify for tax-exempt status. Interpretations of these state laws may follow the rationale of the *Eastern Kentucky* decision cited above, or they may agree with the lower court in that same case.

A recent Missouri case took a unique approach to this issue. The local tax authority assessed the property of three nonprofit hospitals for ad valorem (property) tax purposes. The state tax commission, an administrative agency, overruled the local authority. The case was then contested in the courts. The trial level court ruled that in order to be charitable and thus qualify for a tax exemption, nonprofit hospitals must show that they provide a substantial volume of free care to indigent people. The opinion was quite outspoken in its explanation:

> St. Luke's, Baptist, and Research are all managed by highly trained, highly paid and highly efficient hospital administrators, known as Executive Directors. They are business

and financial managers and their purpose, aim and accomplishment is to operate the hospitals as businesses, making money. This they accomplish admirably . . . All patients are expected to pay, and are billed, the prevailing, ever-increasing rates, rates which so greatly exceed actual costs of hospital care that each of the hospitals shows a large and substantial profit running into hundreds of thousands or millions of dollars, even after deductions for depreciation and bad debts. This profit is not, it is true, distributed in dividends or stock to individuals—it is used for debt retirement and for ever increasing expansion of hospital facilities to satisfy an apparently insatiable demand for more wings, more rooms and more equipment. The enlarged facilities in turn will be used to capacity by fully paying patients who in turn will be charged at rates which will generate, along with capital fund donations, more monies for more enlargements for more such fully paying patients and on, apparently, *ad infinitum.* In this structure, the original charitable objective of the hospital is lost, the relief of those unable to pay cannot be accomodated, and this relief to the county for its welfare poor disappears.

The court then found that the actual number of admissions for free services was less than 0.1% of the hospitals' total revenues and ruled that bad debts cannot be considered services to the indigent.

However, on appeal to the Supreme Court of Missouri, the ruling of the lower court was modified substantially. While not abandoning the principle that a nonprofit hospital must actually perform charitable services in order to be tax-exempt, the court adopted a broader interpretation of the term. According to the Supreme Court of Missouri, the correct interpretation of the law is that "providing of hospital facilities for the sick in a nonprofit manner rises to a charitable purpose for tax-exempt status if the same is available to both the rich and the poor."

Thus that court looked to the nonprofit organization of the hospitals and, most importantly, the failure of the local tax authority to show that any indigent person had ever been turned away. The fact that these hospitals did a small volume of free services was not determinative and the use of percentages as benchmarks for performance was specifically rejected. While not denying that nonprofit hospitals must provide free care to the indigent in some way, this court felt that services to the nonpoor were also charitable and that only a showing that indigent people were being turned away would jeopardize their charitable and tax-exempt status. As such, this neither adopts the *Eastern Kentucky* approach nor rejects the position that charitable nonprofit hospitals have an obligation to provide free care to the poor.

Conclusion

Underlying these various issues regarding the obligations of nonprofit hospitals is a more basic issue: To what extent can these institutions be held accountable to the public? As they developed historically, their role was an accepted one, both by the public and by the people who ran them. For many years they voluntarily accepted a responsibility to care for people who could not afford care; it is only in recent years that some hospitals have changed this policy and are no longer willing to define themselves as serving the public, at least in the traditional sense. The accountability of these hospitals, or to state it more correctly, of these hospital boards, appears to be to their own institution, not to the public at large. At least to some extent, this is understandable in light of the ever-increasing costs of medical care and accompanying difficulties in maintaining the solvency of health care institutions. On the other hand, there is a great deal of reason for labeling these institutions "quasi-public" and expecting that they serve both their institutional self-interest and the public interest, to the extent that is possible. While neither the law nor public opinion has been able to clearly define exactly what the public interest is, it is clear that both are less willing to assume that hospital boards are going to give adequate consideration to the public's interest. Thus the issue becomes one of making these boards accountable for their decisions, to require that their decisions be subject to challenge even if they are eventually upheld.

The willingness of the courts in the *Sibley Hospital* and *Newcomb Hospital* cases to assert their inherent authority to intervene in the affairs of hospitals was in large part a reaction to the hospitals' lack of accountability. Until recently, courts had generally refused to permit anyone other than that state's attorney general to challenge the activities of charitable insitutions. More recently, the courts have been willing to let members of the general public or other specific group of individuals challenge the policy of these institutions for sufficient reasons.

In the *Sibley Hospital* case the court phrased the problem in the following manner:

> The management of a non-profit charitable hospital imposes a severe obligation upon its trustees. A hospital such as Sibley is not closely regulated by any public authority, it has no responsibility to file financial reports, and its Board is self-perpetuating. The interests of its patients are funnelled primarily through large group insurers who pay the patients' bills, and the patients lack meaningful participation in the Hospital's affairs.

In *City of Paterson v. Paterson General Hospital,* 97 N.J. Super. 514, 235 A.2d 487 (1967) a court came to similar conclusions:

> It must be conceded that in this State, and throughout the country as a whole, supervision of the administration of charities has been neglected. Charities in this State, whether or not incorporated, are, in general, only subject to the supervision of the Attorney General. The manifold duties of this office make readily understandable the fact that such supervision is necessarily sporadic . . . The whole problem of the limited extent of supervision of charities throughout the United States, with recommendations for improvement, is carefully considered in Karts, "The Efficiency of the Charitable Dollar: An Unfulfilled State Responsibility," 73 Harv. L. Rev. 433 (1960). While public supervision of the administration of charities remains inadequate, a liberal rule as to the standing of a plaintiff to complain about the administration of a charitable trust or charitable corporation seems decidely in the public interest.

There is a mounting pressure being exerted on a somewhat unstable situation. Perceptions of the public interest are changing. The demands of the public are increasing. Yet the focus of this attention is an institution with a somewhat awkward legal status. While the eventual outcome is impossible to predict, the likelihood of major change is practically inevitable.

References

Bromberg, R.: Charitable hospital, Catholic U. L. Rev. **20**:237, 1970.

Coleman, E.: Financial feasibility as it relates to federal regulation of services to the poor under the Hill-Burton Act (published by Accountants for the Public Interest, 1975).

Hayt, E., Hayt, L., and Groeschel, A.: Law of hospital, physician, and patient, Part II, ed. 3, 1972.

Miller, C.: The hospital as a community facility, 1972.

Rose, M: Federal regulation of services to the poor under the Hill-Burton Act: realities and pitfalls, Nw. U.L. Rev. **70**:168, 1975.

Rose, M.: Internal Revenue Service's 'contribution' to the health problems of the poor, Catholic U.L. Rev. **21**:35, 1971.

Somers, H., and Somers, A.: Medicare and the hospitals, 1967.

Epilogue

It was argued in the introduction to this book that we as a society are, as are most other industrialized nations, at a point in time where the public's health, particularly with regard to the delivery of medical care, is becoming a critically important public and political issue. Given the preceding chapters, perhaps it is possible to be a little more specific about what that actually means.

The major basis for this hypothesis is the willingness of our society over the past few decades to make a major investment of resources in health related services and programs. The best evidence of this continuing willingness is the ongoing drive toward some form of national health insurance. No one is sure what that national health insurance scheme will look like, only that we will soon have one; it is as if we have made a societal commitment to pay for a solution to the problem even without knowing the exact nature—or cost—of that solution, or even without having formulated a consensus as to the nature of the problem.

But there is also emerging a feeling that this willingness to invest resources has some limits; of late, this has been accompanied by a rather uncomfortable feeling that the results of our recent massive investment so far have not been quite as rewarding as we might have expected. We are willing to pay, and we are willing to pay a great deal, but we are not satisfied with the return on our current investment.

From this situation has emerged a number of dilemmas that society must deal with at this point in time. Not the least of these dilemmas is the need to set priorities, both in terms of choosing where best to invest our health dollars and in terms of choosing between spending resources on our health or spending for the many other important societal objectives. This has been compounded in the mid-seventies by an economic recession, which, while possibly temporary, has served as a reminder that our resources are not limitless and that relative prosperity is something that can be neither expected nor assumed.

Other dilemmas exist that are equally fundamental. The decision to protect or promote the public's health almost always results in the control or manipulation of the lives of at least some individual members of that public. The history of social welfare programs in this country has given us enough examples of how easy it is for a government that starts with the intention of providing for the welfare of its citizens to end up intruding into their lives and personal affairs. We not only pay for health with our economic resources, we also can pay with our privacy and other individual rights and freedoms. Similarly, any serious proposal to improve the public's health will invariably clash with powerful economic interests and their individual and institutional rights. In the case of the delivery of medical care, the most obvious examples are the institutional changes often cited as necessary to improve that delivery system, including proposals for greater governmental control of health facilities and more outside supervision of the individual practitioner of medical care. Even if society finds the public's health important enough that it warrants the subordination of private providers' interests in these ways, these choices once made are not easily imposed or implemented as a result of the economic and political power of these interests. The same basic dilemma also arises with any one of a number of more subtle but equally important problems, e.g., the redefinition of the delivery of health care to include the concept of protecting the health and safety of the worker in occupational settings, or in trying to identify and eliminate environmental factors that contribute to the public's health problems.

There are also certain dilemmas that, while not necessarily specific to our current situation and concern for the public's health, are probably inherent societal problems at any point in time: there will always be the theory-to-reality problems associated with implementing our goals and objectives into actual changes with real impact; there are in the provision of any valuable human service inherent disputes as to who gets what, where and when, and for how much.

It is in this context that the law as it relates to the public's health has become so important. Whether one thinks of the law in literal terms meaning all laws, in more theoretical terms as sets of legal rights, or in practical terms with the emphasis on the legal system and legal decision makers, the law defines the relationships among the members of a society. It is not the only way to define these relationships, as economists, sociologists, psychologists, or persons with other perspectives will quickly point out, but the law is one way to define these relationships. And when the issue at hand is one that is going to be contested in the public and political arenas of a society, it is a particularly important one. The law involves the formal, sanctioned relationships between individuals and institutions within a society. As the purposes formulated in the introduction to this book reflect, these formal relationships are at the least a set of barriers that must be understood and worked within. They are also a useful, albeit frequently unsuccessful, means of change. One cannot consider the law in a vacuum divorced from the other considerations and barriers that must be dealt with and/or changed, but it is a consideration that is quite distinct and, for a variety of reasons, one that is frequently misunderstood by large portions of our society often including, ironically, those that are the most responsible for protecting and promoting the public's health.

It is for these reasons that the law as it relates to the public's health, more so now than ever before, must be understood by anyone in the public health fields.

It is for these same reasons that the particular approach to law taken by this book was adopted. It is critically important for people working in the public health field to know not only the theory and basis for the law, but also the reality and practice of the law. It is important to understand that law in terms of the legal rights that can and may exist, but also in terms of the legal process that defines and enforces them. Most importantly, the law must be seen as something other than a set of specific answers to specific questions; it is better thought of as a set of rather vague principles that may or may not be applied in a given situation depending upon a number of factors and considerations. It is only with this sort of perspective that a workable knowledge of law can be developed and maintained over time. It is important to know the specific statutory provisions of the Medicaid program, for instance, but it is also necessary to look at it as an example of an entitlement program set up by statute, interpreted by judicial opinions, implemented by regulations, and operating within governmental constraints imposed by the Constitution. Medicaid is undoubtably a crucially important public health program, but it will eventually give way to another program for the poor, a larger national health insurance program, or even a whole new approach to providing for the health of those who cannot afford to pay for medical care—each of which would be best understood form a legal point of view as a kind of statutory entitlement program with all of resulting ramifications and implications.

Similarly, it is important to know the current legal basis for governmental health planning programs, but these too will someday be replaced, and, therefore, one should view them as examples of how legislation is enacted and implemented and for the principles they illustrate as well as for the specific programmatic details and their immediate impact on the public's health. The point is that such an approach is the more useful way to understand the law as it relates to the public's health.

By way of a conclusion, it is perhaps appropriate to make one fundamental point that may have been indirectly brought out in the preceding chapters but has not been specifically clarified in this book: there is a basic conceptual difference between what we often refer to on the one hand as "the law" and what can be referred to on the other as "medicine" or "public health." In many ways they are not comparable, yet they are often compared, and, consequently, the comparisons have resulted in some amount of misunderstanding of each discipline by the other.

Many people have spoken in terms that draw a comparison between law and medicine or law and public health. The difference between the point of view of those involved in the delivery of health care, primarily the medical profession, has been compared with the point of view of those involved in the legal system, primarily lawyers. This is a perfectly valid, somewhat intriguing line of inquiry. There are a number of ways to compare the two professions along a number of parameters. A comparison can also be drawn between the health care delivery system and what could be called, but what rarely is, the legal services delivery system, meaning the various institutions and providers, both public and private, of legal services to those that seek the advice and assistance of legal counsel. Again, the comparison can be an interesting one, with a number of parallels and a number of fundamental differences.

What is conceptually not appropriate is to compare the health care delivery system with the legal system as a whole. The former is a means by which certain kinds of services are delivered to people in need. The latter is quite different; it consists of the institutions and procedures by which a society makes and enforces certain kinds of rules and decisions.

This is more than an exercise in logic and semantics. This point is basic to any understanding of the role that the law plays in providing for and promoting the public's health and the role that people in the fields of public health can play in the legal system. Far too often the law has been seen by those in the health related fields as merely a separate discipline or a system of institutions and activities that are for the most part separate from the institutions and activities of concern to public health. In fact there is often a preference that this other field or other profession be kept separate or "not interfere" with certain issues relating to public health or the delivery of medical care. The physician who thinks—or says—"Let's keep the lawyers out of medical matters," may have a valid point of view; the hospital administrator who claims "Why is it that everyone is concerned about medical malpractice when there is just as much malpractice in the delivery of legal services?" is asking a relevant question. But if either expresses this preference or thinks in terms of "keeping the law out of medicine" or keeping the health care delivery system and the legal system separate, they would not be making any sense, and even worse, they would be avoiding an important reality. As a system by which societal decisions are made and enforced, the legal system very often affects the public's health and the delivery of health care. Whether or not those decisions are made correctly or the public's interests are in fact served, the law, broadly speaking, is our system for making those decisions and the field of public health is inextricably involved with it. And again, we are at a point in time when this is more obviously true than it ever has been before.

For the very same reasons that the law has to be understood in order to work effectively in the field of public health, this difference between the legal system and the health care delivery system must be born in mind. It explains certain kinds of barriers; it helps one to use the law as a tool for change. The law is not a separate discipline or a field exclusively for lawyers, or at least it should not be.

This suggests what should be abundantly obvious: if we are to make progress in the solution to the dilemmas that currently involve the public's health, then the law must be changed in many ways, including some basic institutional changes in the ways that laws are made, interpreted, and enforced. Just as certain pressures have produced a situation where there is likely to be certain fundamental institutional changes in the delivery of health care, pressures are developing that make clear that certain changes must be made in the law and in the legal system. In fact the dilemmas that involve the public's health are themselves pressures in that direction. In the context of this book it is not possible to list in a serial form some of the changes in the law and the legal system that have to be made, but clearly among that list would have to be the need to eliminate some of the economic barriers blocking access to the legal system and preventing the enforcement of the legal rights of people who simply cannot afford to pay the price for equal justice. There is a need to increase the access of the lower and middle-income individual to the courts, and equally pressing, to the legislatures and the executive branch of the government.

There are many serious criticisms that can be levied against the law, the legal system, or our past legal history. There is, however, another side to the coin. There are some very positive things about the law and the legal system, and some of these bear directly on the very public issue at hand, the public's health. It is these positive aspects of the law that can make one speak more optimistically about the fact that the law and the public's health are so interrelated.

Notwithstanding the shortcomings and past failures of the legal system, many of which have been explained throughout this book, the legal system does have some remarkable strengths. Among these strengths is the legal decision making process and some of the concepts that that process has developed, including among them the idea of an adversary process as the means by which some decisions are best made.

In an adversary proceeding, the data gathering and analysis is done not by the ultimate decision maker, but by advocates, one representing each relevant point of view. The final decision is made by a third party who is supposed to be impartial and objective and is supposed to base his or her decision on that which is expressed by the advocates. A lawsuit is one of those situations where the law has recognized that an adversary proceeding is the appropriate decision making process. Each side is represented by legal counsel who explains the facts and the law in terms that best represent his or her client's point of view. It is only after all of these points of view have been expressed that the judge makes the final decision based on a (theoretically) impartial judgment as to which side is correct or more consistent with the law. It is, in essence, a means for seeking "the truth" or "the best decision." It puts a high value on individual integrity and participation; it implies a notion of valuing justice not just in the outcome but in the process; it even takes into account the human tendency toward partiality by ensuring that the final decision is delegated to a person who is supposed to be impartial and apart from the interested parties. It is, as well, a process that is very often time-consuming, tedious, expensive, and simply inappropriate for some kinds of decisions.

This process for making decisions can be contrasted with the one most often employed in the context of the health care delivery system. Very often decisions are made in that context with what could be described as the medical model for decision making: a single expert or group of experts are responsible for gathering the relevant information, analyzing it, and coming to a decision, usually based on their judgment as to what is in the patient's best interest. This, too, is a means for seeking "the truth" or the "best decision." It is often used where the decision requires a great amount of technical expertise or where the decision maker must have an understanding of a great amount of information. It is also relatively efficient in terms of time and resources.

Consequently, we have relied on this kind of decision-making process in many contexts, including some situations within the legal system, but particularly as our usual approach to making many decisions relevant to the public's health.

It would be a virtually imponderable problem to try to justify the adversary system or the medical model for decision making simply on the basis of which approach makes the more accurate decisions in a given context. However, the adversary system has certain advantages that can justify its preference or application is some situations relating to the public's health apart from consideration of the specific decisions that process is likely to make. There are certain aspects of the adversary process that make it the desirable approach to resolving issues, particularly when those issues have been elevated to the level of critically important public issues.

A process that requires that there be an advocate for each point of view not only assures that the combination of these competing advocates will bring out all of the relevant considerations, thereby assisting in making the correct decision, but it increases the likelihood that the participants will accept the decision, whatever it is. In Chapter 3 it was pointed out that the requirement of advance notice and a hearing for people who are to be committed to a mental institution satisfies our sense of justice and fair play. This is much the same point—having one's interests advocated and fairly considered in a decision-making process makes one more likely to be satisfied that the decision is fair, even where it is adverse to our interests. Moreover, particularly where the decision is one that involves some sort of societal resource allocation or any other choice that is a choice of values as much as it is a calculation of something quantifiable or a comparison to a measurable standard, it is doubtful that anything short of allowing full advocacy for a point of view can really assure that the point of view is effectively represented.

This has already happened in many health related decisions. As seen in Chapter 5, some decisions regarding the entitlement to welfare or health care benefits can only be legally made after a fair hearing, i.e., an adversarial hearing, has been allowed to the beneficiary. The process of civil commitment is another example; the law is evolving to the point where it is requiring that many decisions relating to the confinement of civilly committed people be based on adversarial-type procedures; in the not too distant past these decisions were primarily made by physicians and according to the traditional medical model. Decisions as to the allocation of health care resources, e.g., health facilities planning or certificate of need decisions, will also have to include at least in some ways, adversarial proceedings. It has also been recommended that the proper way to ensure that the rights of patients in a hospital setting are really respected is to allow patients some kind of advocate and a forum for airing their grievances to the institution.

In some situations it will be a matter of the law requiring that this adversarial kind of process be used. But the concept and utility of advocates and adversarial hearings is a useful one that should be adopted where appropriate, not simply where it is legally required.

This is not to suggest that miniature courtrooms should be constructed on the wards of health care facilities or that every person seeking health care should be accompanied by an attorney. The point is that the concept of an adversary proceeding, particularly allowing for an advocate for important points of view, could be incorporated into the process for making many of the crucial decisions that affect the public's health. To put it in broader and more general terms, the entire concept of justice or fairness in the process being as important as the justice or fairness of the outcome is a critically important part of the law, at least in theory; the field of public health could benefit greatly if these concepts were more often applied in making important decisions. Simply put, how we decide public issues can be as important as what we decide. In fact if the critical issues involving the public's health that now face society are truly dilemmas—from which any course of action will require the sacrifice of one societal interest or another—then the importance of making those choices in a fair and just manner is even greater. If the concepts that have developed in the legal system such as due process, fundamentally fair procedures, and equal protection are incorporated into making a decision, then, even apart from our satisfaction with the final decision, there is some assurance that we have acted correctly.

These basic changes in behavior, both personal and institutional, will be, of course, difficult to bring about. At least we are at a point in time when some basic changes in the delivery of health care are being predicted, and some changes are inevitable. Whether or not the way that decisions are made will be revised, however, will depend upon a number of things. Certainly there will have to be an increase in the amount of dialogue between two professions that have never been particularly compatible. It will also require a clarification of our real commitment to such values as individual integrity and procedural fairness. Even with regard to the decisions in the legal system where these values have been explicitly defined, our ability and willingness to actually carry them out in practice have not always been impressive. Above all, it will require an understanding by those in the field of public health of the procedures utilized and the reasons why this approach to decision making has been developed.